SPENSER'S *FAERIE QUEENE*

A CRITICAL COMMENTARY
ON BOOKS I AND II

FOR DEAREST STEVIE
The influence is thine,
and born of thee

SPENSER'S
Faerie Queene

A critical commentary on Books I and II

DOUGLAS BROOKS-DAVIES

Manchester
University Press

Rowman and Littlefield

Published 1977 by
Manchester University Press
Oxford Road
Manchester M13 9PL

ISBN 0 7190 0683 X (cased)

ISBN 0 7190 0698 8 (paperback)

USA

Rowman and Littlefield
81 Adams Drive
Totowa, N.J. 07512

ISBN 087471 829 5

Printed in Great Britain at
The Pitman Press, Bath

Computerised Phototypesetting by
G C Typeset Ltd., Bolton, Lancashire

CONTENTS

ILLUSTRATIONS

PREFACE

When I first read *The Faerie Queene* I enjoyed bits of it but had little idea what it meant. My own students usually have similar reactions, and it is my rather incoherent attempts to explain in tutorials what I think its meaning broadly is that has led to this commentary. There are many good books and articles on Spenser from which I have learned a great deal. There are, equally, good annotated texts. But both have their limitations, since the books tend to discuss, say, Book I in some twenty or thirty pages, inevitably leaving many things unsaid; while the annotated editions need so much room for text that the notes tend to shrink to the bare functional minimum. This commentary tries to get over the problem by offering a full stanza-by-stanza reading or gloss which can be used alongside any of the available texts of the poem. It is limited to the first two books only because these tend to be the most frequently read and also to keep the volume down to a manageable size. Even so there are many things I have had to leave out: this is a purely interpretative account which contains few textual and stylistic comments and no glossary. It is not an attempt to synthesise current views on these books of *The Faerie Queene*. It is, simply, an attempt to explain Spenser's images and allusions in terms of sixteenth-century symbolic modes of thought. At the same time I have tried to avoid making it formidable by relying as little as possible on more obscure sources. I doubt, for instance, if many undergraduate students will go searching for Landino's Commentary on Vergil or for the *Patrologia Latina* to verify my references. But they might want to check references to D. C. Allen's excellent book on Renaissance mythography, *Mysteriously Meant* (1970); or to Edgar Wind's *Pagan Mysteries* (1967); or Jean Seznec's *Survival of the Pagan Gods* (1953); and so I have used these and other authoritative secondary sources where practicable. Among these, incidentally, is Dewitt T. Starnes's and E. W. Talbert's *Classical Myth and Legend in Renaissance Dictionaries* (1955), which shows how much Spenser himself got at second hand.

I have found the *Variorum Spenser* invaluable. All Spenser

quotations are from this edition except that here and in all other relevant cases I have expanded contractions and normalised *i, j, u,* and *v*. All Chaucer quotations are from *The Works of Geoffrey Chaucer*, ed. F. N. Robinson, second edn., 1957; and all Biblical quotations are from the Geneva Bible (1560).

Mary Syner typed the manuscript beautifully, and I am most grateful for her patience and good sense; John Jump encouraged me more than he perhaps realised and I would like this book to be a tribute, however small and unworthy, to his memory; Stevie Davies gave me knowledge and understanding.

ABBREVIATIONS

PERIODICALS

E.C.—*Essays in Criticism*
E.L.H.—*A Journal of English Literary History*
H.L.Q.—*Huntington Library Quarterly*
J.W.I.—*Journal of the Warburg Institute*
M.L.N.—*Modern Language Notes*
M.P.—*Modern Philology*
P.Q.—*Philological Quarterly*
R.E.S.—*Review of English Studies*
S.P.—*Studies in Philology*

OTHER WORKS
(books included here are not mentioned in the Select Bibliography)

Agrippa—H. C. Agrippa. *Three Books of Occult Philosophy,* tr. J. F. London, 1651.

Allen—D. C. Allen. *Mysteriously Meant: The Rediscovery of Pagan Symbolism and Allegorical Interpretation in the Renaissance.* Baltimore and London, 1970.

Alpers—P. J. Alpers. *The Poetry of 'The Faerie Queene'.* Princeton, N. J., 1967.

Ansell Robin—P. Ansell Robin. *Animal Lore in English Literature.* London, 1932.

Berger—H. Berger. *The Allegorical Temper: Vision and Reality in Book II of Spenser's 'Faerie Queene'.* Yale Studies in English, CXXXVII. New Haven and London, 1957.

Chew—S. C. Chew. *The Pilgrimage of Life.* New Haven and London, 1962.

Cullen—P. Cullen. *Infernal Triad: The Flesh, The World, and the Devil in Spenser and Milton.* Princeton, N.J., 1974.

Curtius—E. R. Curtius. *European Literature and the Latin Middle Ages,* tr. W. R. Trask. Bollingen Series, XXXVI. Princeton, N. J., 1967.

de Vries—A. de Vries. *Dictionary of Symbols and Imagery.* Amsterdam and London, 1974.

Evans—E. P. Evans. *Animal Symbolism in Ecclesiastical Architecture.* London, 1896.

Fowler—A. D. S. Fowler. *Spenser and the Numbers of Time.* London, 1964.

F.Q.—*The Faerie Queene.*

Ger. Lib.—Torquato Tasso. *Gerusalemme Liberata.* 1581.

Hamilton—A. C. Hamilton. *The Structure of Allegory in 'The Faerie Queene'.* Oxford, 1961.

Hankins—J. E. Hankins. *Source and Meaning in Spenser's Allegory: A Study of 'The Faerie Queene'.* Oxford, 1971.

Katzenellenbogen—A. Katzenellenbogen. *Allegories of the Virtues and Vices in Mediaeval Art.* London, 1939.

Kermode—F. Kermode. *Shakespeare, Spenser, Donne.* London, 1971.

Klibansky—R. Klibansky, E. Panofsky, F. Saxl. *Saturn and Melancholy.* London, 1964.

Lotspeich—H. G. Lotspeich. *Classical Mythology in the Poetry of Edmund Spenser.* Princeton Studies in English, IX. 1932.

Mâle—E. Mâle. *The Gothic Image: Relgious Art in France of the Thirteenth Century,* tr. Dora Nussey. London, 1961.

Met.—Ovid. *Metamorphoses.*

O.E.D.—*Oxford English Dictionary.*

O.F.—Ludovico Ariosto. *Orlando Furioso.* 1532.

Percival—H. M. Percival, ed. *'The Faerie Queene', Book I.* London, 1921.

Rathborne—I. E. Rathborne. *The Meaning of Spenser's Fairyland.* Columbia University Studies in English and Comparative Literature, CXXXI. Morningside Heights, N.Y., 1937.

Ripa—C. Ripa. *Iconologia.* Rome, 1603.

Smith—W. Smith, ed. *Dictionary of Greek and Roman Biography and Mythology.* 3 vols. London, 1862–4.

Starnes and Talbert—D. T. Starnes and E. W. Talbert. *Classical Myth and Legend in Renaissance Dictionaries.* Chapel Hill, N.C., 1955.

Tervarent—G. de Tervarent. *Attributs et Symboles dans l'Art Profane 1450–1600.* Travaux d'Humanisme et Renaissance, XXIX. Geneva, 1958.

Tuve—R. Tuve. *Allegorical Imagery: Some Mediaeval Books and their Posterity.* Princeton, N.J., 1966.

Var. Sp.—*The Works of Edmund Spenser: A Variorum Edition.* Ed. E. Greenlaw, C. G. Osgood, F. M. Padelford, *et al.* 11 vols. Baltimore, Md., 1932–57.

Wind—E. Wind. *Pagan Mysteries in the Renaissance.* Rev. edn. Harmondsworth, 1967.

Yates—F. A. Yates. *Astraea: The Imperial Theme in the Sixteenth Century.* London and Boston, 1975.

GENERAL INTRODUCTION

Spenser begins *The Faerie Queene*, as Vergil began his *Aeneid*, by looking back to his earlier achievements in pastoral poetry. With traditional but nevertheless genuine humility the shepherd-poet Colin Clout of *The Shepheardes Calender* of 1579 affirms his unworthiness of his epic task and implores his 'sacred Muse' for aid. Yet for Spenser as for Vergil there were clear similarities in theme between pastoral and epic, for both deal with the golden age; and the similarities are made clearer in the case of *The Faerie Queene* by the language that Spenser adopted for his epic, a language showing evidence of dialect and archaic, Middle English, forms. It is very like the language of *The Shepheardes Calender*; but there it fulfilled the simple demands of decorum: rustic-sounding language for a rustic poem. In his epic it fulfils a more subtle decorum, since it is designed to take the reader back linguistically to the Middle Ages of chivalric, Arthurian romance and so imply that the chivalric ideal had actually been revived in Elizabeth's court and that Elizabeth was herself the second Arthur (see Introduction to Book II). And in being remote the poem's language reinforces what the topographical setting implies, which is, in fact, the opposite of the above: that fairyland is a world remote from immediate mundane reality and from the diplomatic, political, and sexual intrigues of the Virgin Queen's court; and that it is a place from which the 'real' world is seen as a mist or shadow because fairyland is near enough to the classical and Arthurian golden ages to know what the virtues in their pristine forms really are. From its perspective we see the decay of nature, the running down of the world from its antique strengths, and Elizabeth's court, the moral and cultural heart of the State, as a parody of the ideal.

Spenser's preoccupation with language was not just the poet's natural obsession with his own medium. It was a crucial aspect of his humanism and a carefully-thought-out contribution to Elizabethan nationalism; for he was heir to the study of Graeco-Roman culture that had been increasing in impetus for the last two centuries on the Continent, and particularly in Italy. The humanists

rediscovered and studied seriously for the first time certain aspects
of the achievements of the ancients. Vergil had been known to the
Middle Ages and so had some of Cicero. Now more of Cicero was
discovered (together with previously 'lost' authors like Lucretius,
Tacitus, and Manilius) and Greek and the literature of Greece,
previously little known, became widely studied, though usually in
Latin translation. The study of the humanities was the study of the
grammar, rhetoric, literature, history, and moral philosophy of the
ancients. In them the humanist scholars found a complete
programme for living well in the world (see J. A. Mazzeo,
Renaissance and Revolution (1967)).

   The study of the ancients for their moral wisdom was
accompanied by the development of a cyclical view of history. The
glories of the ancient world in letters, sculpture, and architecture
that had faded in the medieval darkness were now to be rekindled:
redeunt Saturnia regna (Saturn's golden age kingdoms were to be
restored; Vergil's *Eclogues*, IV). Hence the imitation of classical
models in literature and other arts in the Renaissance. At the same
time the secular and religious hegemony of the Pope was breaking
down more than it had done already, and while the scholars and the
schools were harking back to antique models in their reaction to
medieval scholasticism there was a simultaneous and fierce
assertion of independent nationhood. In religion this was marked in
part by the Reformation. In the world of letters it showed itself in a
proud championing of the vernacular tongues. Although this
movement in favour of the vernacular had been well under way in
the fourteenth century (Petrarch, Dante, Boccaccio) it now
increased under the influence of the linguistic disciplines forged by
the humanists to enable them to understand the languages of the
ancients without the accretions, misunderstandings, and
misinterpretations that had developed during the intervening
centuries. (This also included the study of the Hebrew and Greek
Biblical texts, and a consequent diminishing of the influence and
authority of the Vulgate which was now, for example, no longer the
text used for the most important English translations of the Bible.)
The fostering of ancient languages and literatures, therefore,
encouraged the development of native languages and literatures.
Spenser's case is typical. His main model for *The Faerie Queene* is
the *Aeneid*, but he also has his eyes set firmly on his great English
predecessor Chaucer, 'well of English undefyled' (*F.Q.*, IV.ii.32); so

that in him the native tradition fuses with the Graeco-Roman tradition to produce the first recognisably English epic poem.

The purpose of this poem is political: to celebrate England under Elizabeth, whose grandfather Henry VII had brought peace to England after civil war as the Emperor Augustus had brought peace to Rome after civil war. Augustus and Elizabeth were both, popular mythology said, restorers of the golden age, and this is one example of how the humanist view of historical cycles underlines *The Faerie Queene* (though, as I have said, the Tudors, who regarded themselves as being descended from Arthur, saw themselves primarily as the restorers of the Arthurian golden age. More than that, they were the revivers of New Troy, since they also traced their ancestry back to Brutus, Aeneas's great-grandson, who, it was said, had given his name to Britain and established Troy novant as its capital city. See notes to Book II, canto x).

The Faerie Queene of the poem is Gloriana, by whom, Spenser tells us in his prefatory *Letter of the Authors*, 'I meane glory in my generall intention, but in my particular I conceive the most excellent and glorious person of our soveraine the Queene'. The overall story of the poem is Prince Arthur's quest for Gloriana, whom he has seen in a vision (I.ix.13–15). In the incomplete poem as we have it (six books only were finished: I–III were published in 1590; the last three were added to, and published together with, the first three, in 1596) Arthur never finds Gloriana. When he did at last find her, their coming together would presumably have signified on the political level that Elizabeth was literally the second Arthur. On the spiritual level his attainment of her would have meant that he had reached a state of contemplative ecstasy: Gloriana as an emanation of the divine sun. Clearly Spenser is obliged here to the medieval idealisation of woman, seen in the cult of the Virgin Mary and Dante's Beatrice; but in *The Faerie Queene* Spenser's informing philosophy is Neoplatonic, since Gloriana is blazing light, and so a reminder of the ideal world where all is perfect, light, and stable. Spenser had read the Florentine Neoplatonists Marsilio Ficino and Pico della Mirandola, who flourished a century earlier, but he was in any case an instinctive Platonist, rarely writing more personally and movingly than when, having contemplated this world of change and death, he pauses to imagine God's world of ultimate light and rest, as in the last two stanzas of the *Two Cantos of Mutabilitie* or in the *Hymne of Heavenly Beautie*, which might well be the best possible commentary on virtually every poem he wrote.

'Neoplatonism' is shorthand for the individual philosophies of those many thinkers and writers from Antiquity through the early Christian centuries to the Renaissance and beyond who have espoused aspects of Plato's writings while at the same time modifying them in accordance with their own emotions, religions, and insights. The main Neoplatonic ideas at work in *The Faerie Queene*, though, can be summarised briefly. They are (1) the belief that there is an ideal world of spirit, stasis, and perfection beyond the earth which is material and imperfect, receiving divine influence only as it has been attenuated by its journey through the celestial (planetary) spheres; (2) the belief that the soul is immortal and belongs to and comes from the ideal world and that it is imprisoned in the body which, with its appetites, seeks constantly to drag it down to its own, bestial, level; (3) nevertheless, the soul still participates in the pure *mens* (mind, intellect) of God, retains a memory of its divine origins, and so, even while in the body, can purge itself of surrounding material dross and contemplate divine beauty. The Platonic and Neoplatonic symbol for this beauty is the heavenly Venus, or Venus Urania. To devote oneself to contemplating her is to pursue the contemplative life. But there is another Venus, the natural or worldly Venus Pandemos, who is the embodiment of ultimate beauty in the material world and who, rather than appealing to mind, the contemplative faculty, appeals instead to lower human powers, imagination, reason, and the senses. Finally, there is sensuality pure and simple – bestial love, or lust. This is desire unmotivated by the quest for beauty and is what Phaedria and Acrasia represent in Book II. (See Erwin Panofsky, *Studies in Iconology* (1962), 141ff.; and Wind, 138ff.)

In fact, the Neoplatonic universe is bound together by love which emanates from God and descends to earth whence it returns in a perpetual cycle. The individual human being, moreover, can participate in this cycle (Arthur questing for Gloriana; Redcrosse seeking Una). The cycle is triadic, and the terms for its parts are *emanatio* (the overflowing of divine love), *raptio* (the soul moved to rapture by the recognition of that love), and *remeatio* (the return to God in a state of joy: this is both the final return at death and the momentary return of a contemplative ecstasy).

A related Neoplatonic concept is that of the One and the Many, which Spenser utilises in many places in his poem and notably in his descriptions of Una in Book I and Belphoebe in Book II; for they are composite characters, combining attributes of two planetary deities, Venus and Diana (see I.vi.16n., and II.iii.21–30n.). The philosophical implications of this simple-seeming detail are considerable. To the Neoplatonist the One is ultimate, infinite, and unknowable; all we can perceive of it on earth is fragmentary. But in itself it reconciles all opposites, and so intellectual images for the divine in Neoplatonic thought (as in the symbolic languages of all religions) are based on paradox and the reconciliation of opposites: a Venus (love) combined with a Diana (virginity) or a Mars (war). This union of contraries images the final union in the One; and the planetary deities feature in Neoplatonism so frequently because they, together with other mythological figures, were regarded as symbols of divine wisdom, preserved in riddling form to protect them from the uncomprehending common herd. The truth, it was believed, must be veiled (see Wind, Introduction).

One of the difficulties of reading a Renaissance poet, then, is to understand his thematic vocabulary. Spenser, for instance, alludes to a large number of mythological figures; but it is not enough for us to go to classical sources alone to understand what he is getting at. We have, instead, to try to recover current interpretations from encyclopedias, mythological dictionaries, and emblem books. Similarly, we have to remember that allusions to Vergil are to the poems as filtered through the lengthy commentaries of exegetes like Servius (late fourth century), Fulgentius (sixth century), Bernardus Silvestris (twelfth century), and Landino (fifteenth century). It is the same with Homer and Ovid. (See Allen, *passim*.)

Medieval astrology was given new impetus by Neoplatonism, too, which saw each planetary sphere as being imbued with divine energy which it then imparted to the earth and its inhabitants – mineral, vegetable, animal – as influences. This led to the perpetuation of the notion of classifying material phenomena in terms of planetary characteristics and to a perpetuation, too, of the analogical world-view: the lion was a solar creature and therefore 'meant' (symbolically) the attributes accorded to the sun by astrologers, and so forth. Hence everything is potentially emblematic, and often has a multiplicity of meanings which a good poet like Spenser uses to the full as in, for example, the description of Arthur and his shield at I.vii.29ff. My source for much of this information has been Henry Cornelius Agrippa's *Three Books of Occult Philosophy* (Latin edn, 1531; English translation, 1651); this was a well-known work and is to a large extent an orthodox compendium of Renaissance esoteric lore repeated time and again in other such treatises.

In addition I have used particularly Cesare Ripa's *Iconologia* (1593; enlarged edition 1603), an invaluable mine of information about contemporary symbolism which includes allegories of the virtues and vices, mythological figures, countries, the seasons, etc.; descriptions which are the result of humanist scholarship, since they are frequently based on information found in Greek and Roman writers, statues, coins, and medals, as well as bestiaries, encyclopedias and the work of other mythographers. It was intended as a handbook for poets, painters, and sculptors; and Ben Jonson was glad enough of it when he wrote his court masques. It appeared too late for Spenser to have used it in *The Faerie Queene*, of course; nevertheless its material, too, is commonplace, and I have cited it in this commentary as a useful compendium of details which Spenser would have known from other sources.

So far I have not mentioned the word 'allegory'. But since Spenser, in his prefatory *Letter*, calls the poem 'a continued Allegory', a few words should be said here on the problem of allegorical levels. Spenser and his contemporaries were still familiar with the habit of multiple allegory applied to the Bible by the Church Fathers in their attempts to hear every nuance of God's Word. Its basis was typological: that is, the people and events in the Old Testament were understood as foreshadowings of Christ who comprehended within himself the whole of human history. They are the types; Christ is the antitype in whom human history is fulfilled (hence classical heroes – Hercules, Orpheus, and so on – could also become types of Christ). A characteristic medieval view – the one voiced by Aquinas – was that God himself had made the Bible allegorical, and that the allegory made sense only in the light of Christ and the new law. Allegory is the first symbolic (or spiritual) sense and this is the sense that shows the Old Testament foreshadowing the New; the second spiritual sense is the tropological or moral (showing us how we ought to behave); and the third is the anagogical, which relates to eternal glory and the after life. The primary sense is the literal or historical; and the best-known illustrative example is the often repeated interpretation of Jerusalem, which historically is the Jewish city; allegorically is the Church of Christ; tropologically is the soul of man; and anagogically is the heavenly city. (See Mâle, IV.i, and Joseph A. Galdon, *Typology and Seventeenth-Century Literature* (The Hague, 1975) for general background. Aquinas's statement is in the *Summa Theologica*, Pt I, Q.i, Art. 10. Dante explains the process in his 'Letter to the Can Grande della Scala'.)

Protestantism asserted the primacy of the literal level while at the same time retaining typological readings and, in a slightly different form and with different emphases, the old three spiritual levels (Barbara Lewalski, 'Typology and Poetry: A Consideration of Herbert, Vaughan, and Marvell', in Earl Miner (ed.), *Illustrious Evidence* (Berkeley and Los Angeles, 1975), 41–69). In any case the tradition was alive in secular poetry – the *Divine Comedy, Piers Plowman*, Tasso and Ariosto – and the work of contemporary mythographers who frequently explained myths in terms of their spiritual and moral significance and their hypothetical historical meaning.

The senses were never regarded as operating simultaneously all the time by Biblical exegetes; nor do they do so in secular poetry. In fact in the case of *The Faerie Queene* the question really arises only in connection with Book I, since this is the book that starts the poem, announces its main theme, and embodies its theological content by defining holiness, the ideal of Christian knighthood and sanctification in the light of which the other knights in the subsequent books undertake their quests. (See Introduction to Book I, below.) For many Protestant Englishmen, incidentally, their understanding of the Bible's hidden message would have been that of the explanatory marginal glosses in the Geneva Bible of 1560. I have relied heavily on these particularly in annotating Book I to illustrate an accepted Protestant interpretation of any given Biblical passage Spenser might be alluding to.

Lastly, I should mention Spenser's indebtedness to contemporary Italian writers of epic, especially Tasso and Ariosto. They had preceded him in producing vernacular epics which combined classical and medieval chivalric elements and it was only natural that he should turn to them for ideas and inspiration. Sometimes the borrowings are incidental; sometimes more extensive, as is the case with Acrasia's Bower in II.xii, which is modelled closely on Tasso's *Gerusalemme Liberata*, XV and XVI. But in imitating the Italians (including Vergil) Spenser was trying to outdo them, and to remind his audience that the Muses, whose lamentations he had recorded in *The Teares of the Muses* of 1591, no longer needed to weep.

The Legende of the Knight of the Red Crosse, or Of Holinesse

INTRODUCTION

Book I is about spiritual regeneration: the quest, as far as mortal, fallen man can fulfil it, for the Christian virtues, which are embodied in Dame Caelia's House of Holiness in canto x. These, after the recognition of sin and repentance, replace the concupiscence and pride inherited from the Fall. It is at this stage in his development — in canto x — that Redcrosse, the questing knight of the first book, comes to recognise and assume his role as an instrument of divine grace; a role that will lead, as he finds out, to his sanctification. At the beginning we see him in company with Una. It is his task to liberate her parents, the king and queen of Eden, from a brazen tower in which they are kept imprisoned by a dragon. The quest is complicated by the intrusion of Archimago and Duessa (called Fidessa for most of the book) who test Redcrosse by confronting him with the fundamental Satanic attributes of darkness and doubleness. Deceived by Archimago (a metaphor for his own, fallen, spiritual inadequacy: even saints are human) Redcrosse abandons Una for her parody, Duessa. He then proceeds to Lucifera's worldly House of Pride in canto iv (the structural and moral opposite to Dame Caelia's house) and succumbs to the giant Orgoglio (another form of pride) and then Despair (cantos vii to ix). Viewed tropologically, his progress follows the traditional sequence of temptations with which Satan confronted Christ in the wilderness and which, theologians argued, had also tempted Adam in the Garden of Eden: the Flesh, the World, and the Devil (see Cullen).

As St George (potentially at least), Redcrosse stands for

England; Una is the true Church, the one faith (Elizabethan Anglicanism; that is, the primitive Catholic Church restored, purged of Roman Catholicism's temporal excesses). He is separated from her by Archimago and Duessa (the papal Antichrist) but they are finally reunited and betrothed, thus symbolising the reunion under Elizabeth, after Mary's Catholic interregnum, of country and true faith. This is the allegorical level of Book I; and it is to this level that most of the echoes of Revelation — that Biblical book indispensable to Protestant reformers which seemed in every chapter to be fulminating against and heralding the overthrow of the infernal powers of Roman Catholicism — belong. Allegory becomes, simply but importantly for the contemporary reader, Protestant propaganda. The echoes of Revelation at the end of Book I as Una and Redcrosse are betrothed must also be seen anagogically, as a shadowing forth of the marriage of the Church to her bridegroom, Christ. This is the ultimate vision to which not only this particular book but the poem as a whole (complete or incomplete, it does not matter) tends. It is only Spenser's faith in the inevitability of that marriage and in the Heavenly Jerusalem that makes sense of Redcrosse's painful progress from darkness to light, of Arthur's quest for Gloriana, and the parallel quests of the other knights in *The Faerie Queene*.

It seems, finally, that Spenser wished to underline the inevitable and eventually triumphant journey of Redcrosse in an extra-narrative way by having it unfold, canto by canto, according to a progression governed by number symbolism. (The tradition Spenser used derived from Pythagoras and Plato, was adopted by Christian Biblical exegetes, and was ubiquitous in the Middle Ages and Renaissance: see Vincent F. Hopper, *Medieval Number Symbolism* (New York, 1938); Christopher Butler, *Number Symbolism* (1970); A. D. S. Fowler, *Spenser and the Numbers of Time* (1964); S. K. Heninger, *Touches of Sweet Harmony* (San Marino, Calif., 1974).) In Book I, more so than in the other books, the significance of the canto number sometimes, but not invariably, expresses the meaning of the events within it; for if God had 'ordered all things in measure, number & weight' (Wisdom of Solomon 11:17) why should not, Spenser probably reasoned, Redcrosse's Christian pilgrimage be patterned in the same way? Where such symbolism is likely, I have indicated it briefly in a headnote to the relevant canto.

PROEM

1 Spenser echoes *Aeneid*, I.1–4 (the opening found in Renaissance editions, but now often omitted) in which Vergil surveys his progress as a poet from a writer of pastoral verse through the middle-style *Georgics* to epic: 'I am the man who formerly made the melody of simple poetry with the oaten reed . . . but now I turn to the horrors of Mars'. Spenser consciously models his own progress from the pastoral *Shepheardes Calender* (1579) to the *F.Q.* on Vergil's, thereby making himself Elizabeth's and England's epic poet as Vergil had been Augustus's and Rome's. Other poets' echoes of the passage are discussed by Barbara Lewalski, *Milton's Brief Epic: The Genre, Meaning, and Art of 'Paradise Regained'* (1966), 116–17. The trumpet is Mars's instrument (e.g. Claudian, *Epithalamium* X.195ff.). The last line, balancing the Vergilian opening, affirms Spenser's allegiance to modern as well as ancient Italian epic, since it echoes *O.F.*, I.i ('Of ladies, cavaliers, arms, and loves, of courtesies and bold undertakings I sing') and thereby offers a deliberate modification in the light of chivalric romantic epic of Vergil's subsequent proposition, 'Of arms and the man I sing'. Love and battle were the two chief pursuits of chivalry, but Spenser includes love because of its fundamental significance as a cosmic principle in Neoplatonic thought (see General Introduction, above), and he links war and love to imply the harmonious union of Mars and Venus (on which see st. 3n. below).

2 This is the traditional invocation to the Muse, but, in accordance with the Neoplatonic notion of the union of opposites, Spenser's Muse is a composite figure. He calls upon the 'chiefe' of the nine Muses, usually either Urania, Muse of astronomy and the highest knowledge (Kathi Meyer-Baer, *Music of the Spheres and the Dance of Death*, 33, and fig. 96), or Calliope, Muse of heroic poetry (Hesiod, *Theogony*, 79). But in Spenser's own *Teares of the Muses*, 53, Clio, Muse of fame and history, is the 'eldest Sister' and, incidentally, gives her name to Cleopolis, capital of Spenser's fairyland (see vii.46n.), although, as Lotspeich, 84 reminds us, epic gets its subject matter from history and so the Renaissance did not distinguish carefully between the roles of Calliope and Clio. Thus the trumpet of st. 1, as well as being Mars's emblem, is an attribute of both Muses (Ripa, 346–51, *s.v. Muse*, and Tervarent, col. 279), while a book (the 'antique rolles' of this stanza, which we encounter in II.x.70ff., where Sir Guyon reads the history of fairyland) is the usual attribute of Calliope, shared sometimes by Clio (Ripa, 351; Tervarent, col. 281). The reference to 'holy Virgin' adds religious overtones: Spenser probably means the Virgin Mary in her Dantean role as leader of the nine complementary orders of angels (Meyer-Baer, 194), which is to be read as a compliment to the Virgin Queen Elizabeth, the subject and ultimate inspiration of his epic, since she was regarded as the Virgin of the new Anglican religion (see vii.30n.). For further comments on the Muse of the *F.Q.*, see xi.5–7n. 'Tanaquill' is Elizabeth, as at II.x.76. In classical mythology she was the wife of Tarquinius Priscus and known in the Renaissance as an exemplum of chastity and as a queen of masculine ability (C. B. Millican, 'Spenser's and Drant's Poetic Names for Elizabeth: Tanaquil, Gloria, and Una', *H.L.Q.*, II (1938–9)). The 'Briton Prince' is Arthur, whose quest for Gloriana (note the pun on 'glorious' in the next stanza) is discussed at ix.13–15n.

3   The '<u>impe</u>' is Cupid: for the common notion that Jove was his father, see Starnes and Talbert, 89–90, and on the bow and arrows as his attributes, Tervarent, cols. 31–2, and Erwin Panofsky, *Studies in Iconology*, 101–2, where the tradition of two bows – one white, the other dark – is mentioned. Having inspired Arthur with his passionate love for Gloriana (ix.16) he can now lay aside his dark, ebony bow, symbolising love's pains (ebony is associated with sleep and hence with death: *Met.*, XI.610) and, without it, together with Venus, become the symbol of cosmic love, of which Gloriana is herself an embodiment (the unarmed Cupid as symbol of cosmic love appears in Spenser's *Hymne in Honour of Love*, 57ff. Because they represent the pangs of 'base desire' rather than divine love, Cupid's arrows and bow are also rejected at II.iii.23, II.ix.34, and III.vi.49, where, in the paradisal Garden of Adonis, he is reunited with Psyche, expressing the union of divine love and the human soul: see ix.13–15n.) In invoking 'triumphant *Mart* / In loves and gentle jollities arrayd', Spenser alludes to the taming of Mars by Venus, an ancient emblem of harmony that was of particular importance to Renaissance Neoplatonists since it expressed their vision of the Divine as a union of contraries (see II.iv.16–17n. and II.vi.29–37n.).

4 The 'Great Lady' is Elizabeth. The comparison of the monarch with the sun (Phoebus) is traditional (see II.ii.40–2n.), and the image presented in this stanza as a whole receives a pictorial gloss in the chronologically later picture in the National Portrait Gallery by Marcus Gheeraerts the Younger, known as the 'Ditchley' portrait, of Queen Elizabeth standing on a map of England with black clouds behind her, light before her, accompanied by a verse which describes her as 'The prince of light' (Yates, plate 13). But the reference to her as 'Goddesse' in connection with an island implies that she is also Venus, who was especially associated with the islands of Cythera and Cyprus; and she is 'heavenly bright' because she is the Venus Urania, celestial beauty, which is contemplated by man's highest faculty (see General Introduction). Elizabeth appears implicitly as Venus in *F.Q.*, VI.x.11ff. (and compare the 'April' eclogue in *The Shepheardes Calender*). For Venus symbolism in Book I, see i.48n., ii.36–8n., iv.6–7n. and 8–10n., vi.16n., vii.30n., x.4n. and 29–31n., xi.33–4n., and xii.21–3n. The emphasis on light in this stanza is Neoplatonic; and the 'glorious type' – i.e. image – of Elizabeth at l.7 is Una as well as Gloriana herself.

CANTO I

1 On the level of theological allegory Redcrosse's armour is 'the whole armour of God' that enables the Christian 'to stand against the assauts of the devil' (Ephesians 6:11ff.; the identification is made by Spenser in his prefatory *Letter of the Authors*; and Chew, 140–3 discusses the influence of the Pauline passage on the concept of the Christian knight in the sixteenth century). St George's shield was traditionally silver (or white) with a red cross, though the allusion to Ephesians 6 continues: it is 'the shield of faith, wherewith ye may quench all the fyrie dartes of the wicked', the supreme item of equipment in the Christian's armoury and one which receives the particular attention of the dragon at xi.40–3 (see n.). Redcrosse learns his identity as St George at x.66, though it is made explicit to the reader at ii.11–12. Apocalyptic overtones are present, too: at his initial appearance Redcrosse recalls the battling Christ with white shield emblazoned with a red cross found in medieval illustrations of Revelation (Kermode, 14 and n.). The 'angry steede' symbolises the untamed passions (e.g., Wind, 145 and n., 147n., and fig. 41; cf. Sansloy at iii.33) – a reminder that the knight is in quest of holiness and as yet no more than a fallen, intemperate man. See v.8n., viii.38–41n., and ix.37n. on his irascible or choleric tendencies, which raise the perennial problem of the relationship between culpable wrath and knightly heroism (discussed by Alpers, 337ff., and Curtius, 171). The problem is particularly crucial to the writer of Christian epic, since epic was traditionally concerned with warfare but anger was the sin that was opposed to – and answered by – patience, Christ's own virtue (see viii.38–41n., and x.23n.). On the irascible faculty in the soul, see Introduction to Book II, and II.ix.33–5n.

2   The opening lines recall Revelation 1:18: 'I . . . am alive, but I was dead: & beholde, I am alive for evermore'. 'Faithfull true' is a reminder of the traditional linking of *fides* (faith) and *veritas* (truth), mentioned by Tuve, 121ff., and cf. vi.31, but 'too solemne sad' implies a self-sufficient pride which will confront him in the joyless Sansjoy in I.iv and v and, more horrifyingly, in his temptation by the melancholic Despair at I.ix (see esp. 33–4n. and 35–6n.). The theme has its origins in 2 Corinthians 7:10: 'For godlie sorowe causeth repentance unto salvacion, not to be repented of: but the worldlie sorowe causeth death'. There might, in addition, be a suggestion of the kind of puritan joylessness satirised in Sir Huddibras at II.ii.12–20n. Anger and sadness are two of Gregory the Great's five spiritual vices (the others are vainglory – encountered in cantos iv and v in the person of Lucifera – envy and avarice: an indication of how long and hard Redcrosse's journey will be (Katzenellenbogen, 11)).

3   On Gloriana, see Introduction and vii.46n. and ix.13–15n. The dragon, finally encountered in canto xi, is based on Revelation 12:9 and 20:2 – 'And he toke the dragon that olde serpent, which is the devil and Satan' – conflated with the dragon of the St George legend (on which see st. 4n.).

4   The 'lovely Ladie' is named as Una at st. 45. She represents Truth and Oneness in contrast to the multiplicity of evil as well as the one true Anglican Church which, to Elizabethans, was the primitive Catholic Church restored (see ii.22n.). As head of the Church as well as the State Elizabeth united in herself, as the One Monarch, the two roles of religious and secular sovereign. Her oneness in this respect contrasts with the long–standing battle for supremacy on the Continent between Pope and Emperor – a two-ness symbolised by Duessa on her appearance in canto ii. Una as a cult name for Elizabeth is discussed by Yates, 47, 51, 65–6, 72–3, and Millican, 'Spenser's and Drant's Poetic Names for Elizabeth'; see also Roy C. Strong, 'The Popular Celebration of the Accession Day of Queen Elizabeth I', *J.W.I.*, XXI (1958). Fowler, 3–8, considers Una's name from the point of view of Pythagorean–Platonic number symbolism (see headnote to canto ii, below).

The simplicity of Una's appearance suggests Protestantism's rejection of Catholicism's splendid trappings of temporal power: in this respect she is opposed by Fidessa–Duessa at ii.13 (see n.) and Lucifera in canto iv. Her ass is an emblem of humility (Zechariah 9:9: 'beholde, thy King cometh unto thee: he is juste & saved, poore and riding upon an asse'; identified typologically in the Geneva gloss as Christ, which compares Matthew 21:5ff., Christ's entry into Jerusalem on an ass. It is an important aspect of Book I's circular structure that the Matthew passage should be recalled at the beginning of the final canto when Una's parents are released after Redcrosse's victory over the dragon: see xii. 6–8n.). The ass's whiteness, emblematic of purity, comes from Judges 5:10, 'Speake ye that ride on white asses' (i.e., the governors, according to the Geneva gloss). For additional symbolic implications, see vi.19n. Relevant meanings of the lamb are – as well as innocence – patience, gentleness, and humility (Tervarent, cols. 2–3). It is also a symbol of Christ, as in John 1:29 ('the lambe of God, which taketh away the sinne of the worlde'). In the St George story as told in Jacobus de Voragine's late-thirteenth-century *Legenda Aurea* (translated and published by Caxton in 1487 as *The Golden Legend*) sheep were offered as sacrifices to a dragon which was terrorising a city. When the supply grew short children were sacrificed, and one day the king's daughter was chosen by lot. As she was standing waiting to be devoured (in some versions of the tale she is accompanied by a lamb) St George rode up, wounded the dragon, led it to the city, and killed it (see *Var. Sp.*, I, appendix iv, and S. Baring Gould, *Curious Myths of the Middle Ages*, ch.

XIII). An engraving by Marcus Gheeraerts the Elder shows St George fighting the dragon accompanied by the girl and a lamb in which the lamb is identified as 'Ecclesia Christi', the (Protestant) Church of Christ (Tervarent, col. 3, citing A. M. Hind, *Engraving in England in the 16th and 17th Centuries* (Cambridge, 1952), I. 121, plate 51). For the Neoplatonic significance of Una's veil, see iii.4n.

5 The girl in the St George legend is a princess; but Una's lineage alludes to Isaiah 49:23: 'And Kings shalbe thy nourcing fathers, and Quenes shalbe thy nources' (Geneva gloss: 'Meaning, that Kings shalbe converted to ye Gospel and bestow their power, & autoritie for the preservation of the Church'). Spenser's own meaning is primarily political (see ii.22n.) with the further implication, made explicit at vii.43, that Una is the daughter of Adam and Eve, rulers 'over all the earth' (Genesis 1:26) until their fall into sin.

6 There seems little justification for an allegorical reading of the dwarf (Prudence was suggested by Kitchin, *Var. Sp.*, I.178; the Flesh by Morley: see Percival, 161). Jove puring rain down on to the earth is a classical commonplace (e.g. Vergil, *Georgics*, II.325–6), though the suggestion here is that this is a divinely-ordained test for Redcrosse.

7–9 Redcrosse and Una find themselves in 'the wandring wood' (st. 13) of Error (Latin *errare* = to wander). The episode anticipates in little the overall pattern of Book I, where the notion of straying is ever-present after Redcrosse has abandoned Una (e.g., iii.8) and culminates in Despair's temptation at ix.43–4. Specifically, the escape into this 'shadie grove' looks forward to 'the coole shade' of ii.29, and to vii.2ff. where Redcrosse, as in canto ii, is accompanied by Duessa and rests in 'a gloomy glade' listening to the singing of birds (the birdsong as included here is one of the six often deliberately seductive charms of landscape recognised by rhetoricians since late Antiquity: Curtius, 197; the implication is that the wood is in the tradition of the *locus amoenus* or pleasant place, on which see vii.2–4n.). The 'pathes and alleies wide, / With footing worne' anticipate the 'broad high way . . . / All bare through peoples feet' which leads to Lucifera's palace (iv.2n.) and both contrast with the 'streight and narrow' way into the House of

Holiness (x.5n.). There are additional suggestions of the wild and gloomy wood away from the true path in which Dante finds himself at the beginning of the *Divine Comedy* (*Inferno*, I; the parallel is discussed by Hamilton, 35 ff., who also cites Ecclesiasticus 4:17–18: 'she wil walke with him by croked waies and bring him unto feare, and drede, and torment him with her discipline until she have tryed his soule . . .') and of the ancient forest which Aeneas enters before passing into the underworld (glossed in Servius's late fourth or early fifth-century commentary on the *Aeneid* as the area where beastliness and the passions predominate: see William Nelson, *The Poetry of Edmund Spenser*, 159). A useful general gloss on the Error episode comes from St Augustine's *Soliloquies*, ch. IV: 'O Lord; who art the Light, the Way, the Truth, the Life; in whom there is no darkness, errour, vanity nor death: the Light, without which there is darkness; the Way, without which there is wandring; the Truth, without which there is errour; the Life, without which there is death: say, Lord, let there be light, and I shall see Light, and eschew darkness; I shall see the way and avoid wandring; I shall see the truth, and shun errour; I shall see Life, and escape death: Illuminate, O illuminate my blind soul, which sitteth in darkness, and the shadow of death: and direct my feet in the way of peace' (cited in Francis Quarles, *Emblemes* (1635), IV.ii in connection with Psalms 119:5, 'Oh that my waies were directed to kepe thy statutes').

The catalogue of trees is a rhetorical commonplace that comes from *Met.*, X.90ff. and other classical sources (Curtius, 194–5; *Var. Sp.*, I.179–80) and was followed by Chaucer, *Parlement of Foules*, 176ff. to which, as Chaucer's conscious successor, Spenser is most indebted here. (Chaucer's narrator enters this wood overcome by error, ll. 146ff., as do Dante and Redcrosse.) The attributes of the trees are traditional and express for the most part worldly preoccupations which 'delight' but lead one astray (st. 10): as Cullen, 28–9, reminds us, Eve fell through admiring a tree. The wandering is Redcrosse's rather than Una's (st. 12–13) and his error is embodied in the monstrous Error herself. The 'sayling Pine' recalls, among others, Horace, *Epodes*, XVI.57 (ship of pine) and *Parlement of Foules*, 179 ('The saylynge fyr'); the 'Cedar proud and tall' conflates Isaiah 37:24 (the 'hie cedres' of Lebanon; the same verse mentions 'faire fyrre trees', incidentally) with Ezekiel 31:3ff. (cedar as an emblem of temporal pride); the 'vine-prop

Elme' is in Ovid and the Chaucer passage ('piler elm', l.177) but
was an emblematic commonplace signifying fidelity in love
(Whitney, *A Choice of Emblemes*, 62; Wind, 112 and n.); the
poplar is associated with weeping, as in *Met.*, II.346ff. and X.91
(the mourning Heliades changed into poplars, their tears turned to
amber); the 'builder Oake' is straight from Chaucer, l. 176, as is the
aspen, l. 180 ('the asp for shaftes pleyne'); the connection of the
cypress with death is common and ancient (cf. vi.13–14n.; *Aeneid*,
VI.216, 'funeral cypresses'); the laurel, reward for military prowess,
is also dedicated to Apollo, god of poetry, and awarded to poets
(*Met.*, I.553ff., Tervarent, cols. 231–3); the fir weeps resin; the
willow is traditionally associated with unhappiness in love, as in
Merchant of Venice, V.i.9–12; Chaucer, 180, has 'The shetere
[shooter] ew', though he follows this with the aspen 'for shaftes'
(see above) rather than 'The Birch'; the sallow is a shrubby willow
that likes wet ground, which is why Spenser connects it with water
mills; like the fir, the myrrh bleeds gum (for the story of Myrrha see
Met., X.312ff., esp. 499ff.): Spenser alludes either to the gum
oozing from the wounded tree or to the medicinal effects of that
gum when used by physicians, who regarded it as 'good against
Tumors, old Ulcers, green Wounds, Gangrenes, Fistula's &c.'
(William Salmon, *Pharmacopoeia Londinensis; or, the New
London Dispensatory*, I.viii,166); the beech is perhaps 'warlike'
because occasionally used in victory garlands (de Vries, 43); the
ash was used for many purposes, hence it is 'for nothing ill';
Chaucer, 181, has the traditional 'olyve of pes', and Spenser may
allude to fruitfulness as a consequence of peace (see II.ii.31n. in
connection with II Proem 2n.); or more probably he translates
Aeneid, VI.230 ('fertile olive tree'). The 'Platane round' (i.e., plane
tree with large circumference) is known for its largeness and
magnificence (Pausanias, *Description of Greece*, IV.xxxiv.4); the
holm-oak provides wood good for carving (see *O.E.D.*); Spenser's
reference to the internal rottenness of the maple (perhaps recalled
at viii.47) is illuminated by John Lyly, *Euphues* (1579), ed. Arber
(1900), 100: 'Is not . . . dunge [taken] out of the Maple tree by the
Scorpion?'.

10–11   The multiplicity of paths symbolises the difficulty of moral
choice and the manifold nature of error; the labyrinth, too, is a
symbol of moral perplexity (Jonson, *Pleasure Reconciled to Virtue*

(1618), 232–3, in *Complete Masques*, ed. Orgel, 272). The forest–labyrinth as a symbol of error and worldly pleasures, sin and (by extension) the empty speculations of secular philosophers, is considered by John M. Steadman, 'Spenser's *Errour* and the Renaissance Allegorical Tradition', *Neuphilologische Mitteilungen*, LXII (1961), 23 and 30ff. For the maze of pleasure, see *Ger. Lib.*, XIV.76 and XVI.1, 8, and 35.

13–16   Error is a complex figure. She derives ultimately from the monster Echidna, half woman, half snake, who dwells in a cave (Hesiod, *Theogony*, 295ff.) and whose offspring were dedicated to the destruction of mankind. Spenser has her, together with Typhon (on whom see vii.8–10n), as the mother of the slanderous Blatant Beast at VI.vi.9ff.; and she is similar to the half human, half bestial Duessa (ii.40–1, viii.46–8). Echidna was interpreted in the Renaissance as learned error (Steadman, *art.cit.*, 23–9, quoting among other authorities, Valeriano, *Hieroglyphica*, who associates the serpentine coils of the Chimaera's lower body with 'variety of arguments'); but Spenser also has in mind the convention, deriving from Bede and popular in the Middle Ages and Renaissance, of depicting the serpent in representations of the Fall with the face, or face and torso, of a virgin (J. B. Trapp, 'The Iconography of the Fall of Man', in C. A. Patrides (ed.), *Approaches to 'Paradise Lost'* (1968), 262–3). On this level the encounter with Error is a reminder that, as children of Adam, we are constantly faced with the consequences of the Fall and the means of avoiding them. Related images are Ripa's *Inganno* (Deceit), who has serpents' tails instead of legs (*Iconologia*, 228) and is also found in Henry Peacham's *Minerva Britanna* (1612),47; and Peacham's emblem 146, *Icon Peccati* (image of sin), which shows a young man, naked, and with a serpent gnawing at his heart and another wound round his waist. The accompanying verse explains 'Hell's power the Serpent, which his loines doth girt, / A Conscience bad, the other eates his heart'. To sum up: Error represents false learning (secular and religious; as the latter she embodies Catholic doctrine: see D. Douglas Waters, 'Errour's Den and Archimago's Hermitage: Symbolic Lust and Symbolic Witchcraft', *E.L.H.*, XXXIII (1966)), original sin, and fraud or deceit. The climactic battle with the dragon, which this encounter anticipates, occurs in canto xi; for other dragon-serpents in Book I, see vii.31n. In the spatial symbolism of the book Error's cave is echoed in Morpheus's house (i.39ff.), Night's cave at v.21, the dungeons of Lucifera's palace (v.45ff.) and of Orgoglio's castle (viii.37ff.), and Despair's cave at ix.33, which all contrast with the mountain of x.53ff. The basic movement of the book is from depth to height, dark to light, and their moral equivalents, the blindness of ignorance and intellectual and spiritual illumination. On the cave as spiritual blindness, see Hankins, 74, discussing the deep cave of *Aeneid*, VI, in the forest round lake Avernus (ll. 237ff; cf. st. 7–9n. above). But at the beginning of *Aeneid*, VI the Sibyl inhabits a cave and prophesies from it (ll. 42ff.) – symbolising, according to Renaissance interpreters, that truth is hidden (Allen, 152); so that Redcrosse is, initially at least, not so silly to ignore Una and enter the cave. He might well have found truth there, a possibility supported by a familiar variant on the 'Truth unveiled by Time' motif in which Time brings forth his daughter, Truth, from the cave or dungeon in which she has been imprisoned by the forces of Envy, Strife, and Slander (see Plate 1). On at least one occasion (a procession in 1559) the Truth led from her cave was holding an English Bible, symbolising the triumph of the true faith after the death of the Catholic Mary (Chew, 19–20).

17–18   For the significance of Redcrosse's comparison with a lion, see iii.5–9n. and 10–20n., and x.28n. Error's 'speckled taile' is from Hesiod's Echidna, who has speckled skin (*Theogony*, 299). Redcrosse strikes at her with 'the sworde of ye Spirit' (Ephesians 6:17) but she winds herself around him in an attempt to assert herself against his 'loines gir[t] . . . with veritie' (*ibid.*, 6:14).

19   Una's 'Add faith' at the point at which Error has seized his 'shield of faith' recalls Article XI of the Anglican Articles of Religion: 'We are accounted righteous before God, only for the merit of our Lord and Saviour Jesus Christ by Faith, and not for our own works or deservings'; while 'force' is to be understood in its sense of moral and spiritual strength (*fortitudo*): see Tuve, 59, 84–5 and 96–7. The strangling of Error may recall Hercules's strangling of the fire-vomiting giant Cacus in his cave (*Aeneid*, VIII.192ff.): Hercules was traditionally a type of heroic virtue (see xi.26–8n., where Redcrosse is compared explicitly with Hercules; and, for other possible allusions, ii.36–8n. and vii.5n.), while Cacus, as a giant, is associated with rebellion and pride (see vii.8–10n.)

THREE furies fell, which turne the worlde to ruthe,
Both Enuie, Strife, and Slaunder, heare appeare,
In dungeon darke they longe inclosed truthe,
But Time at lengthe, did loose his daughter deare,
 And setts alofte, that sacred ladie brighte,
  Whoe things longe hidd, reueales, and bringes to lighte.

Thoughe strife make fier, thoughe Enuie eate hir harte,
The innocent though Slaunder rente, and spoile:
Yet Time will comme, and take this ladies parte,
And breake her bandes, and bring her foes to foile.
  Dispaire not then, thoughe truthe be hidden ofte,
  Bycause at lengthe, shee shall bee sett alofte.

and was identified as Satan himself in Pierre Bersuire's fourteenth-century *Moralised Ovid* (cit. Allen, 173).

20   The 'vomit full of bookes and papers' is, specifically, false Catholic doctrine and anti-Protestant propaganda; the 'frogs and toades' allude to Revelation 16:13: 'And I sawe three uncleane spirits like frogges come out of the mouth of the dragon' (Geneva gloss: 'That is, a strong number of this great devil ye Popes ambassadours which are ever crying and croking like frogs and come out of Antichrists mouth, because they shulde speake nothing but lies . . .'). The toad was generally believed to be poisonous (*F.Q.*, III.x.59; Ansell Robin, 135–6), symbolised the vices in general (Mâle, 377), and was identified with the devil (*Paradise Lost*, IV.800; de Vries, 468). The frogs and toads lack eyes as a sign of their spiritual blindness (cf. Corceca at iii.10–20n.).

21   On spontaneous generation from the Nile mud, see especially *Met.*, I.416–37 (the combination of the sun's heat and moisture produces creatures that are in various stages of completeness). Here the simile suggests chaotic confusion (compare the comparison of Duessa with the Nile at v.18 and n.; and note the pun on *pride* as at st. 7) in contrast to its more positive use at III.vi.8 (the sun's impregnation of Chrysogone). This stanza links thematically with the description of the earth-born Orgoglio (vii.8–10n.) and the Biblical 'man of earth' at x.52n. and 64–6n. The 'ten thousand kindes of creatures' symbolise the multiplicity of evil in contrast to the oneness of Una: compare Error's 'thousand young ones' (st. 15) and II.ix.13.

22   The 'spawne of serpents' which are at present unable to harm the knight are perhaps the lusts of the flesh (concupiscence: see st. 47n.): Virgil K. Whitaker, 'The Theological Structure of *The Faerie Queene*, Book I', *E.L.H.*, XIX (1952). They are rendered ineffectual by God's grace, the implication of 'more then manly force' at st. 24. As a gloss on the episode as a whole Whitaker compares St Augustine's account of the two stages in his conversion: the rejection of false doctrine and the overcoming of the flesh (*Confessions*, VIII).

23   The simile is modelled on Homer (*Iliad*, II.469ff., e.g., flies round a herdsman) and is a favourite with Spenser – see II.ix.16 and VI.xi.48, both in an evil context. Its immediate source is

Spenser's own experience in Ireland, though there are symbolic allusions to the diseases and sins which flew from Pandora's box (Starnes and Talbert, 270) and to the fly as a symbol of evil: Beelzebub, 'prince of devils' (Matthew 12:24) is Lord of the Flies. See also i.36n.

25–6 Young vipers were believed to kill their mother by bursting open her womb (Pliny, *Natural History*, X.lxxxii; Ansell Robin, 29–31); but their action of sucking her blood 'Making her death their life' is a parody of Christ's salvific blood answered structurally at xi.46–8n. The consequent bursting of 'th'unkindly [unnatural] Impes' expresses the ultimate self-defeatingness of sin by recalling the suicide of Christ's betrayer, Judas Iscariot, in the field he bought with his betrayal money: 'when he had throwne downe him selfe head long he brast a sondre in the middes, and all his bowels gushed out' (Acts 1:18).

29 Having encountered and defeated Error in an emblematic confrontation, Redcrosse, as the wayfaring Christian still prone to sin, is tested by more insidious temptations. Archimago – identified as Hypocrisy in the Argument to canto i and named at st. 43 – is ultimately Satan, father of illusion, who constantly appeals to 'our deceivable imaginations' (Richard Hooker, 'A Learned and Comfortable Sermon', in *Of the Laws of Ecclesiastical Polity*, Everyman's Library, I.11). He is the Arch image-maker who tries to mislead with 'false beauties' and 'vaine deceiptfull shadowes' and so obscure 'that soveraine light, / From whose pure beams al perfect beauty springs' (Spenser's *Hymne of Heavenly Beautie*, 290ff.). The thought underlying Archimago is both Christian and Neoplatonic. He is also the Arch-image, the 'image of the beast' of Revelation 13:14, predictably identified in the Geneva gloss as the papal empire, image of the first Roman empire. Note that Archimago first appears as a hermit talking 'of Saintes and Popes' (st. 35). The Biblical source for religious hypocrisy is Christ's attack in Matthew 23; and the hypocrite with prayer book and rosary is familiar in the emblem tradition: Ripa, 200–1, and Peacham, *Minerva Britanna*, 198 (an old man with his pilgrim's scallop shell, his rosary and staff). As a hermit Archimago parodies the contemplative life, the alternative to the active heroism manifested in Redcrosse's earlier encounter with Error (Cullen, 32): the true hermit Contemplation is encountered at x.46ff. (and see x.59–63n. on the contemplative and active lives). Moreover, Archimago compounds his evil by being the Arch-magus, the arch black-magician, as his evocation of evil spirits at st. 38 confirms: on the Protestant use of sorcery and witchcraft as a symbol for Catholic doctrine, see Waters, 'Errour's Den and Archimago's Hermitage', and for the accusation that many of the popes were themselves necromancers, see Kermode, 44–5. Finally, his appearance at this point in the narrative recalls the hermit–magician in *O.F.*, II.12ff.

32–33 Note the comparison of Redcrosse with the sun: his solar role is discussed at iii.5–9n. He will fall into spiritual darkness with the coming of night; will escape the sun's heat at ii.28ff. (see notes); at v.2 he will be a false sun; at viii.38-41 he will be unable to bear the sight of the sun (the consequence of his action at vii.2ff.). Finally, in canto xi, his solar role will be restored.

34 The 'Christall streame' and 'sacred fountaine' anticipate vii.2–6 and parody xi.29–30 and 48 (see notes for Biblical references).

36 'Sad humour' = heavy moisture (but on *sad* see also st. 2n. above). Morpheus is the god of dreams. Archimago's black magic begins here and, in accordance with Renaissance theories of demonology, he calls up his 'Legions of Sprights', which also suggest the man called Legion because he was possessed by many devils (Luke 8:30; see II.xi.46n.). For their comparison to 'little flyes' see st. 23n. above. They can seduce Redcrosse while he is asleep because during sleep judgement and reason are suspended, leaving the fancy (phantasy) free: see II.ix.49–58. At II.ix.50–1 Phantastes is seated in a 'chamber filled . . . with flyes' which represent 'idle thoughts and fantasies, / Devices, dreames, opinions unsound'. Robert Burton, *Anatomy of Melancholy* (1621), I.i.2.7 remarks of phantasy: 'In time of sleep this faculty is free, and many times conceives strange, stupend, absurd shapes' (ed. Floyd Dell and P. Jordan-Smith, 139), and the devil was believed to be able to operate through it (see W. B. Hunter, 'Eve's Demonic Dream', *E.L.H.*, XIII (1946)). Klibansky, 302n. mentions a seventeenth-century engraving which shows a sleeping woman having delusions blown into her brain by a demon with batlike wings: the delusions are symbolised by swarming insects.

37 Pluto is king of the underworld and Proserpina is his 'griesly Dame' (cf. II.vii.53). As an aspect of the moon goddess, Proserpina is an antitype to the Faerie Queene of Spenser's poem since the Queen of Fairies was herself understood to be the moon goddess, Diana (Rathborne, 161). One reason why Proserpina is Lucifera's mother (iv.11) is that Lucifera too is a parody of Gloriana. 'Great *Gorgon*' is Demogorgon, the primal deity coeternal with Chaos, grandfather of the gods and daemon of the earth: cf. IV.ii.47 and Lotspeich, 51–2. His is the unmentionable name of *Ger. Lib.*, XIII.10, and cf. Statius, *Thebaid*, IV.514–18. Cocytus and Styx are two of the rivers of the underworld: the former is associated with weeping and grief, the latter is the river over which souls have to pass to enter Hades. It is traditionally 'hateful' (Lotspeich, 48, 108–9).

39 Tethys is the wife of Oceanus, but here she represents the ocean itself. Cynthia is another name for the moon goddess. Morpheus's house is based on *Met.*, XI.592ff. (Sleep's cave, never penetrated by the rays of the sun), though there are many other antecedents, not least Chaucer's *Book of the Duchesse*, 136ff. and *House of Fame*, I.66ff.

40 The gates are based on *Odyssey*, XIX.562ff. and *Aeneid*, VI.893ff., the twin gates of sleep, one made of horn, through which pass true shadows or dreams, the other of ivory, through which come visions false in the light of day. Spenser would have inherited from Macrobius's late-fourth-century *Commentary on the Dream of Scipio*, I.iii.17–20 the idea that the soul, partly disengaged from the body during sleep, gazes at the truth through a veil. Sometimes the veil allows truth to be perceived, in which case it is said to be made of horn (which can be so thin as to be transparent); sometimes the truth is not allowed to be seen – hence the alternative opaque ivory (tr. and ed. W. H. Stahl, 92). Instead of horn, Spenser has silver, symbol of purity (e.g., Psalms 12:6). The sprite returns with his dream through the ivory gate at st. 44. Compare II.xii.44–5 and n.

42 Troubled sleep was believed to be caused by deficiency of moisture in the brain, since sleep itself was caused by vapour ascending to the brain from digesting food and the bodily humours: W. C. Curry, *Chaucer and the Mediaeval Sciences*, 204ff.

43   Hecate is queen of the underworld (and as such identified with Proserpina) and of witchcraft (Starnes and Talbert, 163–4). She is also goddess of dreams (Lotspeich, 67).

45   The false Una is made of air to show that she is in fact a product of the imagination (cf. *Paradise Lost*, V.105) and of the devil: Burton, *Anatomy*, I.ii.1.2 (*ed.cit.*, 159–60). Her creation echoes *Aeneid*, X.637ff., where Juno creates a phantom Aeneas like a shape in a dream; and *Ger. Lib.*, VII.99–100, where a phantom Clorinda is made out of a cloud. Spenser might have had particularly in mind the story that a phantom Helen made of clouds accompanied Paris to Troy, while the real Helen went to Egypt, thus retaining her chastity (Apollodorus, *Epitome*, III.v.). See also v.35n.

46   'Borne without her dew': i.e., unnaturally.

47   With Redcrosse's reason suspended in sleep, the sprite activates his phantasy with a dream which is directed at arousing concupiscent desires, since the devil appeals to the most vulnerable point (Burton, *Anatomy*, I.ii.1.2: he 'suggests . . . envy, lust, anger, &c., as he sees men inclined'; *ed.cit.*, 174). Concupiscence, according to the ninth of the Thirty-nine Articles (see II.ii.1–4n.) remains even after baptism and requires constant combatting by the reason and will (see ii.4–6n. and II.v.1n.), which operate again when he wakes at st. 49 and control his reaction to the false Una. The third, successful, stage of the temptation occurs at the beginning of canto ii. Redcrosse's dream contrasts with Arthur's dream of the Faerie Queene at ix.13–15n. In terms of the dream lore inherited by the Renaissance from the Middle Ages, both dreams are visions or revelations, the results of spiritual forces impressing themsleves upon the phantasy in the form of sense-images. But Arthur's, caused by good spirits, is a *revelation*; Redcrosse's, caused by evil spirits, is an *illusion* (Curry, *Chaucer and the Mediaeval Sciences*, 213–14, citing St Augustine and Vincent de Beauvais). In Neoplatonic terms, Arthur has a glimpse of ideal beauty, Redcrosse becomes involved in the world of 'vaine deceiptfull shadowes' (see st. 29n.). Lust is one of the two fleshly (as opposed to spiritual) vices: see i.2n. and Katzenellenbogen, 11. The other is gluttony.

48 Venus, with her attendant Graces, seems to bring Una to Redcrosse's bed. But this is a debased Venus Pandemos (see General Introduction) in contrast to the chastely Venerean Una of vi.16 (see n.) and xii.21–3 and n. Like Elizabeth at Proem 4n., Una is a manifestation of celestial beauty, a Venus Urania. By arousing Redcrosse's lust, anger, and jealousy, Archimago is persuading him to see her as Fradubio sees Fraelissa at ii.36–7 and as Sansloy sees Una at vi.4 (see notes). The cry of *Hymen io Hymen* (Hymen was the god of marriage) was traditional at weddings (cf. Catullus's *Epithalamium*, LXI, and Spenser's own *Epithalamion*, 140); and so this stanza offers a false vision of the betrothal of Redcrosse and Una at xii.36ff. (a further instance of the circular structure of Book I: cf. st. 4n. above). The three Graces, Aglaia, Thalia, and Euphrosyne, symbolise reciprocity of benefits (*F.Q.*, VI.x.24) and, ultimately, cosmic love, the outgoing from the One into the Many and the return to the One (see Introduction, and Wind, ch. II and III). These parody Graces are answered by the three theological virtues at x.4n. Flora is the Roman goddess of spring; but the Flora who crowns this Una with an 'Yvie girlond' (signifying intemperance through its association with Bacchus: Tervarent, cols. 240–1; and contrast the garlands of vi.13 and esp. xii.8) is the 'famous harlot, which with the abuse of her body having gotten great riches, made the people of Rome her heyre: who in remembraunce of so great beneficence, appointed a yearely feste for the memoriall of her . . . making her the Goddesse of all floures' (E. K.'s gloss on *Shepheardes Calender*, 'March', 16, following Thomas Cooper's *Thesaurus*: Starnes and Talbert, 44–5). Her connection with Rome links her firmly with the Catholic Archimago and Duessa.

51 The 'blind God', like the 'false winged boy' of st. 47, is Cupid. The false Una's reference to him is in itself a give-away: the medieval blind Cupid signifies subjection to passion (Panofsky, *Studies in Iconology*, 105ff.). Contrast the Cupid of Proem 3n. and II.viii.3–6n.

54 The first line contains an ironic echo of 1 Samuel 3:19: 'And Samuel grewe, and the Lord was with him, and let none of his

wordes fall to the ground' (Geneva gloss: 'The Lord accomplished
whatsoever he had said').

CANTO II

As the Argument stanza points out, Redcrosse is now separated
from Una and follows Duessa, 'faire falshood'. The separation is in
accordance with the symbolic significance of 2; for since 1 is
associated with the 'one Lord, one Faith, one Baptism, one God', 2
in its bad sense signifies 'the beginning of division . . . discord, and
confusion'. Hence 'it was not spoken in the second day of the
creation of the world, and God said, That it was good, because the
number of two is evill' (Agrippa, II.iv and v,175 and 177–8,
repeating a commonplace of medieval and Renaissance
numerology).

1 The 'sevenfold teme' is the seven stars in the hinder part and tail
of Ursa major, the Great Bear (known as the *septentriones*). The
Bear is also known as Charles's Wain, so the adjacent northern
constellation Boötes was called the Waggoner: cf. *Met.*, II.176–7
and Milton's *Elegia quinta*, 35–6 ('Now northern Boötes no longer
wearily follows his celestial waggon'). The 'steadfast starre' is the
Pole Star, symbol of constancy (see also II.x.1–4n., and Yates, 51
citing Fulke Greville's *Caelica*, sonnet 82 which refers to Elizabeth
as 'star of the north'). In view of this and the fact that the tail of
Ursa major was associated astrologically with safety in travelling
(Agrippa, II.xlvii,308), it is not surprising that Archimago's night
temptations have failed. Chaunticlere is the cock (cf. Chaucer's
Nonnes Preestes Tale) whose crowing heralds the coming of light
and hence, traditionally, the end of black magic ceremonies: see
Ben Jonson's note to his *Masque of Queens*, 150 (*Complete
Masques*, ed. Orgel, 127). The reference in l.7 is to the chariot of
the sun god.

4–6 The third illusion works when Hesperus, the morning star, is
'in highest skie'; for the morning star is the planet Venus (cf.
xi.33–4n., xii.21–3n., where Una is compared with it) and so
symbolises the reality that Redcrosse is blinded to by the false
Venus–Una, or, in the more precise terminology of moral
psychology, when his reason fails to govern his passions and his

corrupted will acquiesces: 'But in spiritual things we will no good, prone to evil (except we be regenerate, and led by the Spirit), we are egged on by our natural concupiscence' (Burton, *Anatomy*, I.i.2.11, *ed.cit.*, 146).

7 'Rosy-fingred' as an epithet of Aurora, the dawn goddess, is traditional; Tithonus is her husband, whose immortality she obtained from Jove while forgetting to ask for perpetual youth – hence his age. 'Purple' is also a traditional epithet (e.g., *Met.*, III.184). Cf. xi.51. Titan is the sun. Una's search for Redcrosse recalls the Song of Solomon 5:6: 'my welbeloved was gone, & past . . . I soght him, but I colde not finde him: I called him, but he answered me not' (Hankins, 107–8). The Song was allegorised in terms of the Church's love for Christ.

9 'Divided into double parts' confirms the two-ness now operating (see headnote, above). Duessa herself is named at st. 34, and note that Archimago called forth 'the falsest twoo' sprites at i.38.

10 Proteus, a sea god, could assume whatever form he pleased: e.g. *Met.*, VIII.730–7. From one point of view this indicates formlessness and so he could become identified with the disordered passions (Lotspeich, 104, citing Boccaccio's *De Genealogia Deorum*, VII.9), with primitive matter (Allen, 92) and hypocrisy (Allen, 173). In the latter connection, see Abraham Fraunce, *The third part of the Countess of Pembrokes Yvychurch* (1592), sigs. F4^v–G: 'Plato compareth him to the wrangling of brabling sophisters: and some there be that hereby understand, the truth of things obscured by so many deceavable apparences'. He was also interpreted as a wizard or magician (Lotspeich, 104; Allen, 92). The metamorphoses itemised in this stanza suggest Archimago's demonic ability to inhabit the elements (air, water, earth, fire): see Burton, *Anatomy*, I.ii.1.2, *ed. cit.*, 166ff.; R. Kellogg and A. Steele, *Books I and II of 'The Faerie Queene'* (New York, 1965), 96n. This would tie up with Proteus's identification with primitive matter or chaos and might have been suggested by the Ovid passage (where changes into serpent, water, and fire are listed among others) or similar lists by mythographers and dictionary writers (Starnes and Talbert, 72). The fox is a symbol of the devil and of hypocrisy (Evans, 209–12); Satan can adopt whatever shape he pleases: 'Thus the Devil reigns, and in a thousand several shapes' (Burton, *ibid.*, 171).

11 Archimago takes on the appearance of Redcrosse perhaps in allusion to the beast from the earth of Revelation 13:11 disguising itself as the Lamb of God but speaking 'like the dragon'. The beast is 'ye Popes kingdome [which] is of ye earth' (Geneva gloss).

12 Redcrosse encounters Sansfoy (Faithlessness), the typical pagan of medieval romance and Italian Renaissance epic. He overcomes him (st. 19) because he has not deviated so far spiritually as to espouse his ethic of caring 'not for God or man a point'. But he succumbs to the next worse thing, his mistress Fidessa (Duessa in disguise: see st. 44) who contrasts with Una and with Fidelia at x.12–13. Duessa has the two names for the larger part of Book I to confirm her doubleness; she is also physically double, like Error (see st. 40–1 below).

13 Fidessa's appearance is that of the great whore of Babylon of Revelation 17:4 who sits on a scarlet beast: 'the woman was araied in purple & skarlat, & guilded with golde, & precious stones, and pearles'. The Geneva gloss states: 'This woman is the Antichrist, that is, the Pope with ye whole bodie of his filthie creatures . . . whose beautie onely standeth in outwarde pompe & impudencie and craft like a strumpet'. Compare Lucifera at iv.7ff.; Fidessa herself reappears in I.vii and viii. See Waters, 'Errour's Den and Archimago's Hermitage', for the Protestant conception of the Catholic Mass as both witch and whore which probably influenced Spenser here. The contrast is with Una as described at i.4, an opposition based in part on Revelation 17:14, where it is prophesied that the Lamb (Christ) will overcome the whore and her beast, and on Revelation 12:1, the 'woman clothed with the sunne' (on whom see iii.4n.), who is the antithesis of the great whore. Henry Bullinger, *A Hundred Sermons upon the Apocalipse* (1573 edn, Bl^v), explains that in Revelation God 'first . . . brought foorth an honest & noble matrone, to weete, the very spouse of Christ. Now as it were by opposition he setteth against her a proude whore, that false new start up Romishe Church' (cit. S. K. Heninger, 'The Orgoglio Episode in *The Faerie Queene*', *E.L.H.*, XXVI (1959)). The '*Persian* mitre' identifies the papal mitre with pagan religion and temporal pride (an accusation made, for example, by Bishop Jewel: Yates, 72 and n.); while the palfrey's wantonness makes it the horse of the passions (i.1n. above). Its superficial ('tinsell') trappings are 'woven like a wave' to link Fidessa with the Protean Archimago and to confirm her moral instability (see II.v.25–8n.). Cullen, 36–7, analysing the first part of Redcrosse's quest in terms of the temptations Flesh, World, and Devil, sees Duessa as embodying the flesh, which in Protestant readings included doubt, unbelief, and despair, as well as intemperance.

16 The ram simile is a commonplace: e.g., *Ger. Lib.*, VII.88. Note that it fails to differentiate between the two opponents: Redcrosse, like Sansfoy, is filled with 'ambitious pride' and is spiritually very near pagan faithlessness.

19 The phrase 'mother earth' associates Sansfoy with earthly unregeneracy (see i.21n. above) and also with Revelation 13:11 as cited at ii.1ln. above: the papal kingdom 'is of ye earth' but 'the kingdome of Christ is from heaven'.

20 The fall of Sansfoy like 'a broken towre' anticipates Orgoglio's fall, compared to the undermining of a castle at viii.23, and, less immediately, Lucifera's palace at iv.4–5. The tower is an emblem of pride (II.ix.21n.).

22 The Emperor who rules the west from Rome ('where *Tiberis* doth pas') is the Pope, whose empire was regarded as a continuation of the Roman empire. See, e.g., the Geneva glosses on Revelation 13:12: 'For the Pope in ambition, crueltie, idolatrie, & blasphemie did folow & imitate the ancient Romaines' and 13:14: 'the first empire Romaine was as the paterne, & this seconde empire is but an image & shadowe thereof'. The Pope's limited rule of the west contrasts with Una's 'Royall lynage . . . Of ancient Kings and Queenes, that had of yore / Their scepters stretcht from East to Westerne shore' (i.5) just as Una herself contrasts with the specious Fidessa, the Emperor's *one* daughter. (Jonson's *Hymenaei*, 808, describes Truth as having arms that 'reach from east to west'; *Masques*, ed. Orgel, 105). Spenser's specific allusion is to the claim of the reformed, Anglican, Church to be the true uncorrupt Catholic Church, and to the directly related imperial claims of Elizabeth which, ignoring papal imperialism, she traced directly back to the English-born Christian Roman Emperor

Constantine the Great, who, in 330, renamed Byzantium Constantinople and made it the seat of the empire instead of Rome. Constantine's victories in 323 over Licinius, master of the eastern part of the empire, had given him control over east and west. Byzantium was the gateway to the two. See Kermode, 40–3; Yates, 39ff., 42–3, and 49, citing Bishop Jewel and Foxe's *Acts and Monuments*; and Roy Strong, 'The Popular Celebration of the Accession Day'.

23–4 Fidessa is talking of the death of Christ (Kathleen Williams, *Spenser's 'Faerie Queene': The World of Glass* (1966), 10) and her separation from her dead beloved and ignorance of His resurrection signifies Catholicism's deviation from true Christian doctrine – a deviation so extreme as to ally her with Sansfoy. The passage looks back to, and parodies, ii.7–8, Una's search for Redcrosse and its allegorical implications, and looks forward to xii.36ff., the union of the two which is, anagogically, the union of the Church with Christ. Significantly, Fidessa's 'day of spousall' never arrives (and see her last-ditch attempt at xii.26–8); significantly, too, ll. 6–9 of st. 24 echo *Aeneid*, IV.68–9, in which the unhappy Dido wanders distraught through Carthage like a wounded doe, on fire with her love for Aeneas (*Var. Sp.*, I.201). For the usual pejorative interpretation of Dido as intemperance and passion, see II.i.35–56n.

25 The three brothers parody the three theological virtues of x.4 (see n.). Sansloy appears at iii.33ff., and Sansjoy at iv.38ff. Their parentage is revealed at v.22ff.

28–32 Redcrosse, with Fidessa, escapes from the heat of the sun (presumably, since it is 'now ymounted hie', the midday sun) into shade, anticipating his similar action at vii.2ff. He mistakes the heat for 'the plague that destroyeth at noone daye' (Psalms 91:6), and fails to have faith in God's providence (*ibid.*, verses 1–2). From another point of view, he prefers the shadow of ignorance to the sun of the true religion (see iii.4n.) and the blazing *Sol iustitiae*, the sun of justice and righteousness which has its Biblical origin in Malachi 4 and was allegorised as follows by Pierre Bersuire: 'as the sun, when in the centre of his orbit, that is to say, at the midday point, is hottest, so shall Christ be when He shall appear in the centre of heaven and earth, that is to say, in Judgment' (Erwin

Panofsky, *Meaning in the Visual Arts*, 262). See also iii.5–9n. The
'two goodly trees' anticipate, and contrast with, the two trees of
xi.46–8 which are based on the trees in Genesis 2:9 and the
redemptive tree of Christ's cross (see note). The bleeding of the tree
and the reproachful voice have many precedents: *Aeneid*, III.22ff.
(the metamorphosed Polydorus); Dante, *Inferno*, XIII.34ff.; *O.F.*,
VI.26ff.; *Ger. Lib.*, XIII.41ff. The moral implication of the
metamorphosis is that, in succumbing to Duessa, Fradubio has lost
his faith and reason and become, literally, nothing more than a
vegetable soul (see II.ix.27n.). The structural counterpart to this
episode at the beginning of Book II is the encounter with Mordant
and Amavia at i.35ff. On the attempt to crown Duessa with a
garland (an ambiguous gesture, since the garland can be a symbol
of honour and of vice: see Tervarent, col. 126), see i.48n.

33 Fradubio (Brother Doubt, a meaning made explicit at st. 37;
friar continues the anti-Catholic propaganda) has undergone a
similar fall to Redcrosse; and the symbolism of the trees as of the
'living well' of st. 43 (on which see st. 40–1n.) is a reminder that
both falls have re-enacted the first Fall. But Redcrosse is too
involved with Duessa to see how closely Fradubio's tale parallels
his own situation. Boreas is the north wind; the north is
traditionally associated with evil (see II.iii.19n.), and the north wind
with the devil: Evans, 259 cites the fifth-century Bishop Eucherius's
interpretation of the north wind in Song of Solomon 4:16 as Satan,
in contrast to the south wind, which is the Holy Spirit. Fradubio is
exposed to climatic extremes as a punishment for and reminder of
his fallen condition, since before the Fall the climate was temperate:
see II.xii.51n.

36–8 Fradubio's lady, like Una (see ii.4–6n.), shines like the
morning star; by raising a 'foggy mist' Duessa manages to outshine
her as Lucifera, too, tries to outshine Una (see iv.8–10n.). The
garland is made of roses because the rose was dedicated to Venus
(Tervarent, cols. 323–4, and see II.xii.74–5n.) and symbolises
Fradubio's readiness to succumb to concupiscence, like Redcrosse
at i.47–8nn. Fradubio's dilemma recalls the well-known 'Choice of
Hercules', in which the young Hercules seats himself at a
crossroads and is confronted by two women, one representing
Pleasure (Venus) and one Virtue (Diana). Unlike Fradubio,
Hercules, after listening to their arguments, chooses Virtue. The

tale is recounted in Xenophon's *Memorabilia*, II.i.21–33, and the theme is discussed by Erwin Panofsky, *Hercules am Scheidewege* (Leipzig, 1930). See also vi.16n. and Plate 2. In addition the roses – by attraction to Fraelissa's name (= Italian *fralezza*, frailty) – symbolise frailty and mutability (Valeriano, *Hieroglyphica*, LV.i, *s.v. Imbecillitas humana*): though morally preferable to Duessa she is in the same fallen, frail, moral state as all of us. There might, too, be a suggestion of the Tudor rose, connected expecially with Elizabeth (see II.iii.21–30n.): Fradubio abandons his true sovereign mistress for the usurper (the Catholic Mary Queen of Scots). Finally, Fraelissa suggests *Elissa*, a name of Dido: see above, st. 23–4n. (Dido as intemperance) and II.ii.12–20n. This would confirm Fradubio's predisposition to concupiscence.

40–1 *Prime* here is spring, as at vi.13. The annual or periodic penance of witches is a folklore commonplace (cf. *Paradise Lost*, X.574–7). Duessa's misshapen and monstrous lower parts recall Error (i.13–16n.) and are revealed to Redcrosse at viii.46ff. Upton (*Var. Sp.*, I.205) notes the parallel with *O.F.*, VII.72ff., where Ruggiero, with the aid of the magic ring (reason) sees the apparently beautiful Alcina (false pleasure) for the frail and repulsive hag she really is. Fradubio and Fraelissa can be restored only by bathing 'in a living well': see John 4:14: 'the water that I shal give him, shalbe in him a well of water, springing up into everlasting life' (the Geneva gloss identifies this water as 'spiritual grace'), and compare the 'pure river of water of life' of Revelation 22:1. This water contrasts with the physical purging Duessa undergoes in her herbal bath 'in origane and thyme': the former, wild marjoram, was believed to be a cure for the 'scabs, itch, [and] scurvy' (Salmon's *Dispensatory*, I.iv,83: cf. Duessa's symptoms at viii.47), and thyme, applied externally, 'is good against cold Tumors' (*ibid.*, 109).

43–4 In referring to 'suffised [satisfied] fates' Fradubio still uses pagan terminology. Redcrosse tries to avoid identifying himself with Fradubio's failings by thrusting the bleeding bough into the ground (compare the way Fradubio tried to slip away in st. 41): the parallel is with Ruddymane's indelible blood of inherited guilt at II.ii.1–4n., and the clay is a reminder of his origins from earth (see i.21n., and cf. Genesis 2:7, where Adam is made 'of the dust of the

Binium virtutis & vitij.

WHEN HERCVLES, was dowtfull of his waie,
  Inclosed rounde, with vertue, and with vice:
With reasons firste, did vertue him assaie,
The other, did with pleasures him entice:
  They longe did striue, before he coulde be wonne,
  Till at the lengthe, ALCIDES thus begonne.

Oh pleasure, thoughe thie waie bee smoothe, and faire,
And sweete delightes in all thy courtes abounde:
Yet can I heare, of none that haue bene there,
That after life, with fame haue bene renoumde:
  For honor hates, with pleasure to remaine,
  Then houlde thy peace, thow wastes thie winde in vaine.

But heare, I yeelde oh vertue to thie will,
And vowe my selfe, all labour to indure,
For to ascende the steepe, and craggie hill,
The toppe whereof, whoe so attaines, is sure
  For his rewarde, to haue a crowne of fame:
  Thus HERCVLES, obey'd this sacred dame.

grounde' so that he 'shulde not glorie in the excellencie of his owne
nature' (Geneva gloss)).

CANTO III

The narrative returns to Una at this point perhaps because 'the
number of three is . . . a holy number, a number of perfection'
(Agrippa, II.vi,179). It signifies the return to unity in the
Neoplatonic triple rhythm *emanatio, raptio, remeatio* (see General
Introduction).

3 On Una's quest for Redcrosse, see ii.7n. above.

4 Una unveils herself voluntarily here, is unveiled by force at vi.4,
and again unveils herself voluntarily at xii.22. Compare the effect
of the unveiling of Arthur's shield at vii.33–5n. She is compared to
the sun (traditionally the 'eye of heaven': Fowler, 74n.) as the
image of God and Truth (who holds a sun in her right hand, Ripa,
499–501) and is opposed by the solar Lucifera at iv.8ff. On
Elizabeth as the sun who sheds the beams of the true religion, see
Strong, 'The Popular Celebration of the Accession Day'. The
symbolism of the unveiling is largely Neoplatonic: unveiled, Una is
an emanation of the divine glory (cf. Proem 4n.); but that glory
expressed through her is too bright to be revealed to the man whose
eye of reason (ii.5) is obscured by concupiscence. Cf. st. 10–20n.
The solar comparison is also apocalyptic: Una is the 'woman
clothed with the sunne' of Revelation 12:1 who, like Una here (st.
3), flees 'into the wildernes' (verse 6) when persecuted by 'a great
red dragon having seven heades' (verse 3; compare Duessa's beast
at vii.16–18n., and ii.13n.). The Geneva gloss identifies the woman
in the usual Protestant way as 'ye Church which is compassed
about with Jesus Christ the Sonne of righteousnes' and which 'is
persecuted of Antichrist'.

5–9 Lions traditionally reverence virgins and royalty, as in *1
Henry IV*, II.iv, where Falstaff is the 'valiant lion' who 'will not
touch the true prince'. The knight with a lion protector is a
commonplace in romances and folktales: *Var. Sp.*, I.396ff.; the
virgin with a lion protector is discussed by Irving Ribner, 'Una's
Lion: A Folklore Analogue', *Notes and Queries*, CXCVI (1951),

114–15. Spenser's emblem of the lion and virgin has two main meanings. Firstly, it signifies justice: Valeriano's *Hieroglyphica*, I.xxx describes a woman seated on a lion as justice's power to subdue violent passions (Fowler, 68 and n. and plate 2b; cf. Tervarent, col. 244: the zodiacal sign Virgo – i.e., Astraea, goddess of justice – is placed next to Leo because a just judge should have an intrepid and valiant soul so that he can withstand any threat. For Elizabeth as Astraea, see II Proem 2n.). Una, then, is outlawed justice, with the additiona implication that, as Truth, she is acknowledged by the natural world but not by man (cf. the instinctive worship of her by the satyrs at vi.9ff.). Nelson, *The Poetry of Edmund Spenser*, 156, cites Hooker's 'Learned and Comfortable Sermon' (*Laws*, I.12), where the lion is used as an argument for faith: 'concerning the man that trusteth in God, . . . if lions, beasts ravenous by nature and keen with hunger, being set to devour, have as it were religiously adored the very flesh of the faithful man; what is there in the world that shall change his heart, overthrow his faith, alter his affection towards God, or the affection of God to him?' Secondly, the lion relates to the solar symbolism of Book I (on which see Fowler, ch. VIII, *passim*). Leo is the sun's zodiacal house, and this led Bersuire in his commentary on Malachi 4, quoted in part above, ii.28–32n., to associate not only the midday but also the midsummer sun with the Sun of justice: 'In summer, when he is in the Lion, the sun withers the herbs, which have blossomed in the spring, by his heat. So shall Christ, in that heat of the Judgment, appear as a man fierce and leonine; He shall wither the sinners' (Panofsky, *Meaning in the Visual Arts*, 262). Una therefore becomes herself an avenging and apocalyptic Sun of justice – the full meaning of Revelation 12:1 (see st. 4n. above). In st. 7 (cf. i.17 and x.28) Redcrosse is a lion who has abandoned his role and has had to be replaced by this tamed wrathful lion (on the lion and wrath, see st. 33–6n. below). The function of the metaphor is to confirm his solar role and suggest that he is potentially the Christ-like Sun of justice. When he assumes this role, Una becomes the morning star to his sun: see xi.33–4n.; at which point he is also the heraldic lion supporting the royal coat of arms (e.g., Yates, plates 8a, b, and d).

10–20 Spenser now deals with common ecclesiastical abuses: Corceca (blind heart) represents spiritual blindness in its specific

form of blind devotion and superstition (see Argument stanza, and
st. 13–14): compare her penance with Duessa's at ii.40–1n. and
Redcrosse's in canto x. Upton (*Var. Sp.*, I.208) relates her to
Romans 1:21 ('their foolish heart was ful of darkenes') and
Ephesians 4:18: 'Having their cogitation darkened, and being
strangers from the life of God through the ignorance that is in
them, because of the hardenes of their heart'. On the ashes and
sackcloth, see x.24–7n. Abessa, her daughter (named at st. 18)
suggests *abbess* but also absenteeism (Latin *abesse*, depart); while
Kirkrapine, the church robber (st. 17), embodies abuses which
originated in the Roman Church but have been continued into the
English Church: cf. the ecclesiastical satire in the 'September'
eclogue of *The Shepheardes Calender*; Kermode, 46–7; and M. R.
Falls, 'Spenser's Kirkrapine and the Elizabethans', *S.P.*, L (1953).
The reference to 'blind Devotions mart' in the Argument stanza, in
conjunction with Kirkrapine's activities, suggests a further allusion
to Christ's ejection of the merchants from the temple: e.g., Matthew
21:12–13: 'And Jesus went into the Temple of God, and cast out
all them that solde & boght in the Temple, and overthrew the tables
of the money changers . . . and said to them, It is written, Mine
house shalbe called the house of prayer: but ye have made it a
denne of thieves' (Geneva gloss: 'Under the pretence of religion
hypocrites seke their owne gaine, and spoyle God of his true
worship'). The irruption of the wrathful lion at st. 13 hints at
apocalyptic judgement and, specifically, the avenging Christ ('the
lion which is of the tribe of Juda' of Revelation 5:5) in the temple.
Among many other appropriate Biblical references, cf. Job 10:16
('hunt thou me as a lyon'), and Proverbs 28:1: 'The wicked flee
when none pursueth [which is what Abessa does in st. 11]: but the
righteous are bolde as a lyon'. Corceca recalls the iconographical
tradition of blind (or blindfolded) figures whose blindness signifies
sin: e.g., Greed (Ripa, *Cupidita*, 99), Error (*ibid.*, 133), Idolatry
(*ibid.*, 219), and Ignorance (*ibid.*, 221–3). On the tradition, see
Panofsky, *Studies in Iconology*, 109–12 and cf. i.51n. As Upton
(*Var. Sp.*, I.208) noted, l.6 of st. 18, 'And fed her fat with feast of
offerings', echoes 1 Samuel 2:29 where God accuses Eli and his
sons of making themselves 'fat of the first frutes of all the offrings
of Israel', just as Kirkrapine's 'whoredome' with Abessa echoes the
earlier verse 22 where Eli hears how his sons 'laye with the women
that assembled at the doore of the Tabernacle of the

Congregacion'. Spenser therefore establishes a continuity of corruption going back to the Old Testament; so that the symbolic opposition of Una–Truth–Day (she departs with the solar lion at dawn in st. 21) and blind Corceca, Kirkrapine with his Old Testament corruptions, and Night, brings to mind the medieval opposition documented by Panofsky, *op.cit.*, 110–12 of Day – Sun – Life – New Testament – Church and Night – Moon – Death – Old Testament – Synagogue (which is blindfold: contrast Una's necessary veil – st. 4n. above – the removal of which is illuminated by the phrase which traditionally described the opposition of Old and New Testaments, the old law and the new: *Vetus testamentum velatum, novum testamentum revelatum*: the Old Testament is veiled (dark), the new testament is revelation (unveiling)). Note the irony of Una's verbal playing on night–death–shadow and day–light–sight as she addresses the false Redcrosse in st. 27.

16 Aldeboran is a star in Taurus. Spenser intends the allusion symbolically: Kirkrapine the church despoiler enters as '*Aldeboran* was mounted hie' since the star 'causeth the destruction and hindrances of buildings ... and begetteth discord' (Agrippa, II. xxxiii,286). As a good influence 'it giveth riches and honor' (*ibid.*, II.xlvii,307). Cassiopeia boasted that she was more beautiful than the Nereids (sea nymphs) and for her pride was changed into the constellation known as Cassiopeia's chair (Starnes and Talbert, 245–6). Since Una is the sea traveller (see st. 21n. and 31n.) she is, by implication, the Nereids; Cassiopeia is Corceca, triumphant at night and, specifically, black, because she was the wife of the Ethiopian king Cepheus and, on the authority of Ptolemy, Ethiopians 'have black skins' (*Tetrabiblos*, II.2, Loeb edn, 123).

21 Significantly, in view of the oppostion of day and night in this canto, 1.2 recalls Chaucer's *Knight's Tale*, 2273: 'Up roos the sonne, and up roos Emelye' (Upton, *Var. Sp.*, I.208). Lines 4–5 remind us that Una's travels, in addition to their Biblical prototype (ii.7n.), parallel the journeys of Odysseus who, because of his love for Penelope, refused Calypso's offer of immortality (*Odyssey*, V.209) because he had to pursue virtue as a human being (Allen, 93): i.e., Una's quest is an earthly, allegorical one; only at the end is it anagogical.

31 Another epic simile: cf. *Odyssey*, XXIII.233ff. and *Ger. Lib.*,
III.4 (on mariners' rejoicing when they see land and forgetfulness of
the dangers of the voyage). On Tethys, see i.39n. 'Fierce *Orions*
hound' is Sirius, the Dog Star; Nereus – who is here offered a
libation – is father of the Nereids, a sea god known as the old man
(or ancient one) of the sea: e.g., *Iliad*, XVIII.141. He was known
also for his integrity and prophetic powers (*F.Q.*, IV.xi.18–19) and
for his Protean ability to change shape (Apollodorus, *Library*,
II.v.11). The allusive function of the simile is clear: the scorching
midsummer heat of the Dog Star ('blazing': Horace, *Odes*, III.xiii)
recalls the burning heat of the *Sol iustitiae* (st. 5–9n. above),
especially since Orion itself is the bringer of storms (*Aeneid*, I.539;
Amos 5:8; *F.Q.*, IV.xi.13), and storms traditionally signify God's
wrath and judgement on sinners (cf. II.ii.46n. on Orion, and
I.vii.8–10n. for the similar symbolism accorded to earthquakes).
Una, representative of the *Sol iustitiae*, abandons her arduous role
as, deceived by hypocrisy, she thinks the end of her journey has
come (compare Redcrosse's own escapes from the sun, ii.28–32n.).
Nereus recalls the aged Protean Archimago of i.29 and ii.10.

33–6 Sansloy (Lawless, i.e., the denier of natural and divine law)
is an emblem of choler or irascibility, anticipating Wrath at iv.33–5
and Pyrochles at II.iv.37–42n. and v.2–14n. The usual attributes of
choler are a burning sword, a wrathful lion, and flames (Klibansky,
295–6, plate 120; Ripa, 75, which is virtually identical to Peacham's
emblem 128 from *Minerva Britanna*, reproduced as our Plate 3).
At st. 36 he voices the old law 'eie for eie, tothe for tothe' (Exodus
21:24 etc. but especially verse 12: 'He that smiteth a man, and he
dye, shal dye the death'), predictably ignoring the new law of
Matthew 5:38–9: 'Ye have heard that it hath bene said, An eye for
an eye, & a tooth for a tooth. But I say unto you, Resist not evil:
but whosoever shal smite thee on thy right cheke, turn to him the
other also' (Geneva gloss on verse 38: 'Albeit this was spoken for
the judges, yet everie man applied it to revenge his private quarrel'.)
Furthermore, Sansloy uses the language of paganism in his
reference to Lethe (the underworld river of forgetfulness confused
long before Spenser with the Styx over which the souls of the dead
were ferried) and to the three Furies, goddesses of vengeance and
'Authors of all evill and mischiefe' (E.K.'s gloss on *Shepheardes
Calender*, 'November', 164, which refers to 'fyrie furies forse'). For

Cholera.

NEXT *Choller* standes, resembling most the fire,
  Of swarthie yeallow, and a meager face;
With Sword a late, vnsheathed in his Ire:
Neere whome, there lies, within a little space,
  A sterne ei'de Lion, and by him a sheild,
  Charg'd with a flame, vpon a crimson feild.

We paint him young, to shew that passions raigne,
The most in heedles, and vnstaied youth:
That Lion showes, he seldome can refraine,
From cruell deede, devoide of gentle ruth:
  Or hath perhaps, this beast to him assign'd,
  As bearing most, the braue and bounteous mind.

the custom of burning enemies on the funeral pyre of a dead man to propitiate his ghost, see *Aeneid*, X.519–20. Sansloy overcomes Archimago–Redcrosse because he himself originates with lawlessness and so has succumbed to the first principle of his being; it is also a satirical image of an England gone astray under the false religion.

40–4 The canto ends with a pessimistic vision of Truth held hostage by lawlessness. The lion is killed by Sansloy because emblematically there is little difference between them – the lion is wrathful, like Sansloy (for Una's lion's wrath see st. 5, 13, 19–20), even though it is the agent of God's vengeance: it dies to show how violent reformation within the reformed Church can itself easily turn into the evil of lawlessness (Fowler, 68–9 following Ruskin, *Stones of Venice*, III, appendix ii). Sansloy, 'Lord of the field' (st. 43), is given the phrase first used by Una to her lion at st. 7; but for the lion to violate instead of reverencing a virgin, as Sansloy does (canto vi), is to deny natural law (see st. 5–9n.). The combination of Sansloy and Una parodies the reunion of Una with Redcrosse in canto viii, her true lion (iii.7).

CANTO IV

Redcrosse enters Lucifera's palace which is 'built of squared bricke' to parody the quadrate of virtue (see st. 4n.), thereby suggesting that the subject-matter of the canto again accords symbolically with its number. It is, too, the palace of earthly pride, which reminds us that 4 is the number of the earth and the created universe, because of the four elements, humours, qualities (cold, hot, dry, moist), seasons, winds, etc.: see Agrippa, II.vii,183–7 and S. K. Heninger, 'Some Renaissance Versions of the Pythagorean Tetrad', *Studies in the Renaissance*, VIII (1961).

2 Still under the influence of Duessa, Redcrosse confronts the temptation of the World (Cullen, 40): worldly pride in general and the temporal pride of Catholicism (the imperial claims of the Pope, on which see ii.22n.) in particular. Lucifera's palace is Babylon, the type of Augustine's earthly city formed by pride, love of self (*City of God*, XIV.xxviii, XVIII.xxii) parodying the New Jerusalem that awaits Redcrosse at the end of canto x. The 'broad high way' echoes Matthew 7:13: 'it is the wide gate, and broad waye that leadeth to destruction: and manie there be which go in thereat'; and cf. i.7–9n. In terms of Gregory the Great's spiritual and fleshly vices (see i.2n. and 47n.), all of which stem from *superbia* (pride), she represents vainglory (*inanis gloria*): Katzenellenbogen, 11.

4 The description of the palace is influenced by the city of the Circe-like Alcina, surrounded by bastions which appear to be of gold and again approached by a broad highway, in *O.F.*, VI.59ff.; by Chaucer's *House of Fame* which (cf. st. 5) has weak foundations, this time of ice (III.lllOff.); and by the house of Fortune in the *Romance of the Rose*, built on a slope, apparently always about to fall down, and with some walls of gold, silver, and precious stones, and others of mud. Sometimes (like Lucifera) Fortune dresses up like a queen and regards herself as the most important person on earth (see the Isle of Fortune section, 5921ff.). There is an additional suggestion of Solomon's temple (e.g., 1 Kings 6:22: 'And he overlaied the house with golde, until all the house was made perfit') as well as a satirical glance at what John Summerson has called the Elizabethan 'prodigy house' – the extravagant country houses built by Elizabeth's wealthy courtiers to entertain her in on her royal progresses (*Architecture in Britain 1530–1830*, ch. IV). The 'squared bricke' parodies the square or quadrate as a symbol of virtue (the square is virtuous because 'the rightnesse of the angles, is a plain embleme of erectnesse or uprightnesse of mind': Henry More, *Philosophicall Poems* (Cambridge, 1647), 432; cf. Aristotle's *homo quadratus* in the *Nicomachean Ethics*, I.x.11 (1100B)). The square is also (ironically in view of st. 5) a symbol of constancy and stability in opposition to Fortune's rolling sphere or wheel (Tervarent, cols. 136–7; George Puttenham, *The Arte of English Poesie* (1589), II.xii); while the lack of mortar confirms the instability and alludes to Ezekiel 13:10ff., the wall daubed with untempered mortar which will be destroyed in 'a stormie winde' of God's wrath (Hamilton, 67). The gilded walls probably hark back to the palace of the sun, the columns of which glitter with gold (*Met.*, II.lff.; compare the description of the Roman Colosseum, a sun temple 'covered with a heaven of gilded brass', in the twelfth-century *Mirabilia urbis Romae*, cit. Rathborne, 25); the 'many loftie towres' are emblems of aspiration and relate to the tower of ii.20n.; and the 'Diall' which

tells 'the timely howres' is a reminder that Lucifera is involved in
the vainglorious and mutable fallen world (Hamilton, *ibid.*) and a
feature of the Elizabethan great house: e.g., Summerson,
Architecture in Britain, plate 40, showing the clock tower in the
courtyard of William Cecil's Burghley House (1577–85). A watch
or hourglass was an emblem of Truth (Ripa, 501), the clock was a
well-known emblem of Temperance (Tervarent, col. 220): Lucifera
probably parodies both of these. While, finally, Fowler, 74–5n.
suggests that the choice of the word *dial* relates to the 'Dial of
Ahaz' motif in 2 Kings 20 and Isaiah 38: this is the sundial on
which the shadow retrograded ten degrees as a sign to Hezekiah
from God that he would be cured of a near-fatal sickness and that
Jerusalem would be delivered from Sennacherib, King of the
Assyrians, who had been besieging it. This delivering of Jerusalem
from the tyrant was given prophetic significance by Protestant
polemicists and so would suggest further apocalyptic content in
Book I: Lucifera is another manifestation of the Antichrist whose
time is nearly up.

5   The 'sandie hill' alludes to Matthew 7:26–7 (the 'foolish man,
which hathe buylded his house upon the sand'), though the general
description seems to contrast with 2 Samuel 22:2–3: 'The Lord is
my rocke and my forteresse, and he that delivereth me. God is my
strength . . . my hie towre and my refuge'. It was an emblematic
commonplace to identify the rock of Matthew 7 with constant,
stable Virtue and the sand with fickle Fortune (Chew, 66–7);
Chew's fig. 65 is a Lutheran antipapal engraving which identifies
the house built on sand with the fall of the papal Babylon complete
with the seven-headed beast; and see *ibid.*, 126 for another instance
of the identification of the house built on sand with the Catholic
Church. In terms of the book's internal structure, the sandy
instability of the palace contrasts with the 'Diamond stedfast' Una
at vi.4 (and cf. vii.33); while its 'ruinous . . . hinder parts' recall
Duessa at ii.40–1 and viii.46ff. as well as echoing Chaucer's *House
of Fame*, III.1136ff., where on the north face of the ice rock the
names of famous men are engraved, but on the south face they are
melting away.

6–7   The palace with its gates and porter, presided over by
Lucifera, is modelled on the medieval court of love, itself a
combination of the classical temple with resident god (e.g. the

temples of Venus, Mars and Diana in Chaucer's *Knight's Tale*, 1918ff.) and the medieval castle. For an example of the tradition, see the castle of Jealousy in the *Romance of the Rose*, 3797ff. The porter Malvenu (Ill-come) is the antithesis of the Belacueil (Fair-welcoming) of the courtly love allegory (e.g., *Romance of the Rose*, 2765ff.), while there is a probably intentional parallel between Lucifera's palace and the Castle Joyous in *F.Q.*, III.i, since Lucifera is a Venerean figure (see st. 8–10n.), so complementing the unchaste Venerean Malecasta, who glitters like 'the proud *Persian* Queenes' (III.i.41). On Persian pride, which links Lucifera with Duessa, cf. ii.13n.

8–10 Lucifera (named at st. 12) gains her name from Lucifer (light-bringer), the morning star and the planet Venus. Cf. E.K.'s gloss on *Shepheardes Calender*, 'December', 84: 'Venus starre otherwise called Hesperus and Vesper and Lucifer, both because he seemeth to be one of the brightest starres, and also first ryseth and setteth last'. It was the name given to Satan by patristic commentators on Isaiah 14:12 ('How art thou fallen from heaven, o Lucifer, sonne of the morning?'; originally applied to Nebuchadnezzar, tyrannical king of Babylon. The Geneva gloss interprets: 'Thou that thoughtest thyself most glorious, and as it were, placed in ye heaven'). Lucifera's function as an embodiment of Satanic pride is confirmed by her comparison with Phaethon, son of Phoebus Apollo, who presumed to control the chariot of the sun and nearly set the heavens and earth on fire (*Met.*, II.47ff.) and whose story had since the Middle Ages been interpreted as an allegory of Lucifer's rebellion against God (Jean Seznec, *The Survival of the Pagan Gods*, tr. Barbara F. Sessions (1961), 93). Spenser uses the Phaethon myth at V.viii.40–1 to signify political usurpation, since it is applied to the Sultan in his chariot, who represents Philip of Spain in his opposition to Elizabeth. Similarly, she shines 'as *Titans* ray' because she is a parody sun (cf. ii.7 and Proem 4n.) and also to underline her rebellious pride, since the giant Titans fought against the Olympian gods and were thrown out of heaven: cf. III.vii.47, V.i.9, and Lotspeich, 63–4. The giant Disdayne, porter to the Lucifera-like Philotime at II.vii.41, is 'Like an huge Gyant of the *Titans* race'. The notion of the giant Titan links Lucifera with her complementary symbol of pride, Orgoglio, at vii.8ff. Her claim to solar supremacy is clearly a Duessa-like

attempt to emulate the solar Una (iii.4n.), just as her name parodies
Una as the morning star (ii.4–6n., 36–8n.); and note that in posing
as 'a mayden Queene' she not only parodies Una at xii.8 but also
Elizabeth, the Virgin Queen. Hankins, 103 links this phrase with
the 'virgine, daughter Babel' of Isaiah 47:1, probably rightly in
view of Lucifera's dragon (st.10) which recalls Duessa on her beast
(vii.16ff., viii.12ff.) and the whore of Babylon (ii.13n.). The phrase
'exceeding shone' anticipates Arthur's shield at vii.34, which
legitimately outshines the sun (see n.), and contrast also the sunny
Fidelia of x.12–13, who bears a cup with a serpent in it. The mirror
which Lucifera holds emphasises her narcissism: 'her selfe-lov'd'
reflection is an attempt to negate the Neoplatonic theme of the *F.Q.*
as a whole – the search for the One above and beyond the self.
Iconographically, the mirror was an emblem of Venus and Luxuria
(Lechery): Seznec, *Survival of the Pagan Gods*, 107, 197;
Tervarent, cols. 273–4; Meg Twycross, *The Medieval
Anadyomene*, 84ff., where it signifies vanity. And since it became,
by slight extension, the mirror of the harlot, there are signs that it
was, in pictorial art, an attribute of the whore of Revelation 17
(Twycross, 84n.). Again, the mirror was an emblem of pride,
because the proud see only things to admire in themselves (Ripa,
479, *s.v. Superbia*, described as a tall and beautiful woman, dressed
in red, with a gold crown, and holding a mirror in her left hand and
a peacock in her right hand; see also Tervarent, col. 273; Chew,
96–7). The sun and a mirror are emblems of Truth (Ripa, 500–1;
Tervarent, *ibid.*, and cf. iii.4n.): further instances of Lucifera's
parody of Una. The dragon links her with the other evil dragons in
Book I (e.g. i.3n.) but it was in addition sometimes an emblem of
pride, presumably because of its identification with the Satanic
serpent (Chew, 97).

11 Lucifera's origins, like Duessa's (v.27), are from hell and
darkness. On Pluto and Proserpina, see i.37n. Jupiter, against
whom the Titans fought (III.vii.47) is ruler of the gods and
traditionally and significantly judge and law giver (Seznec, 156,
158; Curry, *Chaucer and the Mediaeval Seiences*, 127).

12 Lucifera is self-elected to temporal power, like the Pope (see
st. 2n.), like Milton's Satan after her, and above all like Mary
Queen of Scots. Mary's trial for alleged treason (1586–7) is
depicted in V.ix, where Duessa is Mary and Mercilla is the merciful

and just Elizabeth. The description of Mercilla on her throne in her palace (ix.21ff.) closely resembles that of Lucifera. Mercilla, too, is a maiden queen at V.viii.17. Cullen, 41–2 notes the parallel between Lucifera and Satan's temptation of Christ in the wilderness to 'all the kingdomes of the worlde' (Matthew 4:8). But they aren't Satan's (or Lucifera's) in the first place: cf. II.vii.13. 'Pollicie' implies Machiavellian cunning rather than orthodox statesmanship; and the six advisers together with Lucifera make up the total of the seven sins, of which Pride is chief: contrast the seven beadsmen at x.36ff.

13 Vanity looks back to Lucifera's mirror (st. 8–10n.) and was, significantly, sometimes added to the list of deadly sins: Chew, 79, 93; Morton W. Bloomfield, *The Seven Deadly Sins*, 104.

14 The 'loftie eyes' probably come from Proverbs 30:13: 'There is a generacion, whose eyes are hautie, and their eye liddes are lifted up'.

16–17 Lucifera is associated with the dawn goddess as is Una (ii.7n.), who is also linked with the spring goddess Flora at xii.21–3n. (but see i.48n. for adverse comments on Flora). Juno, Jupiter's consort and queen of heaven, is traditionally shown with a chariot drawn by peacocks (*Met.*, II.531–3; Tervarent, cols. 297–8), the eyes on whose tails originally belonged to hundred-eyed Argus and were placed there by Juno when Argus was killed by Mercury (*Met.*, I.717–23). The peacock is an emblem of pride (Ripa, above, st. 8–10n.; Tervarent, cols. 298–9). Aurora has a golden chariot (Allan H. Gilbert, *The Symbolic Persons in the Masques of Ben Jonson*, 50); but Fowler, 73–4 is doubtless right to connect Lucifera in her coach with her six advisers with traditional portrayals of the sun with the six lesser planets, where the comparison with a royal progress was inevitable.

18–20 For a pictorial gloss on the procession, see Plate 4. The sins and their attributes are for the most part traditional. The beasts they ride on symbolise the uncontrolled passions that they represent (see i.1n.), and they are 'unequall' to signify imbalance and disharmony (Whitney, *Emblemes*, 99 has an emblem on unequal union in marriage – *Impar coniugium* – which illustrates the same principle). The procession here should be seen as an unfolding of the seven-headed beast of Revelation on which Duessa

48

Dic: homini quâ non clades damnosior vlla est?
Peccatum; excussis in quo sibi plaudit habenis.

Welck is het quaetste quaet; en dat meer schade inheeft?
Der sonde boose daet; daer-gh'ongheducht in leeft.

Dis moy, quelle peste, Soit la plus funeste, Et de plus d'effroy,
Du peché la tache, Au quel on se lache, Sans bride, et sans loy.

rides in cantos vii and viii, and which was usually interpreted as
Satan with the deadly sins (Tuve, 102–3). Although there was no
fixed order for the sins, Spenser follows a scheme based on the
infernal trinity of Flesh, World, and Devil (Chew, 71–2; Cullen,
40–1): Sloth, Gluttony, and Lechery were sins of the flesh, Avarice
was the worldly sin; while Envy, Wrath, and Pride belonged to the
Devil. For Idleness (Sloth) as the 'norice unto vices', see Chaucer's
Prologe of the Seconde Nonnes Tale, 1ff., and Bloomfield, *Seven
Deadly Sins*, 193, 219; and for the ass as an emblem of sloth and
ignorance, Tervarent, cols. 28–9, and Chew, 101–2. The choice of
a monk complete with breviary (portesse) to represent this sin is
typical of medieval and Renaissance ecclesiastical satire: Chew,
92; Bloomfield, 440, n.256. It is related historically to the links
between Sloth and Melancholy and the contemplative life
(Klibansky, 78, 221n., 300–2, 316–17, and plate 93). Each sin was
traditionally associated with a disease (Bloomfield, 233 and n.),
and the 'shaking fever' here is probably palsy, sometimes attributed
to Sloth (Bloomfield, *ibid.*).

21–3 The pig is a usual attribute of Gluttony (Ripa, 193; Tuve,
104, fig. 23), while the eyes echo Psalms 73:7: 'Their eyes stand out
for fatnes'. The cranelike neck is an emblematic commonplace
(Ripa, *ibid.*), as is the vomiting (Tuve, 190). In st. 22 Spenser
expands his picture of Gluttony by conflating it with Silenus, tutor
to Bacchus, old, fat, drunk, sleepy, with wine jug and garland (*Met.*,
IV.26–7; Vergil, *Eclogues*, VI.13ff.). On the Bacchic ivy, see i.48n.
Gluttony was commonly linked with Bacchus (Chew, 91–2, 103)
and dropsy was usually attributed to him (Bloomfield, 373n.).

24–6 Gluttony and Lechery are often connected (e.g., Chaucer,
Parson's Tale, 836–8: 'After Glotonye thanne comth Lecherie, for
thise two synnes been so ny cosyns that ofte tyme they wol nat
departe'), and so Lechery follows. The goat is the usual symbolic
animal for this sin (Tervarent, col. 49); the 'whally eyes' (i.e.,
showing their whites) are the rolling, active eyes of the jealous man
(cf. Malbecco's ever-open eye at III.x.58); the green of the gown is
the green of Venus (Agrippa, I.xxviii,59) and of youth, the lustful
age, together with the sea-coloured gown of Jealousy (Ripa, 181);
while the 'burning hart' combines the traditional emblem of love
(Tervarent, cols. 102–3) with the flames of Lechery (*ibid.*, 183). His

disease is presumably syphilis (Chew, 106), though he usually suffers from leprosy (Bloomfield, 196) or epilepsy (*ibid.*, 373n.).

27–9 The camel is occasionally associated emblematically with Avarice because of, e.g., Matthew 19:24 ('It is easier for a camel to go through the eye of a nedle, then for a riche man to enter into the kingdome of God'). Spenser may also allude to the fact that it was used to carry treasure (Isaiah 30:6). A laden ass usually appears in emblems of Avarice (e.g., Whitney, *Emblemes*, 18). The poor clothing and bad food are typical characteristics (Whitney, *ibid.*; Ripa, 29–33), as are the coffers (Chew, 107–8). The phrase 'whose plenty made him pore' became proverbial after *Met.*, III.466 ('*inopem me copia fecit*'), where it is uttered by the self-loving Narcissus. The water in which Narcissus saw himself reflected was interpreted by some mythographers – e.g., Boccaccio – as worldly delight, which led the way open for the myth to be applied to avarice (those who gazed on wealth without enjoying the world): e.g., Ben Jonson, *Cynthia's Revels*, I.ii.23ff.; Starnes and Talbert, 197, 200–2. Avarice is old (st. 28) because it was regarded as a sin of old age just as gout was a disease of old age (Chew, 108–9).

30–2 Envy follows Avarice because, again, they were often paired (e.g., Whitney, 95). Envy rides on a wolf not only because it is, like Envy, 'ravenous', but because it was traditionally supposed to be envious (Tuve, 9; Chew, 109; Bloomfield, 246). Similarly, he chews a toad because toads and frogs were supposed to swell with envy (Horace, *Satires*, II.iii.314ff.) and to be poisonous (see i.20n.). Here the toad replaces the vipers that Envy eats at *Met.*, II. 768–9 and that accompany her in the emblem books (Ripa, 241–2; our Plate 1; Whitney, 94, and *F.Q.*, V.xii.30–1): Spenser transfers the snake to Envy's bosom. The sin of Envy is often practised through the eye (Gilbert, *Symbolic Persons*, 85–6), but Spenser's Envy with his tunic 'ypainted full of eyes' recalls the garb of Jealousy (Ripa, 181–2; see st. 16–17n. and 24–6n.). For Envy and leprosy, see Bloomfield, 355 and 373.

33–5 On the lion of Wrath and the burning brand, see iii.33–6n. and our Plate 3. The red eyes are in Ripa, 243, and characteristic of the man under the influence of choleric Mars (Curry, *Chaucer and the Mediaeval Sciences*, 132). Spenser's Wrath is ash-pale with anger and also to anticipate the death often inflicted by anger (st. 35), and he swells with choler (cf.Ripa, *ibid.*, where the notion is taken literally and *Ira* has a swollen face). The torn clothes are signs of wrath (cf. Fury at III.xii.17; Chew, 112), and Spenser's linking of repentance with this sin again seems to be traditional (Chew, 112–13 notes two other instances). Iconographically, many of the qualities exhibited by Wrath are attributes of Mars (Klibansky, 127, 187, 397, etc.) and not surprisingly there is a similarity between st. 35 and the misfortunes bestowed by Mars in Chaucer's *Knight's Tale*, 1995ff. The spleen was often regarded as the seat of anger (e.g., *Richard III*, V.iii.350–1); while 'Saint *Fraunces* fire' is perhaps erysipelas, which causes an inflamed skin and is known as St Anthony's fire ('St Francis's distemper' is mentioned in Rabelais, *Gargantua and Pantagruel*, V.xxi, where it means 'poverty': clearly of no relevance here).

36 Satan (Pride) is the driver (cf. Plate 4). For the implications of the 'foggy mist', see ii.36–8n. and iii.10–20n.

38–9 Under the influence of Duessa and Lucifera, Redcrosse has become forgetful of spiritual joy through his immersion in worldly temptations (for the implications of joy cf. John 16:22: 'And ye now therefore are in sorowe: but I wil se you againe, and your hearts shal rejoyce, and your joye shal no man take from you'); and see i.2n.

41 Sansjoy refers to the reins of reason which control the horse of the passions: see i.1n., and Whitney, 6 ('Then bridle will, and reason make thy guide').

44 On Morpheus, see i.36n. The 'leaden mace' is, Lotspeich, 83 suggests, adapted from the sleep-inducing branch or wand carried by Somnus, god of sleep (*Aeneid*, V.854; and cf. Ripa, 464–5, *s.v. Sonno*). It is *lead* because of that metal's weight (hence it was dedicated to the slow planet Saturn and carries Saturn's associations with night, darkness, 'and those things which stupifie': Agrippa, I.xxv,55–6). Duessa rises when night falls; Una rises with daylight (see iii.21n.).

48 Note the inversion of solar imagery here, characteristic of the canto as a whole. On the '*Stygian* shores', see iii.33–6n.

CANTO V

1 Characteristic Renaissance praise of the active life, ultimately deriving from, e.g., Plato, *Symposium* 206C ('All men are pregnant ... both in body and soul: on reaching a certain age our nature yearns to beget ...'; Loeb edn, tr. W. R. M. Lamb (1946), 191). On glory, see vii.46n., and see also x.58ff. and notes.

2 Redcrosse is again identified with the sun: cf. iii. 5–9n. The opening lines allude to Psalms 19:4–5: the sun 'cometh forthe as a bridegrome out of his chambre, and rejoyceth like a mightie man to runne his race'. The allusion works proleptically, anticipating the epithalamic echoes of xii.21ff. and hinting at the emergence of Una from her concealing veil at the same point; for the Geneva gloss on 'chambre' in Psalms 19:5 suggests the alternative reading 'vaile', and explains: 'The maner was that the bride and bridegrome shuld stand under a vaile together, & after come forthe with great solemnitie and rejoycing of ye assemblie'. But Redcrosse is fighting in part for the wrong cause here – Duessa and her approval, which suggests that, like Lucifera before whom he fights, he is a false sun, as, indeed, Sansjoy too has been at iv.48. As a false sun, Redcrosse specifically parodies the Arthur of vii.29, whose function it is to redeem him from the night of Orgoglio's dungeon: see viii.38–41n. The phrase 'runne his race' reminds us that Redcrosse abandons his race at vii.2ff., thereby leaving himself open to Orgoglio.

3–4 The music which 'drive[s] away the dull melancholy' and the 'heavenly melody' of st. 17 parody the details of the celebrations at xii.38–9, confirming Lucifera's palace as an inversion of the palace of Una's parents and suggesting that she is the usurper of their dominion as well as an inversion of Una. There is perhaps a suggestion in st. 4 of Song of Solomon 8:2 ('I wil cause thee to drinke spiced wine'), which would confirm the epithalamic implications here (see ii.7n.). Upton, *Var. Sp.*, I.225–6 noticed that the details of procedure follow those customary in chivalric romance and are in accord with actual practice. More specifically, there is a parody of Elizabeth's Accession Day tilts: see II.ii.40–2n. and Yates, 88ff. See also I.vi.7–10n.

8   Redcrosse is compared to a griffin, Sansjoy to a dragon. To interpret the simile at its simplest level, the former is an emblem of Christ (de Vries, 229; George Ferguson, *Signs and Symbols in Christian Art*, 20), the latter represents Satan. But its implications are probably more complex: the griffin is half eagle and half lion and appropriate to Redcrosse's solar role since both creatures were attributed to the sun (see iii.5–9n., xi.33–4n., and Agrippa, I.xxiii, 53), though in view of his 'flaming corage' (st. 1) and fierceness and 'youthly heat' (st. 7) we should also see Redcrosse as choleric, and the eagle and lion were often associated with that temperament: iii.33–6n. and Klibansky, 378 and plate 120. In one sense, Redcrosse is manifesting the correct temperament for his age (he is 'a tall clownishe younge man' in Spenser's prefatory *Letter of the Authors*): the usual equations in the four ages of man scheme were prime or youth (age twenty to forty)—summer–fire–choleric temperament (Seznec, *Survival of the Pagan Gods*, 47: Klibansky, 369). Nevertheless, although natural from one point of view, Redcrosse's choler is a culpable excess which will be replaced in canto x by its traditional answering virtue, patience (x.23n.). Sansjoy's dragon links him with the other evil dragons in the book and confirms his temperamental joylessness, since the dragon was a Saturnian creature and so associated with the dark, melancholy, and gloomy: Agrippa, I.xxv,56; Ripa, 54; Tervarent, col. 82. Sansjoy's melancholic temperament is also suited to his immediate situation – his grief over his dead brother – though as an avenging warrior he is still choleric and wrathful (st. 10). In terms of moral psychology he is probably a choleric melancholic – a condition, significantly, which Redcrosse himself later suffers from (viii.38–41n.).

10   The redoubling of Sansjoy's wrath when he sees his brother's shield echoes *Aeneid*, XII.938ff., where Aeneas's fury increases when he sees the baldric worn by Turnus, the spoils from Pallas, 'the one whom he loved' (*Var. Sp.*, I.227). On the Styx, see iii.33–6n. and cf. iv.48. The ghosts of those who have not been buried with customary rites are condemned to wander its shores and not pass over into Hades (*Aeneid*, VI.325ff.: see st. 13).

13   Sansjoy is overcome but not, significantly in view of the later encounter with Despair (see i.2n.), finally defeated. The 'darkesome clowd' is a familiar device: e.g., *Iliad*, III.380ff. (Aphrodite

snatching up Paris in thick darkness); *Aeneid*, V.808ff. (Aeneas
wrapped in a cloak of mist); *Ger. Lib.*, VII.43ff., Armida's rescue of
Rambaldo from Tancred by creating a thick gloom (Blanchard in
Var. Sp., I.228). In view of other very general parallels noticed by
Rosenthal (*ibid.*, I.223) between the encounter of Redcrosse and
Sansjoy and Palamon and Arcite in Chaucer's *Knight's Tale*,
2095ff., there may be a reminiscence of the 'furie infernal' sent by
Pluto at Saturn's request to overthrow Arcite (2684). The point of
the Chaucer parallel would presumably lie in the kinship of
Palamon and Arcite (1011ff.) which confirms the affinities at this
point between Redcrosse and his enemy.

15 This time Redcrosse is compared to Aeneas: his search for
Sansjoy parallels Aeneas's search in clouds of dust for Turnus
(*Aeneid*, XII.466–7). Turnus was understood as meaning 'violent
mind' (Allen, 139, citing Fulgentius's medieval commentary on the
Aeneid).

17 The wine and oil are Biblical salves (Luke 10:34: 'and bounde
up his woundes, and powred in oyle and wine'). Contrast these
physical remedies with the spiritual purging in canto x after the
encounter with Despair (Sansjoy in his extreme form); and cf.
ii.40–1n.

18 Duessa is the traditionally hypocritical crocodile, reputed to
weep when it has devoured a man (Ansell Robin, 53–5). Redcrosse
is the traveller by the Nile because of the Biblical associations of
Egypt with bondage and its consequent patristic identification with
the bodily passions (e.g., A. D. S. Fowler, 'The River Guyon',
M.L.N., LXXV (1960), citing Valeriano, *Hieroglyphica*, XXI.xiv,
XXXIV.ix). The Nile's seven mouths (see *Aeneid*, VI.800) relate to
the seven-headed beast of Revelation (see vii.16–18n.) and the
seven deadly sins. Seven also symbolises mortality and mutability:
see I.vii, headnote, and II.ix.22n. For a further, related, allusion to
the Israelites' escape from Egypt, see x.53–4n.

20 The 'blacke ... mantle', chariot, and horses are traditional
details found, e.g., at *Aeneid*, V.721ff. and repeated by Renaissance
mythographers (Lotspeich, 91, citing Natalis Comes, *Mythologiae*).
For the black horses, see Ripa, 59, describing Night's chariot.
Iron is almost invariably associated with the underworld: *Iliad*,
VIII.15 (Tartarus's iron gate); Dante, *Inferno*, VIII.

22–3 Night is 'most auncient Grandmother of all' because she was the offspring of the primal Chaos (Hesiod, *Theogony*, 116ff.; Lotspeich, 91). On Demogorgon, see i.37n. Spenser reveals the ultimate chaotic affinities of the three brothers, Night's 'Nephewes deare' (i.e. grandchildren, Latin *nepos*: Upton in *Var. Sp.*, I.232). *Aveugle* = blind (French), a character invented by Spenser. But see iii.10–20n., and especially the reference to Panofsky, whose pp. 110–11 and n. discuss sightless or blindfold Night (*caeca nox*). The connection noted by Panofsky of Night–Death–Old Testament is confirmed by the echoes in st. 23 of Deuteronomy 28:26: 'And thy carkeis shal be meat unto all foules of the ayre', and 1 Samuel 17:46: 'I wil give the carkeises of the hoste of the Philistims this day unto the foules of the heaven'.

25–6 The 'chayne of strong necessitee' originates with *Iliad*, VIII.18–27 where Zeus tells the other gods to test his might by lowering a golden rope from heaven to earth and trying to drag him down by all pulling on it. This rope or chain was often interpreted as the chain of concord and love binding the universe together (cf. I.ix.1, IV.i.30; and contrast II.vii.44–50n.) and, as here, the chain of necessity. For the history of the idea, see A. O. Lovejoy, *The Great Chain of Being: A Study of the History of an Idea* (New York, 1960), *passim*. Night thus admits the principle of order and cosmos, despite her paternal link with Chaos. Not surprisingly, though, in view of her Old Testament associations, she echoes Sansloy's 'eye for an eye' ethic at st. 26 (see iii.33–6n.). The phrase 'sonnes of Day' recalls 1 Thessalonians 5:5 ('Ye are all the children of light, and the children of the day: we are not of the night nether of darkenes'), as Alpers, 344 has noticed. In view of Redcrosse's Christian armour, and the fact that he and Sansjoy have been fighting over Sansfoy's shield, it is significant that verse 8 reads: 'But let us which of the day, be sober, putting on ye brest plate of faith and love'.

26–7 On Duessa's parentage, compare Hesiod, *Theogony*, 224ff. where Night is described as giving birth to, among others, Deceit, Strife, Lies, and Lawlessness, though Shame is not mentioned.

28 Ripa, 59 has Night's chariot drawn by *two* black horses, but the number here is probably influenced by Pluto's chariot which is drawn by four black horses (Tervarent, col. 76; Seznec, *Survival of* *the Pagan Gods*, 236n.). The unlike colours (black and brown) and unlike pairing recall the 'unequall' team that draws Lucifera's chariot (iv.18–20n.).

30 In Appollonius Rhodius, *Argonautica*, III.1216–17, Hecate makes a terrifying appearance with the dogs of the underworld barking about her. The owl is an emblem of Night and her offspring Death (Tervarent, cols. 96–7; Wind, 165) and the wolf is a symbol of the devil (as in John 10:12) and Night (Genesis 49:27). Spenser is concerned to establish an atmosphere of black magic: cf. Lucan, *Pharsalia*, VI.685ff: 'Her voice, more powerful than any drug to bewitch the powers of Lethe . . . the bark of the dog and the howl of the wolf were in it – it was like the complaint of the scared owl'.

31–4 The descent to the underworld is modelled on Aeneas's descent to Hades in *Aeneid*, VI. Its purpose is the physical restoration of Sansjoy, which is answered by Redcrosse's three-day fight with the dragon in canto xi, his affirmation of his spiritual regeneration and re-enactment of Christ's harrowing of hell (see x.36–43n.). Neoplatonic readings of the *Aeneid* saw Aeneas's visit as an allegory of the soul's descent into matter (Allen 152–3). But Aeneas was also understood to have obtained divine knowledge and renewal (see II.vii.21–5n.); so that Spenser juxtaposes pagan modes with Christian redemption, another specific parallel being between this canto and canto viii, where Redcrosse, imprisoned in Orgoglio's dungeon, is rescued by Arthur and Una (just as Night and Duessa seek Sansjoy's cure here): see Hamilton, 70–1.

The deep cave by Lake Avernus with its poisonous atmosphere, through which entry is made to the underworld, is from *Aeneid*, VI.237ff., and the return through 'heavenly grace' of those who have descended there recalls *ibid.*, 129–31, where the Sibyl tells Aeneas that some who were loved by Jupiter or were excessively heroic have been allowed to return. There is probably a reminiscence here of Juno's visit to Hades at *Met.*, IV.449ff., where she summons the 'Furies, sisters born of Night' (*ibid.*, 451–2). Vergil, *Aeneid*, VI.280 mentions the Furies' iron chambers near the entrance to Hades, but as Lotspeich, 61 notes, their *chains* (mentioned also at ix.24) seem to be original with Spenser, though perhaps influenced by the clanking iron chains heard by Aeneas at VI.558. Acheron is connected with woe (discussed by, e.g., Comes, *Mythologiae*, III.i; Lotspeich, 31), and Phlegethon is the infernal river of fire (*Aeneid*, VI.550–1). 'The house of endlesse paine' perhaps recalls *Aeneid*, VI.554ff., the iron tower where Rhadamanthus and Tisiphone judge and scourge sinners. Three-headed Cerberus is the dog who guards the entrance to the underworld: Vergil mentions his snaky mane (*ibid.*, 419), and his 'flaming tong' is paralleled in Spenser's translation of *Virgils Gnat*, 346, where Cerberus emits flames from his mouth. The final line of st. 34 echoes *Aeneid*, VI.247, where Hecate is 'mighty in heaven and in hell'.

35 The punishments here are familiar from *Odyssey*, XI; *Met.*, IV and X (Orpheus's descent); and *Aeneid*, VI. Ixion was bound to a wheel for trying to win the love of Juno, wife of Jupiter. Jupiter deceived him by making a phantom Juno out of a cloud, on whom Ixion begot the Centaurs (half men, half horse): Starnes and Talbert, 116, and cf. i.45n. (the false Una) and Duessa's deceiving of Fradubio in canto ii. Sisyphus was apparently of generally bad behaviour and various reasons were given for his punishment (Lotspeich, 107–8); on Tantalus see II.vii.57–60n.; Tityus was a giant who, for attacking Latona, was cast into Tartarus, where a vulture devoured his liver (*Aeneid*, VI.595ff.). The perpetual renewing of his tissues is a parody of the symbolism of spiritual renewal at xi.29ff. and 46ff., and his crime against Latona parallels Redcrosse's abuse of Una and Sansloy's attack on her at vi.3ff. As a giant and therefore a son of Earth (e.g., Starnes and Talbert, 281–2) he is associated with Typhoeus/Typhon, who was one of the rebels against Jupiter (Lotspeich, 113, who notes that his punishment here was probably invented by Spenser. On the significance of giants, see vii. 8–10n.). Theseus 'went down to hell with his friend Perithous, to ravish Proserpina, where Perithous was slain, and he put in chains, but was delivered by Hercules' (Alexander Ross, *Mystagogus Poeticus* (1647), 399–400, cit. Starnes and Talbert, 412–13; see also II.vii. 53–4n.). Theseus sits 'hopeless' at *Aeneid*, VI.617–18, but Boccaccio, *De Genealogia Deorum*, I.xiv, paraphrasing the Vergil passage, introduces the word *otium* (sloth): Lotspeich, 111. Spenser perhaps intends a parallel with Redcrosse in Orgoglio's dungeon, rescued by Arthur after being misled into sloth by Duessa at the beginning of canto vii. The 'fifty sisters' are the daughters of Danaus, who killed their husbands on their marriage night at their father's command: their punishment was to pour water into a vessel full of holes (*Met.*, IV.462–3).

36–44 In *Aeneid*, VII.765ff. it is narrated how Hippolytus died by the cunning of his stepmother Phaedra, who was in love with him but was rejected. In her anger she told her husband, Theseus, that Hippolytus had made love to her, and he asked his father, the sea god Poseidon, to kill him, which he did by sending sea calves to frighten the horses pulling Hippolytus's chariot. They dragged him until he died (see also Starnes and Talbert, 215–16). He was cured by Apollo's son Aesculapius (who, for his presumption in reviving a mortal, was thrown by Jupiter into Hades) and subsequently protected by Diana. Spenser again offers an analogue to Redcrosse's history, the parallel being between Hippolytus and Redcrosse, Phaedra and Duessa, and Aesculapius and Arthur. As Fowler, 72–3, notes, Aesculapius is an underworld antitype to the Sun of righteousness which governs the book as a whole, and his herbal cure again contrasts with Redcrosse's spiritual healing in I.x and xi. Moreover, his emblem is a serpent, symbol of renewal since it sloughs its skin (Whitney, *Emblemes*, 212; Agrippa, II.xlv,303; see also Macrobius, *Saturnalia*, I.xx where it is in addition identified as a solar symbol). For the parallel-in-contrast with Fidelia's serpent, see x.12–13n.; and note the significant mention of Phoebus 'recuring' himself beneath the ocean while this infernal therapy goes on (st. 44).

45–6 Redcrosse has fled Lucifera's palace because of his dwarf's vision in its dungeon of classical and Biblical examples of sin. The vision is an ironic reversal of the panorama of Roman worthies seen by Aeneas in *Aeneid*, VI.754ff. (which has its true parallel in *F.Q.*, II.x, and III.iii and ix), and contrasts with Redcrosse's telescoped Christian view of history – the old law succeeded by the new – at I.x.53–4 and n. Spenser's main source is Chaucer's *Monk's Tale*, itself written in the familiar medieval tradition of tales of the falls of famous men and influenced by Boccaccio's fourteenth-century *De Casibus Virorum Illustrium (Concerning the Falls of Great Men)* and his *De Claris Mulieribus (Concerning Famous Women)*, and by the Fortune section of the *Romance of the Rose*, which in turn probably influenced Spenser directly in his depiction of Lucifera's palace: see iv.4n. It is a typical

medieval–Renaissance warning against pride in earthly glory: cf.
Rathborne, ch. I; and see, too, vii.46n. and x.58ff. and notes.

47 Babylon was traditionally associated with pride and
Antichrist. The 'proud king' is Nebuchadnezzar who, in Daniel 3,
set up a golden image for his subjects to worship and punished
those who would not adore it by putting them in a fiery furnace. At
Daniel 4:27ff., as he is contemplating Babylon's might, a voice
from heaven tells him 'Thy kingdome is departed from thee, and
they shal drive thee from men, and thy dwelling shalbe with the
beasts of the field: they shal make thee to eat grasse, as the oxen'.
This punishment is to last until he recognises God's power.
Chaucer has him as an example, *Monk's Tale*, 2143ff. Croesus, the
extremely wealthy last king of Lydia, lived in the sixth century
B.C.; Antiochus (cf. *Monk's Tale*, 2575ff.) was king of Syria in the
second century B.C. He besieged Jerusalem and tried to compel the
Jews to abandon their religion (1 Maccabees 1). Like
Nebuchadnezzar he was regarded as an example of excessive pride.

48 Nimrod was 'mighty in the Earth' (Genesis 10:8). The Geneva
gloss on this phrase is: 'Meaning, a cruel oppressor & tyrant'. His
pride led to the building of the Tower of Babel (Genesis 11), a sign,
according to the Geneva gloss on 11:4, that he preferred his 'own
glorie to God's honour'. Ninus, with his wife Semiramis, was the
mythical founder of the Assyrian empire of Nineveh. Pagan history
was traditionally regarded as beginning with him (Rathborne, 74
and n.). Cf. II.ix.21n. for the connection with Babel. The 'mightie
Monarch' is Alexander the Great (cf. *Monk's Tale*, 2631ff.), son of
Philip II of Macedonia, born 356 B.C. It was in 331, after founding
Alexandria, that he visited the temple of Jupiter Ammon and was
greeted by the priests as that god's son. He died through fever and
excessive drinking or poison. The latter tradition is followed by
Chaucer. His death occurred outside Babylon, which he was
intending to make the capital of his empire.

49 Romulus was the mythical founder of Rome (probably
included here because the papal empire was a continuation of the
original Roman empire: see ii.22n.); Tarquinius Superbus,
tyrannical king of Rome, was banished in 510 B.C. when the
republic was established. He tried unsuccessfully to re-establish his
sovereignty. Lentulus was the name of one of the most arrogant

Roman patrician families; Scipio Africanus, born *c*. 234 B.C., believed he was the special favourite of the gods, and is perhaps best known for his conquest of Hannibal and his Carthaginian forces at Naragra in 202 B.C.; Cornelius Sylla, the dissolute Roman dictator, died in 78 B.C.; the ambitious Marius, Sylla's rival, achieved his seventh consulship after banishment and much bloodshed. He died in 86 B.C. *'Caesar'* is Julius Caesar, assassinated in 44 B.C.; Pompey the Great was defeated by the forces of Caesar, his rival, at Pharsalia in 48 B.C., and was killed the same year when he sought refuge in Egypt; 'fierce *Antonius'*, lover of Cleopatra, was defeated by Octavian at the battle of Actium, 31 B.C. He killed himself the next year when told, falsely, that Cleopatra had committed suicide.

50 The 'yoke' which women are supposed not to forget is, predictably, Pauline: see Ephesians 5:22: 'Wives, submit your selves unto your husbands, as unto the Lord'. Semiramis (see st. 48n.) dressed as a man, restored the city of Babylon, and fell in love with her effeminate son Ninus, who killed her when she tried to make love to him (Boccaccio, *De Claris Mulieribus*, tr. Guido A. Guarino (1964), 4–7). Sthenoboea, wife of Proetus, killed herself when her advances to Bellerophon were rejected and she heard that he had married someone else (Lotspeich, 108). Cleopatra's death by asp sting is given in Plutarch's *Life of Anthony* and is the version preferred by Boccaccio, *ibid.*, 196.

53 On this final view of the 'sad house of *Pride*', so different from its glittering first appearance, see iv.4–5n.

CANTO VI

2–3 The narrative returns to Una and her wanderings in the wilderness, which have included India and the West Indies. She is still in the power of Sansloy who, at the end of canto iii, had replaced the lion (itself a surrogate for Redcrosse) as Una's companion. Sansloy is compared to a lion at st. 7.

4 Sansloy's 'fawning wordes' parody the lion's behaviour at iii.6 ('lickt her lilly hands with fawning tong'); and compare the wood gods at st. 12. Not only is Sansloy's behaviour exactly opposite to that of the lion, in that he fails to respect the royal virgin (iii.5–9n.); he also tears aside her veil (cf. iii.4 and n.). The earlier removal of the veil had suggested the divine nature of Truth that, in a fallen world, can shine only away from the haunts of men. Now Sansloy looks on Una, but governed by appetite rather than reason he is incapable of ascending the Neoplatonic ladder of contemplation: he remains at the level of bestial love with no hope of seeing her as a Venus Urania (see Proem 4n. and i.48n.). On Una as 'rocke of Diamond', see vii.33–5n., and cf. iv.5n.

6 Spenser probably echoes Matthew 24:29, where Christ tells of the omens that will follow the arising of 'false Christs, & false prophetes' (i.e., Sansloy as the false lion): 'And immediately after the tribulations of those dayes, shal the sunne be darkened, . . . and the starres shal fall from heaven.'

7–10 Una is rescued providentially by fauns and satyrs (cf. 2 Timothy 4:17: 'the Lord assisted me, and strengthened me, that by me the preaching might be fully knowen, and that all the Gentiles shulde heare, and I was delivered out of the mouth of the lion'). Significantly, her rescuers are compared to a (good) lion in the simile in st. 10. In contrast to Sansloy they instinctively reverence her. The fauns (half man, half goat) and satyrs (also goat men), the companions of the wood god Sylvanus (identified with Pan and Faunus and himself a goat man: Starnes and Talbert, 80) are to be distinguished from the lawless wild man of whom Orgoglio is the example in Book I (see vii.8–10n.). Although they traditionally symbolise man's lower nature – the dichotomy between appetite and reason (e.g., Ripa, 295, where Faunus is an example of *lussuria*, or lust) – Spenser uses them here in a much less censorious way. In this rather beautiful pastoral episode they represent natural man living in accordance with natural law (contrast Sansloy). Several degrees up the chain of being from the lion, king of the quadrupeds, they are custodians of the wood, perhaps even fulfilling a divine function there: 'The ancients . . . imagined the fauns and Sylvanus as tutelary deities who watched over those who worked in field or forest; for nothing can happen, even in field or forest, without the knowledge of God' (Natalis Comes, *Mythologiae*, X, *De faunis*, cited by Lemmi, *Var. Sp.*, I.240). The episode as a whole touches on the long-standing Renaissance debate over the savage: whether he was to be regarded as innocent or depraved and bestial (see Frank Kermode's Introduction to the New Arden *Tempest*, xxxiv ff., and Richard Bernheimer, *Wild Men in the Middle Ages*, 102ff.). Far from idealising the wood gods, though, Spenser intends us to recall the iconographic tradition in which Ignorance was depicted as a hybrid monster, specifically the Sphinx (human upper parts, leonine nether parts: see Jonson's *Love Freed from Ignorance and Folly*, 5 (*Masques*, ed. Orgel, 174)). For its visual affinities with the satyr-figure, see our Plate 5; and compare the discussion of it in Gilbert, *Symbolic Persons*, 129–31. Una's encounter contrasts with Helenore's enjoyment of the satyrs at III.x.43ff.; with Amoret's abduction in a wood by a lustful wild man at IV.vii.5ff.; and with Serena's abominable treatment by the cannibals at VI.viii.35ff. which, in its religious/erotic details, is in absolute contrast to Una's treatment here. The tableau of the wood gods' worship of Una is a direct answer to Lucifera's presumptuous pardoy of the Accession Day tilts (see v.3–4n.). It is elevated into the pastoral mode in accordance with the imagery of some of those tilts: see Yates, 99–100 on the instance in which a knight in rustic dress introduced country people to the Queen: he and they have been praying for her and wish now to see and admire her.

13–14 On the crowning of Una, cf. i.48n. and ii.36–8n. The possibilities for the 'olive girlond' are several: the olive is sacred to Faunus (*Aeneid*, XII.766) – confirmation of the satyrs' idolatrous paganising of Una; it is the emblem of Athena, the wise virginal goddess who is often associated with Diana (Tervarent, col. 290); it is associated with beauty ('his beautie shalbe as the olive tre': Hosea 14:6); but primarily it is an emblem of peace (see II.ii.31n.), and Spenser intends it to carry the implications that it did in the 'April' eclogue of *The Shepheardes Calender*, the eclogue which celebrates Queen Elizabeth: '*Chloris*, that is the chiefest Nymph of al, / Of Olive braunches beares a Coronall: / Olives bene for peace' (121–3). Chloris was pursued and raped by Zephyrus (Ovid, *Fasti*, V.183ff.) and in compensation she was made Flora, goddess of flowers: on Flora and the false Una, see i.48n.; on the true Una and Flora, see xii.21–3n. The 'doubled Eccho' has its analogue in the refrain to Spenser's *Epithalamion* and symbolises the reciprocity between the satyrs and their surroundings. Spenser also has in mind Lucretius, *De rerum natura*, IV.568ff., where places

IGNORANTIA.

Submouendam ignorantiam.

Διαλογισμός.

Quod mōstrū id? Sphinx est. Cur cādida virginis ore,
    Et volucrum pennas, crura leonis habet?
Hanc faciem assumpsit rerum ignorantia: tanti
    Scilicet est triplex causa & origo mali.
Sunt quos ingeniū leue, sunt quos blanda voluptas,
    Sunt & quos faciunt corda superba rudes.
At quibus est notum, quid Delphica littera possit:
    Præcipitis monstri guttura dira secant.
Nāq, vir ipse, bipesq, tripesq, & quadrupes idē est,
    Primaq, prudentis laurea, nosse virum.

with echoes are reputedly haunted by satyrs, nymphs, and Faunus. Sylvanus is usually depicted as an old man (Smith, III.825–6 with refs.); he carries a cypress branch (Vergil, *Georgics*, I.20; Gilbert, *Symbolic Persons*, 226–7) in memory of the boy Cyparissus, whom he loved but who died of grief when Sylvanus accidentally killed his tame deer. As he grieved, he was metamorphosed into the tree that bears his name. In *Met.*, X.106ff. the story is told of Apollo and Cyparissus, though there the boy kills the deer; but it is commonly told of Sylvanus by the mythographers and dictionary-compilers: Lotspeich, 51; Starnes and Talbert, 80. Contrast the true wild man Orgoglio with his 'snaggy Oke' torn from the earth (vii.10n.). The Bacchic ivy (see i.48n.) suggests revelry without pejorative implications.

15 Cybele, the great earth mother, is said to have taught Dionysus–Bacchus the mysteries (Apollodorus, *Library*, II.v.1) and so her rites had a large Bacchic element in them, being celebrated with howling and a loud noise of cymbals and other instruments (Ovid, *Fasti*, IV.179ff.). Perhpas significantly her chariot is drawn by lions to suggest her power over ungovernable forces (Andrew Tooke, *Pantheon* (1824), 148; Fowler, plate 16a). Dryope is the lover of Faunus at *Aeneid* X.551; while Pholoe, in Ovid, *Fasti*, II.273 a mountain frequented by Pan, is in Statius, *Silvae*, II.iii.8–11 a nymph loved by Pan (Lotspeich, 101). On the identification of Sylvanus, Faunus, and Pan, see st. 7–10n. above.

16 Sylvanus's reaction to Una recalls a Renaissance commonplace which originates with *Aeneid*, I.314ff., where Aeneas encounters his mother, Venus, in a wood but fails to recognise her because she is disguised as a virgin hunter. Aeneas's reaction at 332–3 is that she is 'certainly a goddess' ('*O Dea, certe*') and must be Apollo's sister (Diana). Lines 331–2 gave Spenser his verbal 'emblems' at the close of the 'April' *Shepheardes Calender* in praise of Elizabeth (see st. 13–14n.), and Renaissance mythographers interpreted the mystery of Venus appearing as her opposite, Diana, as a symbol of chaste love. The point in the Spenser passage is that Sylvanus, befogged by pagan ignorance, takes her as one or the other: in fact Una is both, as Spenser confirms at xii.7–8 (where she is Diana) and 21 (where she is the Venerean morning star). In being both she transcends the sum of her parts, embodying the familiar Neoplatonic concept of the Many in the One (see General Introduction, and Wind, 75ff. and 205 with specific reference to Venus–Diana). In combining the two Una also resolves the 'Choice of Hercules' motif which confronts Fradubio (ii.36–8n.): we are reminded of Fradubio by the metamorphosis of Cyparissus, whose story we hear at st. 17. On Venus–Diana see II.iii.21–30n. and cf. III.vi.16ff.

18 Classical nymphs became equated with the native fairy tradition, so that the tree-nymph Hamadryad and fresh-water nymph Naiad became, respectively, 'fayries of the woddes' and 'Elfes or Fayries, haunting ryvers and fountaynes' (Starnes and Talbert, 105, citing Cooper's *Thesaurus*).

19 The idolatrous worship of Una's ass recalls a well-known contemporary emblem of the ass carrying the image of Isis (see our Plate 6) which believes that the crowd is worshipping it and not the image. This was usually, as in the Whitney instance, interpreted as a warning to the clergy against pride, since they are the instruments only of God's word, and have no importance in themselves. Spenser slightly modifies this reading of the emblem to emphasise the related meaning of the ass as the gospel, a meaning which derives from patristic commentaries on Judges 15:16, Samson's slaying of the Philistines with an ass's jawbone from which, when Samson threw it down, water came. In patristic glosses the slaying of the Philistines was seen as a type of Christ's overcoming of the Gentiles and secular philosophy, the jawbone symbolising the Word, the water being wisdom and everlasting life (John Steadman, 'Una and the Clergy: the Ass Symbol in *The Faerie Queene*', *J.W.I.*, XXI (1958), 134–7, citing St Gregory and other Fathers and Cornelius Agrippa's *Of the Vanitie and Uncertaintie of Artes and Sciences* (1530)).

The wood gods probably represent superstitious rustics who retain an intuitive reverence for Truth and the Word during their period of exile (England in the arms of Duessa–Rome). As Steadman, 135 notes, there is an echo of Acts 14:11–18, where the inhabitants of Lystra worship Paul and Barnabas as pagan gods (Mercury and Jove). Paul tells them: 'We are even men ... and preache unto you, that ye shulde turne from these vaine idoles unto the living God'. The wood gods' pagan ignorance of Una's meaning is reinforced by the traditional idea of Isis as veiled Truth (cf. Una's own veil, especially at iii.4n.). Plutarch remarks in this connection

Non tibi, sed Religioni.

THE paſtors good, that doe gladd tidinges preache,
    The godlie ſorte, with reuerence do imbrace:
Though they be men, yet ſince Godds worde they teache,
Wee honor them, and giue them higheſte place,
        Imbaſſadors of princes of the earthe,
        Haue royall Seates, thoughe baſe they are by birthe.

Yet, if throwghe pride they doe them ſelues forgett,
And make accompte that honor, to be theires:
And doe not marke with in whoſe place they ſett,
Let them behowlde the aſſe, that ISIS beares,
        Whoe thowghte the men to honor him, did kneele,
        And ſtaied therfore, till he the ſtaffe did feele.

For, as he paſſ'd with ISIS throughe the ſtreete,
And bare on backe, his holie rites about,
Th'Ægyptians downe fell proſtrate at his feete,
Whereat, the Aſſe, grewe arrogante and ſtowte,
        Then ſaide the guide; oh foole not vnto thee,
        Theiſe people bowe, but vnto that they ſee?

that at Sais the statue of Athena, whom the inhabitants believe to be Isis, has the inscription: 'I am all that has been, and is, and shall be, and my robe no mortal has yet uncovered' (*De Iside et Osiride*, 354C; *Moralia*, tr. F. C. Babbit, Loeb edn, V (1936), 25). Athena and Isis could easily be identified since both were moon goddesses: see Plutarch, *De Facie quae in orbe Lunae apparet*, 938B ('The moon . . . is Athena'), and *F.Q.*, V.vii.4, where we are told '*Isis* doth the Moone portend'. The Una who has just explicitly been identified with the moon goddess Diana (see st. 16n.) is thus literally an Isis who embodies a mystery too dark for the wood gods. As Percival, 249 noted, Una on her ass may be an allusion to the familiar medieval Feast of the Ass which commemorated the Flight into Egypt and the entry into Jerusalem by introducing into the church an ass ridden by a girl, at whom the ass's litany was chanted (*Orientis partibus / Adventavit asinus*: from eastern regions came the ass). Here again the ass is a symbol of Christ: for details, see Evans, 269ff.

20–6 Satyrane (named at st. 28) is the offspring of a lustful satyr (st. 22) and Thyamis (Greek *thumos*, passion, appetite), daughter of Labryde (Greek *labros*, furious, violent, impetuous) and wife of Therion (Greek for 'wild beast': Percival, 250). He originates from brute sexuality and is the conventional wild man, born of a satyr and human girl (see Bernheimer, *Wild Men in the Middle Ages*, 100). He is third in the chain of being which began with the lion and had as its middle link the satyrs themselves, and in controlling his environment by taming wild beasts he contrasts with the lawless giant wild man Orgoglio (see vii.8–10n.). Satyrane is more like Arthegall, the savage knight of IV.iv.39ff. who is the titular knight of Book V and who has tamed wild beasts under the guidance of Astraea, virgin goddess of justice (V.i.6–8; the wild man is traditionally lord of animals: Bernheimer, 27–30). There is an element of the monster-quelling Hercules (often depicted as a wild man: Bernheimer, 101–2) in Satyrane, and, as with Hercules, the overcoming of animals signifies self-restraint, victory over the passions (see i.19n.). The animals are to be interpreted symbolically: the lion signifies wrath, as does the bear (also lust: Tervarent, cols. 291–2); the bull, too, is traditionally fierce (e.g., Psalms 22:12–13, where bulls are compared to lions, and cf. *F.Q.*, IV.x.46). But the riding on a bull might add a Bacchic element (cf.

st. 13–15n.) since Bacchus rode a bull (Theocritus, XX.33). This would confirm Satyrane as a figure symbolising natural energies and also as a tamer of unruly passions, since Bacchus was well known as a lawgiver (see II.x.72–3n., and V.i.2). The leopard (st. 25) is Bacchic (Tervarent, col. 234), as is the panther of st. 26 (Ripa, 59; and cf. 294, where it and the leopard are emblems of lust. By referring specifically to its spots, Spenser perhaps alludes to the panther as a familiar emblem of deceit, attracting its prey with its hide and then attacking them: Ripa, 228–9; Peacham, *Minerva Britanna*, 47.) The 'pardale' is a leopard or panther, and the tiger is Bacchic as well, controlled by Bacchus since it along with the others was often depicted drawing his chariot (Ripa, 59; *Met.*, III.668–9). The boar is associated with lust (Tervarent, col. 335), though it might be anti-Bacchic (and hence the object of Satyrane's attentions) because it destroys the Bacchic vine in Psalms 80:13. The antelope is included for its swiftness, which Satyrane outruns. In subjugating the beasts with 'yron yokes' and constraining them 'in equall teme to draw' Satyrane is imposing an order on the forces of nature and the passions in accordance with Bacchus's role as lawgiver and in contrast to Lucifera (iv.18–20n.). As Upton noted (*Var. Sp.*, I.246), the education of Satyrane recalls the education of Achilles by the wise centaur Cheiron (half man, half horse), and that of Ruggiero by his uncle Atlante in *O.F.*, VII.56ff., where he is taught to overcome tigers, boars, and panthers.

28–30   The transformation of wild man into knight was familiar in the Middle Ages: Bernheimer, 18–19. But Satyrane periodically returns to his origins – the natural energies upon which, properly harnessed, civilisation depends. The theme is developed in Book VI, where Calidore makes a more extended but similar journey in cantos ix and x. See Donald Cheney, *Spenser's Image of Nature*, 63–5.

31   On 'faith and veritie' see i.2n.

33–48   This episode is based on *O.F.*, I and II, in which Angelica entrusts herself to Sacripante as Una does to Satyrane, and Sacripante fights Rinaldo as Satyrane fights Sansloy. The role of Archimago parallels that of Ariosto's hermit (see *Var. Sp.*,

I.246–7). Spenser's handling of Ariostan material is discussed by
Alpers, ch. VI.

35 Archimago, identified at st. 48, appears as a pilgrim complete
with his staff, called 'a *Jacobs* staffe' to single him out as a pilgrim
to the shrine of Santiago (St James) de Compostela in Spain. He
was a hermit at i.29n. (and see the reference there to *Minerva
Britanna*, 198 where the pilgrim is an emblem of hypocrisy); but as
a pilgrim now he parodies Una's own wanderings in the wilderness:
she has wandered 'from one to other *Ynd*' at vi.2.

41 The triangular shield was the commonest type in the medieval
period (*Var. Sp.*, I.247).

44 The simile is common, and used again in connection with
Satyrane at IV.iv.29, when he fights Cambell. Upton (*Var.Sp.*,
I.247–8) draws attention to its appearance in Chaucer's *Knight's
Tale*, 1658–60, where it is applied to a fight between Palamon and
Arcite.

47–8 The fight between Sansloy and Satyrane remains
unresolved because Satyrane is too similar to Sansloy in his wild
and unChristian origins (see Bernheimer, *Wild Men*, 19–20) to be
an outright victor.

CANTO VII

Redcrosse encounters, and is imprisoned by, the giant Orgoglio, to
waste away in the dungeon of his castle (see vii.15 and viii.38ff.).
Spenser also describes Duessa's seven-headed beast here
(vii.17–18). Significantly, as well as being the number of the deadly
sins (symbolised by the heads on the beast), seven is the number of
mortality and mutability, pertaining to man's life governed by
seven planets and seven ages, and whose body, too, develops
according to an elaborate series of sevens so that, in fact, 'his whole
life is regulated by it' (Macrobius, *Commentary on the Dream of
Scipio, ed.cit.*, I.vi.62, p. 112).

2–4 Redcrosse again enters the shade, escaping from the sun of
true religion and justice (see ii. 28–32n.). In this deceptively
harmonious setting – it is a fully fledged *locus amoenus* in the

classical–medieval tradition, with its trees, shade, bird song, and breeze (Curtius, 195–200) – there are sufficient similarities to the entrance to Error's wood to act as a warning (i.7–9n.). The *locus amoenus* is often a place of particular sensuous appeal (Curtius, 198), which indicates that Redcrosse, once more in company with the fleshly Duessa and physically weary, is as yet too committed to the body. Indeed, because of the heat (and weight?) he has even removed the 'armour of God' that is his protection (see i.1n.). The episode's similarity to *O.F.*, VI.19–25 (where Ruggiero disarms himself and drinks from a fountain) is discussed by Alpers, 139–46.

5   The enervating fountain episode (compare the water symbolism of ii.40–1n. and xi.29–30n., 33–4n., and 46–8n.) is Ovidian and probably based on the enfeebling waters of Salmacis's fountain (*Met.*, IV.285ff.): Salmacis was a nymph who refused to hunt with Diana and one day fell in love with Hermaphroditus who, however, rejected her advances. Thinking he was safe he swam in her pool. But she leaped in and clung to him and the gods, in answer to her prayer, joined them together to form a hermaphrodite. In answer to a subsequent prayer of Hermaphroditus, the waters ever after made those who swam in it weak and half-men. The myth was usually given the orthodox moral reading of abandonment to 'luxury, idleness, and effeminate pleasures' (Starnes and Talbert, 403, citing Ross's *Mystagogus Poeticus* of 1647), which would confirm the interpretation of the grove offered above. Like the nymph, Redcrosse has abandoned his quest for the Diana-like Una 'in middest of the race' by avoiding the heat of the sun – a point underlined structurally, since the knight's actual fall (st. 12, 13) occurs at the numerically central stanzas of Book I (Michael Baybak, Paul Delany, A. Kent Hieatt, 'Placement "in the middest" in *The Faerie Queene*', in A. Fowler, ed., *Silent Poetry* (1970), 146, modifying Fowler, 72). On the symbolic importance of the mid-point, see Fowler, *Triumphal Forms* (Cambridge, 1970), ch. II and IV: it was associated especially with sovereignty because of the sun's central position in both the Ptolemaic and Copernican systems, and because the sovereign traditionally takes the sun as his symbol; and with justice because equal divison signifies 'equity'. The 'Choice of Hercules' operates implicitly here as it did in the earlier grove of ii.36–8n. since Venus is goddess of gardens and the grove therefore belongs to her (embodied in the false Venus

Duessa; on Venus and gardens, see II.xii.42n.), and Redcrosse has abandoned Diana–Una for her opposite. Hamilton, 76 notes Redcrosse's symbolic descent here through the elements from fire (sun) through air (bathing his forehead, st. 3), to water and earth (drinking from the fountain as he lies on the ground).

8–10 Orgoglio (Italian for pride; named at st. 14) has complex associations. Like his counterpart Luciferà his meaning is ultimately definable only by all these associations, though Cullen, 54ff. is right to suggest that he embodies the third Biblical temptation of the Devil (rebellious pride; see ii.13n. and iv.2n.). He is the offspring of Earth and the ruler of the winds, and the Titans (often confused with the giants) were traditionally the offspring of Earth and Heaven (Hesiod, *Theogony*, 147ff., Starnes and Talbert, 242), though Spenser probably also has in mind the tradition, found in Hyginus, according to which pride (*Superbia*) is the offspring of Air and Earth (Upton, *Var. Sp.*, I.249). Hamilton, 75 notes a parody of the Biblical creation of man from earth and air (Genesis 2:7). As a giant he embodies pride because of the giants' rebellion against the Olympians (Lotspeich, 63–4) and because of the 'gyantes in the earth' of Genesis 6:4 which, according to the Geneva gloss, 'usurped autoritie over others & did degenerate from ye simplicitie, wherein their fathers lived'. Also relevant, as S. K. Heninger notes ('The Orgoglio Episode in *The Faerie Queene*', *E.L.H.*, XXVI (1959)), is Spenser's friend Gabriel Harvey's *Pleasant and pitthy familiar discourse, of the Earthquake in Aprill last*, where we read: 'The Materiall Cause of Earthquakes ... is no doubt great aboundance of wynde, or stoare of grosse and drye vapors, and spirites, fast shut up, and ... emprysoned in the Caves, and Dungeons of the Earth' which, seeking to free themselves, forcibly erupt (*Var. Sp.* edn, 453). Volcanoes, similarly, were regarded as imprisoned giants and winds (*Aeneid*, III.571ff. on Etna; *Met.*, XV.298ff., which in Golding's 1567 translation, 327ff., tells us that the wind in subterranean caves in struggling to escape 'did stretch the ground and make it swell on hye, / As dooth a bladder that is blowen by mouth'). Typhoeus/Typhon (see v.35n.), one of the main rebels against Jupiter, was regarded as symbolising the power of volcanoes, specifically Etna, under which mountain he had been buried by Jupiter (Heninger, *A Handbook of Renaissance Meteorology*, 126–7), and volcanoes were themselves symbols of rebellion or, like the earthquake, of divine judgement; both of which meanings apply to Orgoglio. The 'snaggy Oke' torn from 'his mothers bowelles' marks him out as the lawless giant wild man, a type found in the cannibal Cyclops of *Odyssey*, IX and *Aeneid*, III.655ff. (the massive and monstrous Polyphemus carrying a pine-trunk. On the tree as an attribute of the wild man, see Bernheimer, *Wild Men*, 1 and *passim*; on the giant wild man, see 46–7, 64–6, 72, 91). Orgoglio doubtless carries with him the associations of the wild man as an earth spirit embodying erotic and destructive power in general (Bernheimer, *passim*) – a demonic inflation of the faun–satyr–centaur of canto vi. The oak cudgel contrasts with Sylvanus's cypress (vi.13–14n.). An engraving by Melchior Lorch, dedicated to Luther, shows the Pope as Antichrist in the form of an animal Satan complete with frogs coming out of his mouth (cf. i.20n.) who is also a wild man carrying a tree trunk which is a papal cross (Norman Cohn, *The Pursuit of the Millenium* (1970), plate 2): a further insight into the apocalyptic meanings of Book I. William Tyndale, incidentally, identified the giants of Numbers 13:33–4 as the Pope and his ecclesiastics, 'giants above all power and authority' (*Doctrinal Treatises*, Parker Society (Cambridge, 1848), 311–12, cit. Rathborne, 146–7). Orgoglio is matched by the wild man who abducts Amoret (IV.vii.5ff.) and who also carries an oak tree, and, structurally, by the giant Disdayne of VI.vii.41ff., 'sib to great *Orgoglio*', who, like his kinsman, and at the end of the poem as Spenser left it, fights Arthur in canto viii.

11   Notes the puns: Recrosse is 'disarmd' (without God's armour), 'disgrast' (without His grace, which arrives only with Arthur), and 'dismayde' (unmade into his component elements: see Hamilton, 76 cited at st. 5n. above). The knight is, literally, flesh here; he cannot, unaided by grace, withstand the embodiment of that flesh in the 'earthly slime' of Orgoglio (Cullen, 57). On the symbolism of earth in the book (which includes Adam, unregenerate man whose name itself means 'earthly'), see i.21n.

13   The notion of the infernal origin of cannon is found in *O.F.*, IX.28ff. and 91, where they are said to have been forged by Beelzebub in Tartarus. On the Furies, see iii.33–6n. and v.31–4n.

16–18   On the apocalyptic significance of Duessa here, see ii.13n. and iii.4n. And compare Lucifera and Ripa's description of *Superbia* with her red garments and gold crown (cited at iv.8–10n.).

The 'triple crowne' is papal, and signifies the Pope's authority as priest, judge, and legislator (Upton on ii.13 in *Var. Sp.*, I.199). The seven-headed beast – recalling Error of canto i – is from Revelation 12:3, the 'great red dragon having seven heades, and ten hornes' which is identified as Satan at verse 9 (the Geneva gloss interprets the seven as the number of the world: 'For he is prince of this worlde'; on seven, see headnote above). It is conflated with Revelation 17:3: 'I sawe a woman sit upon a skarlat coloured beast, full of names of blasphemie, which had seven heads, & ten hornes' (the Geneva gloss identifies the beast as ancient Rome, the woman as 'the newe Rome which is the Papistrie': cf. ii.13n. and contrast Una on her ass at vi.19n. It was a commonplace to identify the seven heads as the seven deadly sins; Tuve, 102–8 and plates 21, 22, 24.) Alciati, *Emblemata* (Lyons, 1551), 12, incidentally, has an emblem of false religion (*Ficta religio*) based on Revelation 17, the woman on the beast, adjacent to an emblem of the image of Isis on the ass (p. 13). The many-headed hydra (snake) slain by Hercules–Alcides, type of heroic virtue (see i.19n.), as the second of his twelve labours was the offspring of Echidna (see i.13–16n.) and Typhon (see v.35n. and also st. 8–10n. above). The heads (nine according to classical tradition) symbolise the multiplicity of error; and Tuve, 17 mentions the tradition in which the water-snake *hydrus* was identified with the Herculean *hydra*, and given seven heads which were then interpreted as the devil with his sins. As Upton (*Var. Sp.*, I.250) notes, the reference to *Stremona* is a mystery. He suggests that Spenser might allude to Strymon in Thrace because of Thrace's connection with warfare and sedition. The iron of st. 17 might come from Daniel 7:7 (Upton, *ibid.*), Daniel's vision of a beast 'feareful and terrible and verie strong. It had great yron teeth . . . it had ten hornes' (identified in the Geneva gloss with the Roman empire, the teeth signifying tyranny and greed, the horns the Roman provinces). But brass and iron are often connected in the Bible, as at Jeremiah 6:28: 'Thei are all rebellious traitors, walking craftely: they are brasse, & yron, they all are destroyers'. The tail throwing stars to the ground comes from Revelation 12:4, where the dragon's 'taile drue the third parte of the starres of heaven, & cast them to the earth', perhaps influenced by Daniel 8:10, the battle between the ram and the goat: 'it grewe up unto the hoste of heaven, and it cast downe some of the hoste, & of the starres to the grounde, and trode upon them'.

22–3   Una refers to the three Fates who spin and then cut the threads of life (cf. *F.Q.*, IV.ii.47–52). Death traditionally has a dart (Tervarent, col. 187; cf. *Paradise Lost*, II.672, XI.491). In st. 23 the allusion is to Genesis 1:4 ('And God sawe ye light that it was good, and God separated the light from the darkenes') with the additional suggestion of the binding and imprisoning of Satan in Revelation 20 (see xii.36n.). The solar Arthur arrives to dispel Una's darkness as he arrives to dispel Redcrosse's darkness at viii.38, where, in a grotesque reversal of Revelation 20 he is 'in baleful darkenesse bound'.

29   The 'goodly knight' is Arthur, identified in Spenser's prefatory *Letter of the Authors* as the virtue of magnificence, 'the perfection of all the rest' of the virtues. Christianised (as here) it is an aspect of the Holy Ghost's gift of *fortitudo*, which answers the sin of sloth. Chaucer's parson, under the heading *fortitudo*, defines it thus: 'magnificence, that is to seyn, whan a man dooth and perfourneth grete werkes of goodnesse; and that is the ende why that men sholde do goode werkes, for in the accomplissynge of grete goode werkes lith the grete gerdoun' (Chaucer, *Parson's Tale*, 251); and this 'gerdoun' is, as Tuve, 134 notes, the 'uncorruptible' crown of 1 Corinthians 9:25 (see also Tuve, 57–60, 77ff., 98, 119–20). On the gifts of the Holy Ghost, see viii.30–4n. Magnificence, since it involves pursuance of virtue to the very end, is specifically associated with grace (Tuve, 84–5, 98, 133), and so Spenser has his Arthur embody the operation of divine grace upon heart and will (see viii.1, and A. S. P. Woodhouse, 'Nature and Grace in *The Faerie Queene*', *E.L.H.*, XVI (1949)). Spenser's characterisation of Arthur is thus in accord with the tradition that he was the greatest of Christian kings (C. B. Millican, *Spenser and the Table Round*, 7–8), and his historical significance in the poem derives its main inspiration from Geoffrey of Monmouth's twelfth-century *History of the Kings of Britain* which was the basis of the Tudor claim to supremacy, since the Tudors traced their pedigree ultimately back to Brutus, great-grandson of Aeneas and mythical founder of Britain, and his supposed descendant, Arthur (Millican, 17 and *passim*; R. F. Brinkley, *Arthurian Legend in the Seventeenth Century* (1967), ch. I; and cf. the genealogies in II.x and III.iii and ix).

Arthur's connection with the sun (Phoebus) is supported by his helmet, 'horrid [bristling] all with gold' (st. 31) which gives him a corona and turns him into a sun god, specifically a *Sol iustitiae* after the manner of Albrecht Dürer's engraving (Panofsky, *Meaning in the Visual Arts*, plate 82, and cf. plate 84). Arthur therefore displays the solar qualities that Redcrosse is still aspiring to (see, e.g., iii.5–9n., and v.2n.). Spenser probably intends an echo of and contrast with the menacing Aeneas who is compared to a comet at *Aeneid*, X.270ff. ('Aeneas' crest blazed on his head and from his plumed crown streamed the flame; his gold shield-centre spouted forth its broad beam, like the sinister, blood-red glow of a comet on some clear night, or Sirius the star that brings thirst and disease to suffering humanity'; Penguin edn, tr. W. F. Jackson Knight (Harmondsworth, 1960), 259). The pagan Argantes, armed for battle, glitters like an ill-portending comet in *Ger. Lib.*, VII.52; and Kermode, 15 sees Arthur here as a chivalric development of the angel of Revelation 18:1ff. who descends from heaven with 'great power, so that the earth was lightened with his glorie' telling of the fall of Babylon. Arthur's shield, at st. 34 brighter than Phoebus, is at viii.20 'sunshiny', relating to (1) Una's solar affinities at iii.4 and xii.23; (2) Redcrosse's 'sunne-bright shield' (xi.40); and (3) Psalms 84:11: 'For the Lord God is the sunne & shield unto us: the Lord wil give grace & glorie'. The 'bauldrick' or belt is an attribute of heroes (*Aeneid*, IX.359–60, Rhamnes's gold-studded sword-belt).

30 The 'one pretious stone ... shapt like a Ladies head' represents Gloriana, the Faerie Queene, and is based on the image of the Virgin Mary which, according to Geoffrey (*History*, IX.4), was painted on Arthur's shield, Pridwen. Elizabeth was often seen as the Virgin of the new religion (Yates, 78–80, 109). Its position 'in the midst' alludes to the central position of sovereignty (see st. 5n. above), while its comparison with Hesperus, the evening star and the planet Venus (see ii.4–6n.) is another strand in the Elizabeth–Una–Venus web of allusion (see Proem 4n.). The 'mortall blade' is the sword Morddure (see II.viii.21): the one that 'bites cruelly', with a pun on *mort*, death. Spenser changes the name from Caliburn–Excalibur (Geoffrey, *History*, IX.4). A sword is an attribute of Justice and the Sun of justice.

31 The description of the helmet is modelled on Turnus's helmet in *Aeneid*, VII.785–6, triple plumed and with a Chimaera on it breathing out Etna's fires (followed by Tasso, *Ger. Lib.*, IX.25, where the Soldan's helmet has a malignant dragon on it), and on Geoffrey's *History*, IX.4, which describes Arthur's gold helmet with its dragon crest: the dragon is the emblem of Cadwallader, last king of the Britons and Henry VII's ancestor (Millican, *Spenser and the Table Round*, 11, 39) and also of Arthur's father, Uther Pendragon, who had a vision of a dragon-shaped ball of fire prophesying his kingship and who, after he was made king, carried a sculpted golden dragon into battle with him which thus became an emblem of war (Geoffrey, *History*, VIII.14–15, 17). The dragon–serpent is also a solar symbol since, like the sun, it undergoes cyclical renewal (see v.36–44n.), and an emblem of *fortitudo* (moral strength): Tervarent, col. 150. Arthur's virtue of magnificence was traditionally one of the parts of fortitude (Tuve, 59–60, 107, 132ff.). And see our Plate 7 for the connection of the Aesculapian dragon–serpent and kingship.

32   Vergil has 'palmy Selinus' at *Aeneid*, III.705, but Spenser probably has in mind Numbers 17:8, Aaron's budding almond rod, which showed that he was to be high priest, and Ecclesiastes 12:5, 'the almonde tre shal florish', which St Gregory interpreted as the beginning of the holy Church which put forth the first flowers of virtue in its preachers, because the almond is an early-flowering tree (*Expositions on Job*, cit. Evans, 166–7). The 'loftie crest' possibly allies Arthur with Minerva, patron of wisdom and chastity, since a high-crested helmet was one of her attributes: Tervarent, cols. 62–3. Arthur's shield is Minervan: see st. 33–5n.

33–5   Arthur's shield, in part relevant to his solar role (see st. 29n.), is based at this point on Atlante's shield of carbuncle in *O.F.*, II.55–6 and XXII.81ff. (where it is used by Ruggiero. The shield is usually kept veiled, but like Arthur's, has blinding and stunning power. Alpers, 166–79 discusses the shields at length.) There is also an allusion to the diamond shield, 'the special safeguard of the Lord God', in *Ger. Lib.*, VII.82 (Hankins, 32, 109), and to 'the shield of faith' of Ephesians 6 (see i.1n.). Compare, too, 2 Samuel 22:31 (God as 'a shield to all that trust in him') and 36 ('the shield of thy salvacion'). It is made of diamond not only in allusion to Tasso but also to express its immutability (the fact that it cannot be split affirms its integrity and associates it with the Una–Duessa symbolism of the book as a whole) and Arthur's own invincibility

Rex medicus patria.

A DRAGON lo, a Scepter grasping fast
Within his paw : doth shew a King should be
Like Æsculapius, ev'er watchfull plac't;
Amongst his subiects, and with skill to see,
   To what ill humors, of th'infectious mind.
   The multitude, are most of all inclind.

And when he findes corruption to abound,
In that Huge body, of all vices ill,
To purge betimes, or else to * launch the wound,
Least more, and more, it ranckles inward still :
   Or when he would, it bring to former state,
   Past all recure, his phisick comes to late.

       Quæ mala contraxit populus contagia morum,
         Ne pigeat medica tot resecâsse manu :
       (Et Reges olim iuvit medicina) venenis,
         Hinc citus occurras quæ valuêre mora.

(adamant = Greek *adamas*, unconquerable). Additional meanings of the diamond are fortitude and good faith (Tervarent, cols. 147–8); it was identified with Christ (Evans, 45 citing the medieval *Physiologus*) and was a solar stone (Agrippa, II.xli,300–1), thus confirming Arthur's Christlike and solar roles (see viii.38–41n.). Martha Craig, 'The Secret Wit of Spenser's Language', in Paul Alpers, ed., *Elizabethan Poetry: Modern Essays in Criticism* (1967), 417n., suggests a pun on *deus-mundus* (god, earth), without, however, hazarding a similar pun on *almond* (*alma-mundi*, world-soul) in the corresponding position in st. 32. The immutable solar diamond shield is set over against the mutable moon (*Cynthia*) in the same way that the 'woman clothed with the sunne' of Revelation 12:1 has 'the moone . . . under her fete' to signify that 'The Church treadeth under fote what soever is mutable' (Geneva gloss). Its religious implications, moreover, are emphasised by the parallel with God's throne in Spenser's *Hymne of Heavenly Beautie*, 153–4: more durable than 'steele or brasse, / Or the hard diamond'; just as its sun- and moon-obscuring brightness recalls God's 'Majestie divine, / In sight of whom both Sun and Moone are darke' (*ibid.*, 124–5). In being moon-eclipsing it also has magic powers, the powers that popular superstition gave to witches: Horace, *Epodes*, V.46–7; *Paradise Lost*, II.665–6. The *veiling* of the shield recalls the Neoplatonic implications of Una's veil (iii.4n.); and its power to turn 'men into stones' is borrowed from Minerva's shield which had on it an image of the Gorgon Medusa who, with her snaky locks, was able to petrify all who gazed on her (*Met.*, IV.769ff.; see III.ix.22 for a reference to Minerva's '*Gorgonian* shield'). The phrase 'exceeding shone' looks back immediately to the stone 'shapt like a Ladies head' of st. 30 which also 'exceeding shone'; both look back further to, and contrast with, Lucifera at iv.8–9 ('exceeding shone'), and forward to x.67, Redcrosse's vision of the New Jerusalem which is too bright for him, and did 'too exceeding shyne'.

36 The making of the shield by Merlin is Spenser's Arthurian romance version of *Iliad*, XVIII.468ff., where Hephaestus makes Achilles' armour: cf. II.viii.20–1 on Arthur's sword. The armour may 'yet . . . be seene' because the Tudors revived the Arthurian golden age. In terms of Spenser's own myth, it is probably to be thought of as hung in Panthea as a sign of enduring fame (see x.58n. and Rathborne, 47).

37 Arthur's squire is Timias (Greek *time*, honour). He has an ebony spear (like the Minervan Britomart at IV.v.8 and vi.6) because of that wood's hardness and indestructibility.

43 Una's parents are the king and queen of Eden (see i.5n., xii.26), which was watered by four rivers, of which Spenser omits Hiddekel (Tigris). In the Genesis account (2:11ff.), Phison 'compasseth the whole land of Havilah, where is golde', and Gihon 'compasseth the whole land of Cush' (Ethiopia). It was common in the Middle Ages, following particularly Philo and St Ambrose, to allegorise the rivers as the cardinal virtues: the Phison, flowing over gold, is Prudence or frugality; the Gihon, flowing by Ethiopia (= vile, impure) is Temperance; the Tigris is Fortitude; and the Euphrates is Justice (A. D. S. Fowler, 'The River Guyon', *M.L.N.*, LXXV (1960); Mâle, 110n.). As Fowler argues, the Gihon gives its name to the hero of Book II, Guyon, the Knight of Temperance; and since in alchemical thought gold is the only tempered metal, because in it the four constituent elements are most perfectly balanced, Spenser transfers the gold, associated in the Bible with the Phison, to the Gihon to reinforce its identification as temperance and to prepare the way, symbolically, for Guyon's quest, which he takes over from Redcrosse, in Book II. The Gihon is identified with the Nile: its additional function here, presumably, is to cancel out the pejorative implications of the Nile at i.21n. and v.18n. (where it is associated with the deadly sins).

44 Tartarus is the lowest place in Hades. The four years were interpreted by Upton, *Var. Sp.*, I.256, as an allusion to Revelation 11:2 (the Gentiles will tread the holy city 'under fote two & fortie moneths') and 12:6 (the 'woman clothed with the sunne' will be in the wilderness 1,260 days, or three and a half years). Percival, 267, suggests an allusion to the four thousand years which, according to Jerome, passed from the Fall of man and Christ's death (as in the carol 'Adam lay I-boundyn'); and cf. the meanings of four cited in the headnote to canto iv above. Lazarus had been dead four days when raised by Christ (John 11:17, 39).

46 The 'noble order' suggests the Order of the Garter (Percival, 267), the patron of which is St George, and whose head is the sovereign. Elizabeth utilised the Order as an important aspect of her glorification: Yates, 108–9 and plates 14a (a portrait of Elizabeth holding the Garter badge) and 14b (procession of Garter Knights). Cleopolis, a refinement of the historical London and an earthly shadow of the Heavenly Jerusalem (see x.55–9), derives its name from Greek *kleos* = fame, glory, and is clearly connected in Spenser's mind with Clio, the Muse of history, invoked at III.iii.4 (and see Proem 2n.). Rathborne, 22ff., notes an earlier sixteenth-century use of Cleopolis, this time for Paris. In schemes which connect the Muses with the planetary spheres, Clio is associated with the sphere of the moon, itself symbolising earthly honour (Meyer-Baer, *Music of the Spheres*, fig. 96; Fowler, 84, citing Valeriano, *Hieroglyphica*, XLIV.xxiii; Shakespeare, *1 Henry IV*, I.iii.202 ('To pluck bright honour from the pale-faced moon'); and II.i.32n.). Cleopolis, then, is the city of knightly honour and noble deeds; its limitations are its reliance on war to promote its causes (Rathborne, 33–4); but its 'great Queene of glory bright', Gloriana, is an emanation of the divine glory, that glory which Redcrosse's 'glorious name' (II.i.32) celebrates at the end of the book and which, in a Neoplatonic *scala*, has secular honour as its starting-point but passes far beyond it to attain the 'heavenly Registers above the Sunne' (*ibid.*). So that Gloriana and her city are an image of the end and, in themselves, a beginning. See x.58n.

CANTO VIII

Redcrosse is redeemed by Arthur from Orgoglio's dungeon, an event according with the meaning of eight as the number of regeneration (Hopper, *Medieval Number Symbolism*, 77, 85, 90, 101, 114, 178). Among various reasons for the symbolism given by arithmologists were: Christ's resurrection on the eighth day after the beginning of Holy Week and the eight souls saved in Noah's ark (Fowler, 53–4 notices the appropriateness of Arthur's rescue in canto viii – a regular feature in all books except III). Arthur's deliverance of Redcrosse from a *dungeon* is perhaps specifically glossed by 1 Peter 3:18–21: 'Christ also hathe once suffred for sinnes, ye just for the unjust, that he might bring us to God, and was put to death concerning the flesh, but was quickened in the spirit. By the which he also went, & preached unto the spirits that

were in prison. Which were in time passed disobedient, when once
the long suffring of God abode in the daies of Noe, while the arke
was preparing, wherein fewe, that is, eight soules were saved in the
water. To the which also the figure that now saveth us, even
Baptisme agreeth ...'. The stanza-total for the canto, fifty,
probably alludes to fifty as the number of the advent of the Holy
Spirit (fiftieth day after the resurrection) and Jubilee (the liberation
of slaves, remission of debts, etc.): Fowler, 54n., and Agrippa,
II.xv,224 ('The number fifty signifies remission of sins, of
servitudes, and also liberty'). See also II.x.5–69n.

1 This stanza makes explicit Arthur's role as an embodiment of
'heavenly grace': cf. II.viii.17–18n.

3–4 The magic horn is modelled on the horn of Roland, via *O.F.*,
XV.14–15 (Upton, *Var. Sp.*, I.257). Upton further identifies it with
the word of God, the sound of which 'went out through all the
earth' (Romans 10:18); and cf. Joshua 6:5: 'And when they make a
long blast with the rams horne, & ye heare the sounde of the
trompet, all the people shal shoute with a great shoute: then shal
the wall of the citie fall downe flat'.

9 The comparison of the wrathful Orgoglio with the just wrath of
Jupiter with his thunderbolts confirms the giant as the proud
usurper of just religious authority. The Giants/Titans fought
against Jupiter: see vii.8–10n.; Lotspeich, 63–4.

10 The wounding of Orgoglio with the blood gushing like water
from rock recalls Exodus 17:5–6 (Moses' smiting of the rock) and
1 Corinthians 10:2–4 where that event is interpreted typologically:
'they dranke of the spiritual Rocke ... and the Rocke was Christ'.
Cf. ii.40–1n. and xi.29–30n. and 46–8n. A related text is John
19:34, on the crucifixion: 'But one of the souldiers with a speare
perced his side, & forthewith came there out blood and water':
further instances of outrageous blasphemous parody on Orgoglio's
part.

11 The giant is compared to a herd of bulls (see vi.20–6n.)
bellowing for lack of a female. Typhon (see vii.8–10n.) bellows like
a furious bull in Hesiod, *Theogony*, 830–2. The Cimbri lived in
Northern Germany, an area later divided between Holstein, Silesia,
and Jutland: Orgoglio is thus associated with the evil north (see
ii.33n.).

12   The phrase 'swolne with bloud' recalls Revelation 17:6: 'And I sawe the woman [the whore of Babylon] drunken with the blood of Saintes, & with the blood of the Martyrs of Jesus'.

14   The 'golden cup' comes from Revelation 17:4: 'And the woman was araied in purple & skarlat . . . and had a cup of golde in her hand, ful of abominations, and filthines of her fornication' (Geneva gloss: 'false doctrines & blasphemies'), conflated with the witch Circe's magic and golden cup (*Odyssey*, X.316). Circe is the evil Venus who has the power to turn Odysseus's sailors into beasts (Acrasia is modelled on her in Book II: see esp. II.i.55 for her cup, and II.xii *passim* for the Circe echoes in the Bower of Bliss). As a Circe–Venus, Duessa is linked again with Lucifera–Venus (iv.6–7n., 8–10n.) and contrasts with the Venerean Una (e.g., ii.4–6n., and Proem 4n. for general references to the Venus theme). Contrast Fidelia's gold cup at x.13.

16   On the striking of the head, cf. Revelation 13:3: 'And I sawe one of his heads as it were wounded to death' (the reference is to the seven-headed, ten-horned beast from the sea; cf. vii.16–18n.).

18–20   On the shield and its effects, see vii.33–5n.

22–3   The tree simile is a commonplace: e.g., *Aeneid*, II.626–8 (Troy falls like an ancient ash tree in the mountains); *Ger. Lib.*, IX.39 (Latinus falls like an Alpine oak blown down). On the castle, cf. ii.20n. and iv.5n.: the parallels imply a thematic link.

30–4   The blind keeper is spiritual Ignorance. Percival, 274 cites Ephesians 4:17–18: 'This I say therefore and testifie in the Lord, that ye henceforthe walke not as other Gentiles walke, in vanitie of their minde, Having their cogitation darkened, and being strangers from the life of God through the ignorance that is in them because of the hardenes of their heart' (Geneva gloss on 'vanitie of their minde': 'Man not regenerat hathe his minde, understanding & heart corrupt'); and cf. Corceca at iii.10–20n. The rusty keys are presumably from Luke 11:52: 'Woe be to you, interpreters of the Law: for ye have taken away the keye of knowledge: ye entred not in your selves, and them that came in, ye forbade' (Geneva gloss: 'They hid & toke away the pure doctrine & true understanding of the Scriptures'). Ignaro relates to Archimago at i.29 and vi.35 and contrasts with Contemplation at x.46ff. Compare and contrast, too, the 'old old man' of II.ix.55, who symbolises memory and the wisdom of age and is related to the tradition of three-headed prudence (*ibid.*, st. 49–58n.). Ignaro's backward-turned face (st. 31) might suggest this tradition, and the punishment of those who dared prophesy future events in Dante's *Inferno*, XX (they have their heads reversed); though the symbolism is obvious enough: Ignaro does not embody the retrospection of memory but, simply, spiritual backwardness. He is 'unlike to men' because such wilful denial of the understanding and reason is inhuman – hence he has foster-fathered the wild-man giant Orgoglio. Contrast the wood gods of vi.7–10n. who are ignorant of revealed religion as Ignaro and Orgoglio are not, but whose ignorance is not willed. Arthur calms 'his wrath with goodly temperance' (st. 34) because in the traditional schemes which correlate the seven gifts of the Holy Ghost with the seven virtues and oppose them to the seven sins, the third gift, *scientia* (knowledge), ousts wrath and replaces it with temperance (Tuve, 94). Significantly, *scientia* can also oppose ignorance (*ignorantia*): *ibid.*, 95. Arthur shows that he possesses already here the virtues only attained by Redcrosse at the House of Holiness in canto x.

35–6 The 'resplendent gold' recalls Lucifera and confirms the Church's secular commitments; while the 'bloud of guiltlesse babes, and innocents trew' turns Orgoglio into a combination of Moloch (to whom children were sacrificed: e.g., 2 Kings 23:10), Pharaoh (Exodus 1:15–22, the order to kill the Jewish boy babies), and Herod (Matthew 2:16, the Massacre of the Innocents). 'Sacred ashes' could mean (1) accursed ashes (as at II.xii.37, 'sacred soile', a common meaning of Latin *sacer*) or (2) the 'sacred [holy] ashes' of those protestants burnt as heretics – either by the Inquisition or by the 'bloody' Mary Tudor (Percival, 276). There must inevitably be an allusion to the Massacre of St Bartholomew which began on 24 August 1572 and in which thousands of Huguenots were killed in Paris and the provinces to the main benefit of Elizabeth's arch-enemy Philip II of Spain; for the Huguenot leader Coligny had been about to assist in an invasion of the Netherlands to redeem them from Spanish tyranny. (Heninger, 'The Orgoglio Episode', *E.L.H.*, XXVI (1959), associates Orgoglio with Philip.) The 'cunning imagery' on the altar suggests Catholicism's use of icons and images in worship, linking them implicitly with splendid pagan

carvings and emblems; it might hint, too, at the association of the
Roman Church with black magic (see i.29n. and II.xii.50n.). The
spirits of the 'holy Martyrs' crying from under the stone recall
Revelation 6:9–10, the victims of persecution revealed when the
fifth seal is opened: 'I sawe under the altar the soules of them, that
were killed for the worde of God, & for ye testimonie which they
mainteined. And they cryed with a lowde voyce, saying, How long,
Lord, holie and true! doest not thou judge & avenge our blood on
them that dwell on the earth?'

38–41 Arthur rescues Redcrosse who has been imprisoned for
three months; Christ harrowed hell for three days (Hamilton, 78;
and see x.36–43n. and headnote to canto xi). Tartarus has an iron
gate (*Iliad*, VIII.15). Redcrosse measures time by the moon –
associated with the underworld since Hecate (i.43n.) is a moon
goddess and, incidentally, called 'three-fold' (e.g., *Aeneid*, IV.511;
Starnes and Talbert, 163–4). His invocation to the moon is further
confirmation of his abandonment of his solar role. See also vii.46n.
Arthur, Christ-like and solar, brings illumination to Redcrosse
who, spiritually lost and eclipsed (cf. vii.22–3n.), 'could not endure
th'unwonted sunne to view'. His physical debility is similar to that
of the Saturnian melancholic Maleger, embodiment of original sin,
at II.xi.20–3n., though it more nearly resembles Chaucer's
description of Arcite in the *Knight's Tale*, 1361ff.: 'lene he wex and
drye as is a shaft; / His eyen holwe ... / So feble eek were his
spiritz, and so lowe, / And chaunged so, that no man koude knowe
/ His speche nor his voys'. This illness is diagnosed by Chaucer as
a 'manye, / Engendred of humour malencolik'; and in fact the term
'mania' was reserved for choleric melancholy only, i.e., melancholy
caused by a mixture of black and yellow bile (Klibansky, 88–90,
citing Avicenna, who remained influential through to the
seventeenth century). So that Redcrosse's symptoms here are
probably the physiological and psychological results of his earlier
tendencies to melancholy (i.2n.) and choler (v.8n.), two of the
spiritual vices. Choleric melancholy typically manifests itself as a
frenzy which is rather similar to despair (itself caused by
melancholy: see ix.33–4n.): see the discussion of Dürer's
Despairing Man (engraving B70) in Klibansky, appendix II,
403–5, which, instead of depicting despair seems rather to depict a
choleric melancholic tearing his hair in his mania. Redcrosse is

now, then, well on the way, clinically speaking, to the very real despair that assails him in the next canto as the result of his full realisation of his fallen nature (implied also by his 'flesh shronk up like withered flowres': see II.i.35–56n. for the significance of this). Note that Arthur counsels 'patient might' in st. 45: in the gifts–virtues–deadly sins schemes (see st. 30–4n. above), patience as well as temperance displaces wrath (Tuve, 95). Redcrosse learns patience at x.23 (see n.).

46–8 Redcrosse now sees Duessa for what she is: compare Fradubio at ii.40–1n.; but with the aid of Arthur and Una he just avoids Fradubio's fate. The revealed Duessa follows the Echidna figure (i.13–16n.); *O.F.*, VII.71–3, where the apparently young and beautiful Alcina is shown to Ruggiero to be a hideous old hag through the magic ring of reason; and Revelation 13:2 ('the beast which I sawe, was like a leopard, and his fete like a beares') and 17:16: 'And the ten hornes which thou sawest upon the beast, are they that shal hate the whore, and shal make her desolate and naked, & shal eat her flesh, & burne her with fyre'. Hankins, 101 notes important parallels in Isaiah 47 on the denunciation of Babylon (e.g., v.3: 'Thy filthines shalbe discovered, and thy shame shalbe sene') and Isaiah 3:17 and 24 (the stripping of the daughters of Jerusalem because of their pride and wantonness): 'Therefore shal the Lord make the heads of the daughters of Zion balde, and the Lord shal discover their secret partes. . . . And in stead of swete savour, there shalbe stinke, and in stead of a girdle, a rent, & in stead of dressing of ye heere, baldnes'. The maple (st. 47) is chosen because it is 'seeldom inward sound' (i.9: Duessa linked with Error again); the fox is traditionally cunning and evil, associated with Herod (Luke 13:32) and the devil (Evans, 209–10) and the corrupt clergy (*ibid.*, 208, 210–12, 214–15, 221; Spenser's *Shepheardes Calender*, 'September'); the bear is presumably the emblem of lust and gluttony here (Tervarent, cols. 291–2) and, again, a type of the devil on account of 1 Samuel 17:36, David slaying a lion and a bear (Evans, 88–9 citing, among others, Augustine, *Sermons*, CXCVII). The eagle's claw is from personifications of Fraud: 'A woman with two faces, one of a beautiful girl, the other of an old hag, naked down to the breasts . . . her feet are like those of an eagle, she has a scorpion's tail. . . . The scorpion's tail and the eagle's feet signify the venom that excites her continually, like a bird of prey, to grab the goods or honour of others' (Ripa, 173–5).

CANTO IX

Redcrosse now undergoes his greatest spiritual temptation: it is literally infernal in its power (at st. 28 Despair is 'a man of hell'). The placing of this episode in the ninth canto is again symbolic, since nine is associated, e.g., with Vergil's Hades which is encircled by the nine-fold Styx (*Aeneid*, VI.439), with the fall of the rebel Titans into Tartarus, which lasted nine days and nights (Hesiod, *Theogony*, 664ff.), and with King Og of Bashan, the last 'of the remnant of the gyants' whose iron bed was nine cubits long (Deuteronomy 3:11). As Agrippa, II.xii, 208 cryptically remarks, 'Neither is the longitude of nine cubits of *Og* King of Basan, who is a type of the divel, without a mysterie'.

1 On the 'golden chaine', see v.25–6n.

3–4 In Malory's *Tale of King Arthur*, Book I, Arthur is taken from his mother Ygerna and given to Sir Ector to foster. Timon (Greek *timē*, honour) is a name invented by Spenser. Rauran is in Merionethshire, one of the ancestral seats of the Penmynydd (North Wales) Tudors from whom Henry VII was directly descended: Millican, *Spenser and the Table Round*, 37, 145–6, 150, n.5. Note that Arthur is brought up in the wilds, because one so brought up is incorruptible (Bernheimer, *Wild Men*, 19). There was a tradition that Merlin himself was a wild man (*ibid.*, 13, 99). Arthur's upbringing thus complements that of Satyrane (vi.20–6n.), giving the roots of the Tudor monarchy a firmly uncorrupt and primitive soil and contrasting him and the monarchy absolutely with the wild-man Antichrist Orgoglio.

7–8 The wound of love theme is developed at length in Book III: e.g., the effects of Britomart's falling in love with Arthegall at ii.31ff. The flame of love is a commonplace; Percival, 280 compares Burton's *Anatomy of Melancholy*, III.ii.3: 'Empedocles the Philosopher was present at the cutting up of one that died for love, his heart was combust, his liver smoky, his lungs dried up, insomuch that he verily believed his soul was either sod or roasted, through the vehemency of Love's fire' (ed. Floyd Dell and P. Jordan Smith, 734).

10   'Their God' is Cupid (see Proem 3n.).

13–15   There is a long tradition according to which a Celtic fairy princess gives herself to a mortal: a noble lineage usually develops from the union (Rathborne, 167ff.) Cf. Chaucer's *Sir Thopas*, 778ff. Arthur's dream contrasts with Redcrosse's dream in canto i (see i.47n. on the difference between the two and their Neoplatonic implications). In terms of classical mythology, Arthur's dream recalls Diana's love for Endymion: the goddess came down to the youth, kissed him and lay with him while he was sleeping in a cave on mount Latmos (e.g., Apollonius Rhodius, *Argonautica*, IV.57ff.). This myth relates to the Neoplatonic aspect of Arthur's vision, since the love of any immortal for a mortal was taken by Neoplatonists as an image of that yearning for eternal bliss that can be achieved only through death (Wind, 154 citing the Diana–Endymion myth, where it is related to St Paul's 'desiring to be losed and to be with Christ' (Philippians 1:23)). In fairy mythology, the Queen of Fairies was identified with Diana, a point which influenced Elizabeth's own mythological role as the Dianan Fairy Queen (Rathborne, 161). Arthur's wanderings echo Una's (ii.7n., vi.2–3n.) but, in connection with this vision, also bring to mind the Cupid and Psyche story as narrated in Apuleius's *Golden Ass*, in which Cupid fell in love with Psyche and visited her nightly and unseen. Against his wishes Psyche tried to discover who he was; he fled, and she then wandered far and wide in search of him. Finally she was made immortal and married him. Since *Psyche* means *soul* in Greek, the tale was interpreted allegorically as the union of the soul after purgation and the sloughing off of mortality with pure love or divine bliss and contemplation (Lotspeich, 104, citing Boccaccio, *De Gen. Deor.*, V.xxii). In view of this, the nine months of Arthur's search probably refers to a common meaning of nine as the number of the soul (see II.ix.22n.).

19   Arthur's diamond box contains healing drops of divine grace; on the diamond, see vii.33–5n.

21   Pegasus is the winged horse that sprang from the blood of Medusa when Perseus beheaded her (*Met.*, IV.785–6).

22–4 The description of the knight is typical of personifications of Fear: cf. Fear in III.xii.12; Ripa, s.v. *Paura* (Dread), 382–3, and *Timore* (Fear), 487; and Sackville's Induction, 232–8, in *The Mirror for Magistrates*, ed. Campbell, 306: 'Next sawe we Dread ... / Benumde of speeche, and with a gastly looke / Searcht every place al pale and dead for feare, / His cap borne up with staring of his heare'. On the 'infernall furies', see v.31–4n. Sir Trevisan (named at st. 32) has had a horrifying vision of Despair – as Redcrosse himself is going to – that is in symbolic contrast with Arthur's vision of Gloriana.

27 Terwin's love for the cruel 'Ladie gent' contrasts with Arthur's for Gloriana and Redcrosse's for Una. Arthur's is as yet unfulfilled, but he has a motivation for his love which saves him from Terwin's suicidal despair.

28 On Despair, see notes on st. 33ff. The concealed snake is a common emblem deriving from Vergil, *Eclogues*, III. 93 ('flee the snake lurking in the grass'). It appears frequently in the emblem books: e.g., Paradin's *Devises Heroiques* (1562), 41, where it is interpreted as a warning against gathering wrong opinions from books and thereby being damned; and Whitney, *Emblemes*, 24, where it is a warning against flattery (both of which are applicable here). Spenser uses it again in connection with deception at III.xi.28.

29 Despair is usually shown with a knife or dagger in the breast (Ripa, 106); though Anger, too, is often depicted stabbing herself with a sword or dagger (Mâle, 115). The notion goes back to Prudentius's fifth-century *Psychomachia*, 150ff., and is a warning to the choleric Redcrosse. The rope as an attribute of Despair derives from Judas Iscariot's suicide (Matthew 27:5; cf. Chew, 222–3, 379, n.44). Compare George Wither, *Abuses Stript and Whipt* (1622), I.xi: Despair stands 'with gastly looks' and 'poysons, ropes, or poyn-yards' in his hands.

30–1 Terwin kills himself because of love melancholy. The words applied to him at line 2 echo those used of the love-lorn Dido, soon to commit suicide, at *Aeneid*, IV.451 ('she prayed for death; the vault of heaven was a wearisome sight to her'). Cf. the suicides (among whom is Dido) at *Aeneid*, VI.435–6, described as those who 'threw away their souls in detestation of the light'. On Dido, see II.i.35–56n. Despair's 'guilefull traine' recalls '*Errours* endlesse traine' at i.18.

33–4 Despair's cave has affinities with Error's (i.13–16n.) and with hell-mouth, as in Sackville's Induction, 204ff. ('An hydeous hole al vaste, withouten shape', etc.; *Mirror for Magistrates, ed.cit.,* 305). But above all this is a Saturnian scene, since Saturn is god of melancholy, solitude, and grave-diggers (Klibansky, 191ff.). As Agrippa puts it (I.xlviii,96): 'all stinking places, dark, underground, ... and mournfull places, as ... solitary dens, caves, and pits ... are appropriated to *Saturne*'. The owl, too, is Saturnian (*ibid.,* I.xxv,56), though Spenser also recalls *Aeneid,* IV.462–3 ('the lonely owl sounding a deathly song'). *Tristitia* (Sadness, Melancholy) leads to, and is sometimes iconographically indistinguishable from, Despair: Mâle, 106; Katzenellenbogen, 13n. And cf. viii.38–41n. The suicide Judas, betrayer of Christ (see st. 29n. and i.25–6n.), was diagnosed as a melancholic (Klibansky, 121, 195n.). Kathrine Koller, 'Art, Rhetoric, and Holy Dying in *The Faerie Queene* with special reference to the Despair canto', *S.P.,* LXI (1964), notes that this is a stock description and compares, e.g., Breughel's *Triumph of Death.*

35–6 Redcrosse's faith is now tested by a confrontation with despair, the denial of God's mercy and His will that man should be saved (as Una has to remind him, st. 53). It is caused by an overriding sense of sinfulness, and is to be contrasted with the repentance which leads to recognition of mercy in canto x (see Hamilton, 81 and n., citing especially Calvin's *Institutes of the Christian Religion*). Despair's physical details here – the emaciated appearance, the rags, etc. – are melancholic (cf. the melancholic Redcrosse at viii.38–41n.) and have affinities with the Dame Melancholy tradition, in which leanness and rags are also to be found (Klibansky, 221ff.): see II.vii.3–6n. Melancholy is traditionally linked with the sin of sloth and displaced in virtues–vices–gifts of the Holy Ghost schemes by the fourth gift, *fortitudo,* which gives the knightly virtue, prowess (Tuve, 96–7; on Arthur's fortitude see vii.31n.) Upton (*Var. Sp.,* I.279) noted that the clothes held together with thorns recall the unkempt stranger who was left in the Cyclops' cave and whose garments are similarly held together, at *Aeneid,* III.594.

37 Line 4 echoes the fourth line of viii.40, where Arthur is rescuing Redcrosse from Orgoglio's dungeon ('with constant zeale, and courage bold'), except that Redcrosse now *burns* with '*firie* zeale', whereas Arthur has the constancy which is traditionally a part of fortitude (Tuve, 60, and cf. 135). Redcrosse still has the fiery choler noted earlier (e.g., v.8n.), which leads him to demand 'eye for an eye' Old Testament justice and ignore the New Testament ethic (cf. the choleric Sansloy at iii.33–6n.). He thus lays himself wide open to Despair's perversion of New Testament doctrine that follows, and his emphasis on God's justice rather His mercy. The stanza ends, ironically, with a parody allusion to Christ's salvific blood (cf. i.25–6n. and viii.10n.). Redcrosse moves symbolically from Sinai (the Law) to the Mount of Olives (the Gospel, mercy) at x.53–4.

38 Despair combines commonplaces of Stoic philosophy used in the Christian 'art of dying' tradition and culled from Plato, Epictetus, Plutarch, Cicero, and Seneca (see Koller, 'Art, Rhetoric, and Holy Dying') with deliberate perversions and suppressions of relevant Biblical texts. The emphasis on *ease* (st. 38, 40) reminds us that this is a temptation to sloth (see st. 35–6n.). St. 38 bases itself on, e.g., Romans 3:20 ('Therefore by the workes of the Law shal no flesh be justified in his sight: for by the Lawe commeth the knowledge of sinne') and 6:23 ('the wages of sinne is death'), ignoring the last part of that verse ('but the gifte of God is eternal life through Jesus Christ our Lord'): see Cullen, 60. Despair's trick of suppressing mercy and emphasising Old Testament justice is discussed by E. Sirluck, 'A Note on the Rhetoric of Spenser's "Despair" ', *M.P.*, XLVII (1949–50).

39–40 Despair recalls, e.g., Psalms 69:1–2 ('Save me, O God: for the waters are entred even to my soule. I sticke fast in the depe myre, where no staie is: I am come into depe waters, and the streames runne over me'), and Cicero, *De Senectute*, XIX: 'The nearer I approach death the more I feel like one who is in sight of land at last and is about to anchor in his home port after a long voyage' (Loeb edn, tr. W. A. Falconer (1923), 83). See Koller, *art.cit.*, on these commonplaces. Suppressed here is the salvific significance of the water of baptism (death leading to life): e.g., Romans 6:3–4: 'Knowe ye not, that all we which have bene baptized into Jesus Christ, have bene baptized into his death? We are buryed then with him by baptisme into his death, that like as Christ was raised up from the dead by the glorie of the Father, so we also shulde walke in newnes of life'. The passing over the river bank to death alludes ironically to the crossing of the Jordan into the Promised Land, a traditonal figure for baptism (Cullen, 60; Tuve, *A Reading of George Herbert* (1952), 184, 197–8).

41   Cf. Cicero, *De Senectute*, XX: 'Pythagoras bids us stand like faithful sentries and not quit our post until God, our Captain, gives the word' (Loeb edn, 85; the allusion is to Plato's *Phaedo*; see Helen Gardner, *The Business of Criticism* (Oxford, 1949), 49). It was a commonplace in the suicide debate.

43   There is truth here: Alpers, 355 notes the similarity with Contemplation's words at x.60 ('For bloud can nought but sin'). Line 6 echoes Genesis 9:6 ('Whoso shedeth mans blood, by man shal his blood be shed') and Matthew 26:52 ('Then said Jesus unto him . . . all that take the sworde, shal perishe with the sworde'). But Despair's 'truth' is only partial: see Una's words at st. 52–3.

44   Cf., e.g., Lucretius, *De rerum natura*, III.943ff.: 'Why not rather make an end of life and labour? Do you expect me to invent some new contrivance for your pleasure? I tell you, there is none. All things are always the same. If your body is not yet withered with age, nor your limbs decrepit and flagging, even so there is nothing to look forward to' (tr. Ronald Latham, Penguin Classics, 124).

47   Cf. Ezekiel 18:4 ('the soule that sinneth, it shal dye').

49–50   A good gloss on this is Burton's *Anatomy of Melancholy*, III.iv.2.6, on the effects and cures of despair: the despairing melancholic has hellish visions but (cf. st. 53) 'where sinne abunded, there grace abunded muche more' (Romans 5:20).

51   The quivering aspen is a traditional symbol of fear; significantly, it was one of the trees believed to have been used to make Christ's cross (de Vries, 26). Redcrosse's hand starts back as a sign of natural revulsion to suicide (Alpers, 357 and n.).

53   Redcrosse is 'chosen': cf. Mark 13:20 ('but for the elects sake, which he hathe chosen, he hathe shortened those dayes'). Tuve, 124 notes that this 'is the fundamental Christian answer to *man*, common to all Christian churches' and warns against reading it as specifically Calvinistic.

CANTO X

Ten is the number of perfection, of the circular return to God, of the commandments: 'the tenth day after the ascension of Christ the Holy Ghost came down ... all things with the number ten, and by the number ten, make a round, as saith *Proclus*, taking their beginning from God, and ending in him' (Agrippa, II.xiii,211). From the evil nine and Despair Redcrosse now moves to ten, the Law, and Holiness. The House of Holiness is the opposite of Lucifer's earthly House of Pride and, like it, based on the medieval court of love tradition which, in turn, conflates the description of the palace of a divinity with the feudal castle. The Elizabethan reader would also have detected in the opposition a juxtaposing of the new 'prodigy house' and the older style of domestic architecture (see iv.2n. and Summerson, *Architecture in Britain 1530–1830*, 30–3, 41–2, 61ff.) – a contemporary version of the contrast between architectural ostentation and simplicity in, e.g., Horace's *Odes*, II.xv and xviii ('Neither ivory nor gilded cornice shines in my house').

1 Cf. Ephesians 2:8–9: 'For by grace are ye saved through faith, and that not of your selves: it is the gifte of God, not of workes, lest any man shulde boaste him self'.

3 Upton (*Var. Sp.*, I.283) compares 1 Peter 2:5: 'And ye as livelie stones, be made a spiritual house'. The 'matrone grave' prays and acts, combining faith and works in accordance with Anglican doctrine (Calvin and Luther emphasised faith alone). Contrast Corceca at iii.10–20n.

4 Caelia = Heavenly One. Her daughters, the three theological virtues, Faith, Hope, Charity, are in the traditional order (1 Corinthians 13:13: 'And now abideth faith, hope, & love, even these thre: but the chiefest of these is love'). It is in fact an ascending order: 'Faith builds the foundations of the spiritual edifice, Hope raises it, and Charity crowns it' (Peter the Precentor, *Verbum abbreviativum*; *Patrologia Latina*, CCV, col. 271, cit.

Mâle, 110). In terms of the structure of Book I, Fidelia displaces Corceca, Fidessa and Sansfoy; Speranza displaces Despair (see Mâle, 112–3 on the opposition of Faith, Idolatry and blind Synagogue and iii.10–20n.; and *ibid.*, 115 and fig. 53 on the opposition of Hope and Despair). Faith and Hope are 'spousd' but only Charity is married, to show that the first two belong solely to this life, the earthly pilgrimage, whereas Charity, the greatest virtue, is fulfilling now and also in the after life (Mâle, 116; cf. Geneva gloss on 1 Corinthians 13:13: love 'serveth bothe here & in the life to come; but faith and hope apperteine onely to this life'). The two plus one scheme is influenced in addition by the usual two plus one portrayal of Venus's three Graces (e.g., *F.Q.*, VI.x.24, and E. K.'s gloss on *Shepheardes Calender*, 'April', 109: the Graces are depicted 'the one having her back toward us, and her face fromwarde, as proceeding from us; the other two toward us, noting double thanke to be due to us for the benefit, we have done'). A usual Neoplatonic reading of the Graces saw them as embodying *Pulchritudo* (Beauty, emanating from God), *Amor* (Love), and *Voluptas* (Pleasure); this last (in Spenserian terms embodied in Charissa) being the ultimate divine joy, or ultimate pleasure (Wind, ch. III, and especially 50–1). This explains why Spenser depicts Charissa as Venus, goddess of pleasure (see st. 29–31n. below): but she is, of course, a *celestial* Venus (see Proem 4n.). On Charissa's fecundity (the 'many pledges'), see st. 29–31n.

5 The opening lines echo Nehemiah 4:9, the day and night watch against the foes of Jerusalem: i.e., Caelia's house is the earthly Jerusalem, allegorically, Christ's Church on earth (Hankins, 116). With Humility, contrast Malvenu (iv.6) and Ignaro (viii.31): he must be the porter to the house in which Redcrosse discovers his true spiritual nature and confronts his fleshly pride, since in the gifts of the Holy Ghost—virtues—vices schemes, the first gift, *timor Domini* (fear of the Lord) destroys pride (*superbia*) and places in its stead the virtue of humility (Tuve, 93–4, 125; Chew, 123). It also correlates with the first beatitude ('Blessed are the poore in spirit, for theirs is the kingdome of heaven': Matthew 5:3; Tuve, 93–4). On the opposition of humility and pride (again in Prudentius's *Psychomachia*), see Katzenellenbogen, 2, 8rl., 9, 12, 16, 17, 18n., 20n. Humility is the most significant characteristic of Christ (*ibid.*, 43) and the root of the seven virtues (10, 34, 53n., 54, 63, 67, 75,

80). The final line recalls Matthew 7:14: 'the gate is streicte, and the way narrowe that leadeth unto life, and fewe there be that finde it' (cf. iv.2n., and cf. st. 35 below). In view of the climb up the mountain with Contemplation to view the Heavenly Jerusalem at the end of the canto, Spenser probably has in mind the various scales or ladders (based on Jacob's dream at Genesis 28:12 of the ladder reaching from heaven to earth with angels going up and down it) called 'ladders of perfection', etc., common in medieval and Renaissance theological treatises, which have each rung labelled as a virtue, beginning, e.g., with Humility and ending with Contemplation (Chew, 201–2; Katzenellenbogen, 22–6, and especially 25 on the Benedictine *scala humilitatis*).

6–7 Arthur has 'constant zeale' at viii.40 (and see ix.37n.). Zeal appears on the elaborate ladder of virtue described by Katzenellenbogen, 23–4n. Reverence is giving superiors their due (Tuve, 68, discussing it as an aspect of justice); his 'sad attire' is dark, or sober, with no pejorative implications.

8–9 Una, 'borne of heavenly berth', seeks the cure of Redcrosse from heavenly Caelia as Duessa, speciously 'sunny bright', seeks the cure of Sansjoy from 'griesly *Night*' (v.20ff.). Sansjoy is choleric and melancholic; Redcrosse is suffering from melancholic despair (v.8n., viii.35ff. and notes).

10 On 'the broad high way', see iv.2n.

12–13 Faith and Hope appear together because they are ultimately different from Charity (see st. 4n. above). Their 'even steps' symbolise the proportion and measure associated with virtue (Tuve, 94; contrast iv.18–20n. and cf. vi.20–6n., Satyrane's 'equall teme'). Fidelia's association with the sun recalls Una (e.g., iii.4.n., where it is among other things an emblem of Truth; see i.2n. on the linking of Faith and Truth) and the solar Arthur (vii.29n.). The 'Christall' might suggest Revelation 21:11, the Heavenly Jerusalem shining 'cleare as cristal'; crystal was also emblematic of purity and the durability of true faith (Kitty Scoular, *Natural Magic* (Oxford, 1965), 178). Her white robe is a traditional sign of her purity (Ripa, 149, *Fede Christiana* (Christian Faith)), and the Eucharistic chalice (contrast viii.14n.) is traditional: Ripa, *ibid.*; Mâle, 113. The 'wine and water' allude to the blood and water that flowed from the wound in Christ's side (viii.10n.), to the mixing of wine and water in the communion service in the primitive Church, and to a familiar emblem of temperance (see II.i.35–56n.). The serpent comes from Numbers 21:8–9, the brazen serpent lifted up by Moses against the plague of serpents, interpreted in John 3:14–15 as a type of Christ's salvific power. Upton, *Var. Sp.*, I.285, links it with the serpent, symbol of renewal and emblem of Aesculapius (see v.36–44n., and compare Arthur's dragon at vii.31n., as well as the serpent of wisdom and prudence at Matthew 10:16). Faith is *constant* (Hebrews 10:23) and holds the New Testament, sealed with Christ's blood and the blood of martyrs, in her left hand (see Ripa, 149; Chew, 128). For the last line of st. 13, see 1 Corinthians 13:12 ('For now we se through a glasse darkely'), and 2 Peter 3:16 (St Paul's Epistles contain 'some things . . . hard to be understood'). St John the Evangelist is traditionally depicted bearing a cup with a snake in it (in allusion to an unsuccessful attempt to kill him with poisoned wine) and a book: Mâle, 300, 309, 311. The cup here again symbolised redemption.

14 Speranza is 'clad in blew', the colour of the heavens at which she traditionally gazes (Mâle, 114; Ripa, 471, s.v. *Speranza divina*). The usual colour of her dress is green (Ripa, 469–70); blue is the colour of Truth (Gilbert, *Symbolic Persons*, 180, 231, 238: because it is the heavenly colour). The anchor (cf. Ripa, 470) derives from Hebrews 6:18–19 (hope 'as an ancre of the soule'), and it is silver as a sign of purity (Psalms 12:6: 'The wordes of the Lord are pure wordes, as ye silver, tryed in a fornace of earth') and wisdom (Proverbs 2:4, seeking wisdom as one seeks silver). Upton (*Var. Sp.*, I.286) suggests that 'she does not seem altogether as chearful as her sister, because hope is attended with some mixture of fear, and 'tis in another world that hope is swallowed up in certainty'.

15 On 'shamefast modestie', see II.ix.40–3n.

16 Charissa is discussed at st. 29–31n.

17 Obedience is fear of God (often exemplified by Abraham's readiness to sacrifice Isaac) and one of the Christian virtues: according to one tradition, it was one of the virtues bestowed by the gifts of the Holy Ghost (Katzenellenbogen, 37–9, 43–4; see also 15, 57).

18 'Opened his dull eyes': cf. iii.10–20n. and Ephesians 1:18: 'That ye eyes of your understanding may be lightened'.

19 Lines 8–9 probably recall 2 Corinthians 3:6, on the contrast between the old law ('the letter') and the new: God 'hathe made us able ministers of the New testament, not of the letter but of the Spirit: for the letter killeth, but the Spirit giveth life' (Geneva gloss on 'Spirit': 'the spiritual doctrine [given by Christ], which is in our hearts').

20 The allusions are to celebrated instances of faith: Joshua 10:12ff. (Joshua commanding the sun to stand still); 2 Kings 20:10ff. (Hezekiah and the dial of Ahaz: see iv.4n.; significantly, a symbol of deliverance); Judges 7 (Gideon's victory over the Midianites with only three hundred men); Exodus 14:21–31 (the passage of the Israelites over the Red Sea, typologically Christ's baptism and His delivery of fallen man from sin: Tuve, *George Herbert*, 112ff.); and Matthew 21:21 (the faith that will move mountains: cf. *ibid.*, 17:20).

21 Redcrosse now, in a context of faith in Christ's redemptive power, undergoes the self-abhorrence and contempt for the world that he had previously undergone with Despair. Repentance follows, and is produced by, faith (Calvin, *Institutes of the Christian Religion*, III.3). Redcrosse begins the process of mortification which, in terms of traditional theology, will lead to spiritual health.

23 *Patientia* (Patience) is the virtue that answers two of the spiritual vices, *Ira* (Wrath) and *Desperatio* (Despair): here Redcrosse purges the tendencies in his nature to choler and melancholic despair (see i.1n. and 2n. for references, also ix.29ff. and notes). On Patience and Wrath, see Katzenellenbogen, 2, 8n., 9n., 11n., 12, 18n., 20n.; on Patience displacing Despair, see Mâle, 115. It is Christ's special version of heroic fortitude (Barbara Lewalski, *Milton's Brief Epic*, 20–6, 254–5) and his Passion is the ultimate example of Patience which, as a personification, traditionally bears the cross as an emblem (Chew, 119–20, 122). There is a hint of the knight's Christ-like 'passion' at the end of st. 24.

24–7 Compare and contrast Redcrosse in Orgoglio's dungeon (viii.38ff.) and Despair's cave. Contrast, too, the physical salves of ii.40–1n. Patience traditionally includes Amendment, Penance, and Repentance (Tuve, 93n.), and Redcrosse is undergoing the 'attrition by mortification' associated with penance, which subdues bodily lusts and develops the mind's contemplative power (Hankins, 118; this is what Contemplation himself has achieved at st. 46ff.). Penance in Ripa, 389 is emaciated, dressed in sackcloth, and holds the whip of self-correction. The 'ashes and sackcloth' recall Job 2:8 (Job sitting 'among the ashes') and 16:15 ('I have sowed a sackecloth upon my skin, and have abased mine horne unto the dust'); and Remorse 'did pricke and nip' because etymologically *remorsus* = biting back. For repentance (*sad* because this is a constructive *tristitia* as opposed to Despair's destructive sadness; and cf. st. 32) see 2 Corinthians 7:10 on 'godly sorowe' causing repentance (cited at i.2n.). The bathing of Redcrosse's body in salt water suggests, e.g., Psalms 51:2 ('Wash me throughly from mine iniquitie, and clene me from my sinne'), but *salt* water is at once the tears of repentance and the salt of purification: Ezekiel 16:4 ('thou wast not washed in water ... thou wast not salted with salt') and 2 Kings 2:21 (salt used to purify a well). On the 'drops of bloud' which 'like a well did play', see st. 12–13n.

28 The roaring lion metaphor expresses the purging of Redcrosse's sin (for the devil as a lion see 1 Peter 5:8) and recalls the lion of wrath, one of his specific spiritual vices, It also reminds us that he is now almost ready to take on his role of the leonine Sun of righteousness (iii.5–9n.).

29–31 Una's kiss is the 'holie kisse' of salutation in the early church (e.g., Romans 16:16; see Hankins, 116) whose ideal primitive Christianity, restored by Elizabeth (ii.22n.), Redcrosse is now worthy to participate in. It is also the kiss of charity of 1 Peter 5:14. He reaches the ultimate virtue of Charity (see st. 4n.), the sign of God's love and mercy. Charity is usually depicted barebreasted, suckling and surrounded by babies (Ripa, 64–5; contrast Error's brood at i.15), though her robe is usually red (*ibid.*, 63–4). Typically, Spenser's Charity is composite and more complex than the usual simple personification: she is conflated with Perfection, usually yellow-robed because gold is the perfect metal and barebreasted to 'signify a very important part of perfection, that of nourishing others ... since it is more perfect to give than to receive benefits' (Ripa, 391–2). The *gold* crown combines Charity's usual crown of flames (Ripa, 63–4; Tervarent, cols. 127–8) with the gold crown of virtue (Tervarent, col. 126), the gold of perfection, and the

'incorruptible crowne of glorie' of 1 Peter 5:4. She is a Venus
Urania, too, (see st. 4n. above, and Proem 4n. for
general references to Venus in Book I): she hates 'Cupids
wanton snare' (see Proem 3n.) like Una, and like Una, who has
'golden heare' (st. 28), she is associated with yellow and gold, not
only for the reasons just mentioned but, in addition, because yellow
is a colour of Venus (Ptolemy, Tetrabiblos, II.ix; Loeb edn, 193).
The two doves are Venerean (Tervarent, cols. 104–5; Ripa, 51) as
is the 'yvorie chaire' (see Andrew Tooke, Pantheon (1824 edn),
IX.i,97 for Venus riding in an ivory chariot). Venus Urania was
identified by Neoplatonists with Christian Charity (Panofsky,
Studies in Iconology, 142, citing Ficino; Wind, plate 76); and
Charissa here contrasts specifically with the earthly Venus Lucifera
(iv.8–10n.). See above, st. 4n., for the possible complementary
identification of Charissa with the third Grace, Voluptas.

34–5 Mercy is the virtue bestowed by the fifth gift of the Holy
Ghost, consilium (counsel), corresponding to the fifth beatitude
(Matthew 5:7: 'Blessed are the merciful: for thei shal obtaine
mercie'): Tuve, 100–1. It imitates God's own mercy (Luke 6:36:
'Be ye therefore merciful, as your Father also is merciful'). Spenser
has Mercy appear exactly in the middle of the canto (st. 34–5 of a
total of 68) because she will be of supreme importance on the Day
of Judgement, which is associated with the central point (see
ii.28–32n. and vii.5n.). The Biblical authority for her role then is
Matthew 25:31ff. (Christ sitting on the 'throne of his glorie'
separating the sheep from the goats and rewarding the charitable
'of his fre mercie' (Geneva gloss on verse 35)). This passage – on
clothing the naked, etc. and receiving the reward of 'life eternal'
(verse 36) – is alluded to in the last line of st. 34 and the stanzas
following.

36–43 Contrasting with the seven sins of the House of Pride are
the seven corporal works of mercy, which have their Biblical base
in the Matthew 25 passage just alluded to (feeding the hungry,
giving drink to the thirsty and hospitality to strangers, clothing the
naked, visiting the sick and those in prison). The care of widows
and orphans comes from James 1:27: 'Pure religion & undefiled
before God, even the Father, is this, to visite the fatherles, and
widdowes in their adversitie'; and the burial of the dead derives
from Tobit 12:12 ('& when thou didest burye the dead, I was with

thee likewise'). These works of mercy were enumerated in the
fourth century by Lactantius and codified definitively by Aquinas
who, however, omitted the care of widows and orphans (Lactantius
himself kept the number to seven by omitting 'giving drink to the
thirsty' and including the widows and orphans). Spenser keeps his
seven by conflating the giving of food and drink (st. 38) so that he,
too, can include the care of widows and orphans. He probably
knew Lactantius on the works of mercy either at first or second
hand and was influenced by him: see Charles E. Mounts, 'Spenser's
Seven Bead-men and the Corporal Works of Mercy', *P.M.L.A.*,
LIV (1939), 974–80. Christ's three-day harrowing of hell (st. 40) is
recounted in the Gospel of Nicodemus, part II (see especially
section vi, where Christ sets free 'the prisoners that are held bound
by original sin': *Excluded Books of the New Testament*, tr. J. B.
Lightfoot, M. R. James, H. B. Swete (London, n.d.), 95).

46–63 On the traditional mountain of meditation and of the
house of the Lord (Isaiah 2:2ff.; contrast Error's cave, Lucifera's
and Orgoglio's dungeons) Redcrosse attains understanding
(*intellectus*) and, for a moment, wisdom (*sapientia*), the last two
gifts of the Holy Ghost which are possessed mainly by
contemplatives and associated with the mystical states of
illumination and perfection, or union with the One (Tuve, 101;
Redcrosse's earlier stay in the House of Holiness can be related to
the first mystical stage of purgation). In Christian Neoplatonic
thought particularly, contemplatives were regarded as being under
the patronage of melancholic Saturn (Klibansky, 254ff.; Agrippa,
I.lx, 133: Saturn 'is the Author of secret contemplation' who
makes the mind withdraw from 'outward businesses' and 'ascend
higher'). Moreover, the gifts, virtues, vices and beatitudes were
correlated with the seven planets; so that the sixth gift,
understanding, was given to Jupiter (sixth counting from earth in
the Ptolemaic system) and the last, wisdom, to Saturn, the seventh
planet, for Saturn is old and therefore wise (Klibansky, 166ff.,
citing Alexander Neckham). Contemplation with his 'litle
Hermitage' cancels out Archimago and his hermitage with its false
vision (i.34ff.), and also Ignaro (canto viii) and the melancholic and
emaciated Despair (ix.33–5). Contemplation is emaciated (st. 48),
but for a different reason: 'his mind was full of spirituall repast'.
Spenser develops the theme of Redcrosse's growth in accordance

with the by now traditional dichotomy between the pathological, self-destructive, and depressive melancholy associated with despair, and contemplative melancholy (see Klibansky, *passim*; Tuve, *Images and Themes in Five Poems by Milton* (Cambridge, Mass., 1967), 15–36). Contemplation recalls, too, the wise counsellor figure as embodied in the Homeric Nestor (Curtius, 170ff.), Good Counsel (depicted in Ripa, 85 as an old man), and Thought (*Pensiero*: an old man, pale, thin, and melancholic; Ripa, 389). The wise hermit was an important aspect of the Elizabethan chivalric tradition: after an active youth, one retires to a contemplative old age (Yates, 106–7).

47–8   The eagle was believed to be able to gaze at the sun without being blinded: a notion related to the rebirth symbolism associated with the bird (xi.33–4n.), and interpreted as the power to contemplate Christ, the Sun of justice (Hankins, 118): contrast Corceca, iii.10–20n. The oak symbolises endurance (rooted in deepest earth, it reaches up to heaven, withstanding strong winds: *Aeneid*, IV.441ff.), and was dedicated to Jupiter (Agrippa, I.xxvi,57; see above on Jupiter and the sixth gift, understanding). Contemplation's mortification is explained by Romans 8:13: 'if ye live after the flesh, ye shal dye: but if ye mortifie the dedes of the bodie by the Spirit, ye shal live'.

50   The keys are those of 'the kingdome of heaven' (Matthew 16:19). Contrast Ignaro's keys (viii.30–4n.).

52   'Man of earth' recalls Genesis 3:19 ('thou art dust, and to dust shalt thou returne') and 1 Corinthians 15:47, contrasting Adam and Christ: 'The first man is of the earth, earthlie: the seconde man is the Lord from heaven'.

53–4   The high mountain – in part the steep hill of virtue (see Plate 2) – is defined by Spenser typologically. It is compared first to Sinai, on which Moses received the tablets of the law (Exodus 24 and 34). The crossing of the Red Sea (Exodus 14:16ff.), referred to at line 3, was a figure for baptism and redemption, and the escape from the Egyptian bondage achieved thereby was seen as a transition from bodily passion to mind (the Promised Land): see, e.g., J. A. Galdon, *Typology and Seventeenth-century Literature* (The Hague, 1975), ch. VIII, 'Exodus Typology'. Noah's flood had lasted forty days, Moses was forty days on the mountain, the

Israelites were in the desert forty years: all were typologically
related to Christ's forty-day sojourn in the wilderness (Matthew
4:2, etc.). The old law then yields to the new law as embodied in
Christ's sermon on the mount (Matthew 5; see Tuve, 88), though
this was not delivered on the Mount of Olives, to which Spenser
refers here. For Christ on the Mount of Olives, see, e.g., Matthew
24:3, and John 8:1. The olive garland is an attribute, appropriately,
of Mercy (Ripa, 328–9). The third element in the comparison is
Mount Parnassus, the home of the nine Muses: Spenser alludes to
the originally Platonic notion of the contemplative power of the
prophet-poet. Compare the Proem to Book VI, where the Muses
are invoked as the guardians of sacred lore; and *Shepheardes
Calender*, 'October', *passim*. There is more than a hint of the
Renaissance concept of the *Musarum sacerdos*, the man dedicated
to the Muses who embodied the new notion of the *vita speculativa*
(the speculative, studious, life), the secular equivalent of the
contemplative life understood in its exclusively religious sense
(Klibansky, 245). Note the reference to Spenser's own poetical
power at st. 55. A mountain that goes unmentioned but that is
obviously in Spenser's mind is that in Revelation 21:10 from which
St John sees the heavenly Jerusalem. It is worth recalling that St
Bonaventura (*Itinerarium mentis in Deum*) related the threefold
pattern of illumination to the progression from the old law to the
new as follows: (i) *Apprehensio*, in which the soul turns from itself
to the outside world to discover signs of the Creator corresponds to
the old law; (ii) *Oblectatio* (delight), the middle meditative stage in
which the mind turns inward and finds within itself patterns of the
Creator corresponds to the new law; (iii) *Diiudicatio* (decision), in
which the contemplative mind moves out to the eternal is compared
to the insight achieved in Revelation (see Russel A. Peck, 'Theme
and Number in Chaucer's *Book of the Duchess*', in A. D. S. Fowler
(ed.), *Silent Poetry* (1970), 93).

55–7 The angles going 'to and fro' come from Jacob's dream
(see st. 5n.); and cf. Hebrews 12:22: 'ye are come unto the mounte
Sion, and to the citie of the living God, the celestial Jerusalem, and
to the company of innumerable Angels'. The 'cursed tree' is
Christ's cross (cf. xi.46–8n.); Christ is 'the lambe of God, which
taketh away the sinne of the world' (John 1:29).

58 On Cleopolis, see vii.46n. Panthea = place of all gods,

identified variously by critics with Westminster Abbey, Greenwich
Palace, *et al.* It recalls the ancient Roman Pantheon (dedicated to
Cybele, the earth mother, and all the other gods) and Capitol,
which has a 'shining Christall' wall in Spenser's *Visions of Bellay*,
II (following, ultimately, the twelfth-century *Mirabilia urbis
Romae*: Rathborne, 27, 35). Rathborne, 25ff. discusses the
relationship of Cleopolis to the Renaissance view of Rome inherited
from the Middle Ages as a city which was at once a monument to
pagan pride (the attitude taken in the Geneva Bible glosses: see,
e.g., vii.16–18n.) and pagan virtue. She discusses in detail the
influence of the *Mirabilia* on Renaissance and earlier writers. For
the symbolic meanings of crystal, see st. 12–13n. above.

59–63 Spenser raises explicitly the problem of the relationship
between the two traditionally opposed modes of life, the active and
heroic (see v.1n.) and the world-denying contemplative. The
allusion in st. 61 is to wisdom, the ultimate gift of the Holy Ghost
belonging to the contemplative (see st. 46–63n. above), which
Redcrosse glimpses but will finally achieve, with his sanctification,
only after death. Its corresponding beatitude is the seventh,
'Blessed are the peace makers' (Matthew 5:9; Tuve, 101): at this
point the contemplative has reached complete unity with God and
himself. Note the reference to *peace* in st. 62. Redcrosse's words in
st. 63 recall Despair's temptation (e.g., ix.40); but he has to return
from mind to the active world of the body in order to complete his
chivalric quest. Now, though, he knows positively what his goal is
and can look forward to the registering of his name 'above the
Sunne' (II.i.32) in the book of Life (e.g., Revelation 21:27) where
the names of the saints of the New Jerusalem are enrolled.
Hankins, 116–7 notes the allusion to Peter's two wishes, the first on
the Mount of Transfiguration, where he wanted to stay (Matthew
17:4), the second at the Last Supper when he wanted to die with
Christ (John 13:36ff.). Like Redcrosse, Peter was refused.

64–6 Knowing his spiritual goal, Redcrosse now finds out his
identity: he is *georgos* (ploughman, husbandman), the root of which
is Greek *gē*, earth. Spenser recalls *Met.*, XV.553ff. and Cicero, *De
divinatione*, II.xxiii, the discovery of the boy soothsayer Tages by a
ploughman. Cf. st. 52n. above, and vii.8–10n. The idea of the
changeling is from folklore; but the tale told here underlines the
nation's aberration as it moved away from truth to error (the

changeling of 'base Elfin brood') until, under Elizabeth–Gloriana, the Arthurian empire can be restored (the process begins with George's arrival at court). See II.x.70ff. and notes. George brought up by a ploughman and then going to court parallels Satyrane's similar progress: see vi.28–30n., and cf. Arthur at ix.3–4n.

CANTO XI

The dragon, climactic image of evil, appears here because eleven is the number of sin since it transgresses the ten of the decalogue: St Augustine, *City of God*, XV.xx; Fowler, 54. In *The Voyage of the Wandering Knight. Showing the whole course of Mans life* (tr. William Goodyear from the French of Jean de Cartigny, 1581), the knight stays in the Palace of Worldly Felicity for eleven days because, the author explains, it is a wicked number in that it exceeds the number of the commandments (see Chew, 211). Cullen, 13ff. claims, with justice, that this work is an important source for Book I of *The Faerie Queene*. Redcrosse's victory occurs on the third day in allusion to Christ's harrowing of hell during the three days between His crucifixion and resurrection.

3 The tower probably recalls the brazen tower in which Danaë was imprisoned by her father Acrisius. Jove visited her as a shower of gold and she bore the child Perseus as a result (see *F.Q.*, III.xi.31; Horace, *Odes*, III.xvi). Perseus killed the snaky-locked Medusa (see vii.33–5n.), exemplifying the overcoming of lust by divine grace and wisdom (Allen, 189). In addition, the brass could suggest the brass doors of hell in the *Gospel of Nicodemus*, II.v (*ed.cit.*, 92), though in a good sense it symbolises durability (vii.33–5n.) and perfection: in Revelation 1:15 the image of Christ has feet of brass (Geneva gloss: indicating that 'His judgements & waies are moste perfect'). The watchman recalls the Old Testament prophets who, in the harrowing of hell tradition, announce Christ's arrival (*Nicodemus, ibid.*, 92–3) and, in the Bible, watch for the good news of the gospel (Carol V. Kaske, 'The Dragon's Spark and Sting and the Structure of Red Cross's Dragon-fight: *The Faerie Queene*, I.xi–xii', *S.P.*, LXVI (1969), citing Isaiah 21:5–11 ('watche in ye watche towre') and Romans 10:15 where, as here, 'glad tydings' = the gospel). Kaske further links the tower from which Una's parents are to be released with the old Mosaic law as described in Galatians 3:23: 'before faith came, we were kept under the Law, and shut up unto the faith, which shulde afterwardes be reveiled'. Redcrosse is, of course, about to enact one of the seven corporal works of mercy, the redeeming of captives (see x.40).

4 The dragon is 'the great dragon, that olde serpent, called the devil and Satan' of Revelation 12:9 defeated by Michael (and cf. vii.16–18n.), and the dragon of the St George legend (see i.4n.). In comparing him to 'a great hill' (he is a mountain in st. 8) and emphasising his roaring that seems to shake the ground, together with the smoke and sulphur of st. 13, Spenser identifies him with a volcano (made explicit at st. 44) and hence with Typhon, the rebel giant who embodies the power of volcanoes (see vii.8–10n. and the Vergil and Ovid passages cited there, and in addition *Ger. Lib.*, IV.8, where Satan is described as a volcano with breath like sulphur, etc.). Cf. the 'great mountaine, burning with fyre' of Revelation 8:8 (Geneva gloss: 'Divers sectes of heretikes were spred abroad in the worlde').

5–7 According to one tradition, the Muses were daughters of Apollo (rather than Jove) and Memory: Lotspeich, 83; Starnes and Talbert, 98; and compare *F.Q.*, III.iii.4, where Clio, Muse of fame and history, is daughter of Phoebus and Memory. It seems likely that Spenser is invoking Calliope–Clio here (see Proem 2n. on their virtual identification at this period); and she must come 'gently' to him and not with the 'mighty rage' appropriate to possible later martial books of the *F.Q.* (st. 7) because Redcrosse has purged his wrath with patience (x.23n.) and is to demonstrate a Christlike fortitude that is much less wrathful than that of the pagan epic heroes (e.g., Achilles). Hence she is to let down the 'haughty string' (i.e., high-pitched string) appropriate to the martial epic and raise instead her 'second tenor'; i.e., supporting voice to Spenser's own, principal, melody. The phrase is from bell-ringing, where the 'second tenor' is the bell next to the tenor, the latter being the largest of a set or peal (*O.E.D.*, Tenor, 4c). The musical imagery derives from the correlation of planetary spheres, Muses, modes and musical scale as found in, e.g. the well-known woodcut from Gafurius's *Practica musice* (1496): see Meyer-Baer, *Music of the Spheres*, fig. 96; Wind, fig. 20; S. K. Heninger, *Touches of Sweet Harmony*, 179ff. In the order given in

this woodcut – a common one, though not necessarily the one
Spenser had in mind – Clio comes at the bottom, corresponding to
the sphere of the moon and the hypodorian mode, and Calliope sits
immediately above her, corresponding to Mercury and the
hypophrygian mode. If Spenser conflates Calliope–Clio, as he
seems to, then he implies a division of labours here. Calliope,
literally a tone higher on Gafurius's octave scale, lowers herself to
Clio's note and mode: martial epic (of which Calliope is Muse)
yields to the province of Clio, the registering of noble deeds
(Spenser's *Teares of the Muses*, 97–8). Even more precisely, Clio's
hypodorian mode is appropriate to Redcrosse, who is now
preparing for battle, since the Dorian modes have a calming effect
on those so preparing: see *Paradise Lost*, I.550–4: 'The *Dorian*
mood / ... such as rais'd/To highth of noblest temper Hero's
old/Arming to Battel, and in stead of rage/Deliberate valour
breath'd'. The appropriateness of the modes to the moods or
passions is discussed in Plato's *Republic*, III.398–9.

8–15 The dragon is like a mountain (st. 4n. above); but even they
can be moved with faith (x. 20n.). The brazen scales like armour
have infernal associations (st. 3n.), and the description as a whole
follows that of the serpent sacred to Mars and vanquished by
Cadmus (*Met.*, III.31ff.): parallels are the eyes flashing fire (st. 14,
Met., III.33), the body swollen with venom (st. 8, *Met.*, *ibid.*), the
triple row of teeth (st. 13, *Met.*, III.34) and hellish mouth (st. 12,
Met., III.75–6). Spenser is influenced, too, by the beast of Daniel
7:7, which has iron teeth, and the Leviathan of Job 41 (which has
strong scales, and 'Out of his mouth go lampes, and sparkes of fyre
leape out'). Both were types of the devil: Hankins, 110. The fight
with the dragon is recapitulatory: through it Redcrosse encounters
again and overcomes, with the aid of grace, the temptations to
wrath and concupiscence that had almost defeated him earlier (e.g.,
i.47n., v.8n., vii.2–5n.). The dragon is particularly emblematic of
wrath, which the knight learned to subdue with patience at x.23n.:
based on Ovid's Martian serpent, it is conpared to the eagle,
emblem of Mars and choler (Agrippa, I.xxvii,58; dragons and
serpents are Martian too: *ibid.*; on the eagle and the choleric
temperament, see Klibansky, 378 and plate 120); the red and black
of st. 11 are Martian colours in combination as here (Curry,
Chaucer and the Mediaeval Sciences, 132), as are the brass of st. 9

and iron of st. 13 (Agrippa, *ibid.*) and the boar of st. 15 (traditionally fierce, and also a symbol of concupiscence: vi.20–6n.). Upton, *Var. Sp.*, I.298, observes the expressions from falconry: the wings as sails, the crop as gorge, the stooping to the prey (st. 18); and cf. the reference to a hawk in st. 19. The usages are deliberate, since the hawk and falcon were dedicated to Mars (Agrippa, *ibid.*). The two stings in the tail (st. 11) probably signify concupiscence, the ineradicable but controllable sin alluded to as 'a pricke in the flesh' in 2 Corinthians 12:7, and death (1 Corinthians 15: 55–6: 'O death, where is thy stinge! ... The sting of death is sinne'); see Kaske, *art.cit.* Kaske explains the sequence of three battles as comprising and recapitulating the threefold progress of human history and development of the individual: (i) Redcrosse as unregenerate man, the old law; (ii) Redcrosse as the regenerate but still sinful Christian; (iii) Redcrosse as the type of the perfect man, Christ.

21   There are no specific sources but many general parallels to this stanza: e.g., *Met.*, V.5–7 (the sea's peaceful waters lashed by the wind into boisterous waves). The important thing is the hint in the dragon's rage of a return to chaotic, elemental strife (he is himself fiery; the other three elements are supplied in this stanza).

26–8   Redcrosse is burned in his armour (1) as a punishment for having already twice escaped from the heat of the sun (ii.28–32n., vii.2–4n.); (2) to remind him of his previous tendency to wrath; and (3) to recall the flames of concupiscence (see Kaske, *art.cit.*, which also suggests that the paradox of the protective armour harming the knight is explained by Augustine's familiar gloss on the first half of Romans 7: 'Sin conquered you with your own arms, with your own arms it slew you' (*Sermo in Scripturis*, CLIII)). The despair death-wish recurs, but he is saved by God's grace (the well), and , before that, compared to Hercules, type of Christ and of heroic virtue (Ripa, 507, where he is described as overcoming a dragon, interpreted as concupiscence. And cf. i.19n.) Spenser refers here to the coat soaked in the poisoned blood of the centaur Nessus which, given to Hercules by his wife Deianira who thought it would act as a love charm, poisoned and burned at his body. The parallel-with-contrast is that the suffering Hercules then committed suicide on Mount Oeta on a funeral pyre, and was taken up onto Olympus and immortalised (*Met.*, IX.101ff.): Redcrosse has overcome

Despair's temptation to suicide (canto ix); and his immortalisation will take the form of sanctification. The burning poison was interpreted by, e.g., Bersuire in the *Moralised Ovid* and Comes, *Mythologiae*, VII.i, as concupiscence (Kaske, *art.cit.*). In Golding's translation (*Met.*, IX.209–10), the 'scalding venim' makes Hercules's blood hiss 'As when a gad of steel red hot in water quenched is': appropriately a common emblem of temperance, acted out when Redcrosse falls into the well (for the emblem, see II.v.2–14n.).

29–30   The well is the river of Paradise (Genesis 2:10: 'And out of Eden went a river to water the garden') and the 'river of water of life' of Revelation 22:1: see ii.40–1n. for references to water as 'spiritual grace'. In addition, it symbolises baptism (see the reference to Redcrosse's 'baptized hands' at st. 36): in the Anglican Article 27 baptism is 'a sign of Regeneration or new Birth whereby ... the promises of the forgiveness of sin, and of our adoption to be sons of God by the Holy Ghost, are visibly signed and sealed; Faith is confirmed, and Grace increased by virtue of prayer unto God'. By washing in the 'poole of Siloam' the blind man was enabled to see (John 9:7ff.): the Geneva gloss interprets the pool as a prefiguring of the Messiah. For Jordan's cleaning and revivifying power, see 2 Kings 5:10–14, and Tuve, *George Herbert*, 184 for Jordan as a type of redemption and baptism. Christ was baptised in the Jordan: Matthew 3:13. Bath had been well established as a Roman spa, known as *Aquae Solis* (waters of the sun: cf. the solar symbolism that recurs with st. 31, and Fowler, 69n. citing Camden's *Britannia*); Spau itself is near Liège; the waters of the Cephisus washed sheep white (Pliny, *Natural History*, II.cvi.230); and the head of the dismembered Orpheus floated down the Hebrus (*Met.*, XI.1–60). It drifted to the shore of Lesbos and was saved from a serpent that was attacking it by Phoebus Apollo (symbols of Satan and Christ respectively). Orpheus himself was a celebrated type of Christ.

31   With the setting of the sun into the sea, Redcrosse also sinks into water: compare i.32–3 and v.2n.

32   Una watches and prays (Matthew 26:36ff., Christ in Gethsemane, and especially 41: 'Watch, and pray'; cf. Mark 14:38): contrast Corceca's vigil at iii.13.

33–4 Una rises before the sun and Redcrosse (who is now assuming his solar role) just as the morning star (Lucifer, Venus) precedes the rising sun (ii.4–6n., iii.5–9n.). For Emelye's parallel action in the *Knight's Tale* (cf. iii.21n.), see D. Brooks and A. Fowler, 'The Meaning of Chaucer's *Knight's Tale*', *Medium Aevum*, XXXIX (1970), 127. Redcrosse is now an eagle – not the Martian eagle of st. 9 but its homoeopathic opposite, the eagle of the sun (Agrippa, I.xxiii, 53). Spenser refers to the well-known tale found in the *Physiologus* that when the eagle grows old and blind it seeks out a spring of water, flies up to the sun, burns off its old feathers and the film over its eyes, returns to earth and dips itself three times in the water and emerges renewed: cf. Psalms 103:5 ('thy youth is renued like the egles'). This was interpreted as putting off the old Adam and putting on the new (Christ) – regeneration by baptism – in the name of Father, Son, and Holy Ghost. The sun is the Sun of righteousness (Evans, 116ff.; Hankins, 117). Fowler, 69 sees the 'newly budded pineons' as an allusion to Malachi 4:2: 'unto you that feare my Name, shal the Sunne of righteousnes arise, and health shalbe under his wings' (Geneva gloss: 'he regenerateth us into righteousnes, cleneth us from the filth of this worlde').

37–9 The lions here are emblems of choler (iii.33–6n.). The second battle recapitulates the first but is now encountered with the aid of grace. The dragon's death sting (st. 8–15n.) provokes a wrath that this time will not be tempered by patience (x.23n.) since it is not an intemperate but a just wrath, as in Romans 13:4–5: 'if thou do evil, feare: for he beareth not the sworde for noght: for he is the minister of God to take vengeance on him that doeth evil'. The severing of the five joints presumably signifies victory over the five senses.

40–3 The dragon now attacks Redcrosse's 'sunne–bright shield' of faith (i.1n.; vii.29n. and 33–5n.) On Cerberus, see v.31–4n. Physical strength alone is insufficient to withstand it, but 'the sworde of ye Spirit, which is the worde of God' (Ephesians 6:17) prevails, though a claw remains (concupiscence as doubt: Kaske, *art.cit.*, quoting Melanchthon). Romans 7 remains a key text for Redcrosse's fight.

44–5 On the volcano, see st. 4n. above. Redcrosse withstands this second attack by fire – symbolising the devil's attempt to frighten him into submission by unleashing fundamental rebellious and chaotic powers – better than the first. But he falls in shame that his heroic fortitude is not strong enough.

46–8 The two trees are 'the tre of life . . . and the tre of knowledge of good and evil' (Genesis 2:9); the first tree recalling in addition Revelation 22:2: 'the tre of life . . . & the leaves of the tre served to heale the nations with' (cf. and ct. ii.28–32n.). Christ himself is the tree of life (St Augustine, *City of God*, XX.xxvi), and the 'goodly tree' is also the tree of His cross (1 Peter 2:24: 'Who his owne self bare our sinnes in his bodie on the tre'; cf. x.55–7n.; Chew, 8; Jean Daniélou, *Primitive Christian Symbols*, ch.II). The apples suggest the Fall, while their redness signifies redemption through Christ's blood and hence the Eucharist (Hankins, 118; Tuve, 23–4). The imagery of st. 48 recalls that of st. 29, and Arthur's gift of 'liquor pure' (ix.19n.), and is parodied by Orgoglio (viii.10n.). Hankins, 118–19 suggests that Spenser also alludes to Extreme Unction, apparently alluded to by Hooker, *Laws of Ecclesiastical Polity*, V.lxviii.11 (Everyman edn., II.347), and to the oil from the tree of mercy (life) with which Seth asks Michael if he can anoint his father, Adam. He is told this cannot be until Christ has been baptised, then 'shall he anoint with the oil of mercy all that believe on him, and that oil of mercy shall be unto all generations of them that shall be born of water and of the Holy Ghost, unto life eternal' (Gospel of Nicodemus, II.iii; *ed.cit.*, 89). There is a visual parallel to the stanzas in Robert Vaughan's title-page engraving for Richard Brathwaite's *Lignum Vitae* (London, 1658), which shows a pilgrim bearing a cross as he travels away from the tree of knowledge up a hill on the top of which is the tree of life. The cross has by it the inscription 'De Ligno Vitae emanavit balsamum omni vulneri Saluferium' (From the Wood of Life flows the balsam that brings health to every wound).

51 Cf. ii.7n.; iii.21n.; iv.16–17n. For the flowers, see Ripa, 60, *s.v. Carro dell'Aurora.*

53–4 Redcrosse is now, anagogically, Christ vanquishing Satan; allegorically, he is the Church Militant. Note the brevity of the battle and the fact that it is the dragon's mouth – hell mouth – that is here destroyed: Christ entered hell mouth and vanquished death

(Hankins,113–14). Compare Revelation 20:14: 'And death and hell were cast into the lake of fyre' (Geneva gloss: 'Hell & death which are the last enemies, shalbe destroied').

CANTO XII

Tropologically, the release of Una's parents into their kingdom of Eden represents the regenerate soul, traditionally seen as a paradise (Tuve, 22ff., 108ff.). Anagogically – the other principal level in the canto – Redcrosse's betrothal is a foreshadowing of the marriage of Christ to the Church at the end of time (Revelation 19:7: 'Let us be glad and rejoyce, and give glorie to him: for the marriage of the Lambe is come', and 21:2, where the Heavenly Jerusalem is 'prepared as a bride trimmed for her husband'. The Geneva gloss explains that Jerusalem is 'the Church, which is married to Christ by faith'). Allegorically, England has returned, after centuries of error and the aberration of Mary Tudor, to the true Church. The number twelve is appropriate to all this: the Heavenly Jerusalem is proportioned by twelve (Revelation 21:12ff.), and so the number is 'divine' (Agrippa, II.xiii,216–17) and 'most perfect' (Pietro Bongo, *Numerorum mysteria*, 289). On the progression ten–eleven–twelve read symbolically in relation to the subject matter of the respective cantos, compare Agrippa, *ibid.*, 216: 'The number eleven as it exceeds the number ten, which is the number of the commandments, so it fals short of the number twelve, which is of grace and perfection, therefore it is called the number of sins'.

1   A common metaphor: Curtius, 128–30, 'Nautical Metaphors'.

4–8   Structurally answering i.4–5 (see n.). The 'sad habiliments' – compare Una's 'blacke stole' and sadness at i.4 – lament man's fall into sin. The laurel is not only an emblem of victory but also of the sun god, Apollo (Tervarent, cols. 231–3). Spenser recalls the entry of Christ into Jerusalem, Matthew 21:8: 'And a great multitude spred their garments in the way: and other cutte downe branches from the trees, and strawed them in the way' (cf. st. 13). The Christian image then yields to an allegorical pagan one – Una as the virginal Diana, image of the Faerie Queene. For documentation see especially vi.13–14n. and 16n. There is a contrast with i.48n. and ii.36–8n.

9–11 Upton, *Var. Sp.*, I.306, compares the reaction to the dead beast with *Aeneid*, VIII.264ff., the reaction to the dead monster Cacus, strangled by Hercules and no longer able to spit fire, etc. (cf. i.19n.), and *Met.*, VIII.420ff. (the reaction to Meleager's killing of the Calydonian boar).

12 On the gifts of ivory and gold, cf. *Aeneid*, III.464 (heavy gifts of gold and carved ivory).

17 The fulfilment of Despair's temptation at ix.40 ('port after stormie seas'); but Redcrosse has learned his lesson (st. 18). Percival, 328 suggests that the six years of servitude allude to the six ages of the world which are to be followed by the eternal sabbath: compare the *Two Cantos of Mutabilitie*, viii.2, and Agrippa, II.x,195–6 on the days of creation: 'to . . . the seventh day is ascribed [rest], which signifies the seven thousandth, wherein (as *John* witnesseth) the Dragon, which is the Divell, and Satan, being bound, men shall be quiet, and lead a peaceable life'. At that time only can the actual marriage take place (st. 19).

21–3 On Una as the morning star, see xi.33–4n. and, on Venus generally, Proem 4n. There is also a reminiscence of Revelation 2:28 ('Even as I received of my Father, so wil I give him the morning starre') and 22:16, where Christ is 'the bright morning starre'. Compare Spenser's *View of the Present State of Ireland*, 137, on 'the morninge starr of truethe'. The image is a commonplace (*Aeneid*, VIII.589, Pallas like the morning star drenched in the ocean; *Ger. Lib.*, XV.60, the rising of the morning star combined with a reference to the birth of Venus from the waves), but this does not detract from its symbolic function here. Her 'sad sober cheare' suggests appropriate solemnity (cf. *Epithalamion*, 234) and perhaps the reluctance traditionally supposed to be felt by virgins at moving from the patronage of Diana (st. 7) to Venus: Brooks and Fowler, 'The Meaning of Chaucer's *Knight's Tale*', 126–8; Jonson, *Hymenaei*, 736ff. (*Masques*, ed. Orgel, 95). The May comparison is again common (*Knight's Tale*, 1035ff., Emelye, fairer than May flowers, going out to perform her May observances), and links Una with Flora, whose festival ended on 3 May (*Shepheardes Calender*, 'May', 31; Ovid, *Fasti*, V.183ff.; compare and contrast i.48n.). Yates, 67 comments on Elizabeth as May and Flora in John Davies's *Hymnes to Astraea*. The white garment recalls the Lamb's bride 'araied with pure fyne linen and shining' (Revelation 19:8) combined with Christ's praise of the church (bride) in the Song of Solomon 4:7 ('there is no spot in thee': Una's garment is 'withouten spot'). A white robe is a sign of purity, and adorns, e.g., personifications of Virginity and Truth (Ripa, 501 and 506). On the 'sunshyny face', see iii.4n. Anagogically Una is the church but also Wisdom, the last gift of the Holy Ghost (x.46–63n.). Compare Spenser's *Hymne of Heavenly Beautie*, 183ff., where Sapience sits in God's bosom 'Clad like a Queene in royall robes'.

26–7   Compare ii.22n. Note the pagan reference to 'burning Altars', as at *Aeneid*, XII.201.

36   The binding of Archimago is the binding of Satan (Revelation 20:2ff.) who shall be bound a thousand years and then 'shalbe losed out of his prison, And shal go out to deceive the people' until finally vanquished. Archimago is thus free to reappear in the poem. But we have already had an apocalyptic vision of the final conquest of the devil at xi.53–4n.

37–8   Although this is a betrothal only, Spenser follows the details of ancient wedding ceremonies followed more elaborately in his *Epithalamion*; and compare Jonson's *Hymenaei, passim*. The fire and water are carried by the *auspices* or marriage sponsors, who also join the hands of the married couple (*Hymenaei*, 53–4 and Jonson's note; and cf. Plutarch, *Quaestiones Romanae*, 263E, where the bride touches the two elements to symbolise the joining of male (fire) and female (water)). The 'teade' or torch is an emblem of Hymen, god of marriage (Catullus, LXI.15); the light driving away evil is found in, e.g., Ovid, *Fasti*, VI.165–8, and compare 129–30. The sprinkling with wine is mentioned by Claudian, *Epithalamium of Honoris and Maria*, 209–10; the perfuming is alluded to there, too; and the music is again traditional: compare and contrast v.3–4n. above.

39   The betrothal music receives an anagogical accompaniment: the multitude rejoicing at the preparation for the marriage of the Lamb in Revelation 19:6–7, combined with the music of the planetary spheres, of which there are nine to accord with the ninefold hierarchy of angels (divided into three groups of three: Meyer-Baer, *Music of the Spheres*, 38ff., 78ff.).

BOOK II

The Legend of
Sir Guyon,
or Of Temperaunce

INTRODUCTION

Temperance is one of the four ancient cardinal virtues (the other three are prudence, fortitude, and justice). In Plato's *Republic*, IV.430–1 it is defined as being like concord or harmony, and it implies self-mastery, the better part of the soul controlling the worse; but Aristotle's definition in the *Nicomachean Ethics* as received by the Renaissance was more influential. The passions are the appetite and anger; they must be controlled by the reason, and are so controlled in the temperate man who knows the just principles of virtue (which Aristotle defined as a mean between the extremes of excess and defect: *ibid.*, II.vi.16; 1106B). The temperate man chooses to be temperate, says Aristotle; in this he is to be distinguished from the continent and incontinent person who, like the temperate, is subject to his appetites but, unlike him, is under their complete sway. Temperance is willed and is a virtue; continence is not.

To Christian moral philosophers, temperance was the virtue which had to be possessed before the other virtues: through it alone could a just balance be apprehended (Tuve, 69); and it was divided into 'parts' (important for the virtues and vices examined by Spenser in Book II) which by the late Middle Ages included continence, chastity, shamefastness (modesty), sobriety, sparingness (moderation), integrity, and restraint (Tuve, appendix).

By the Renaissance an elaborate moral psychology had been worked out which recognised three souls in man: the rational, the sensitive, and the vegetable (see II.ix.27 and 33–5n.). Within the sensitive soul are the concupiscible power (desire, pleasure) and the irascible (anger, fear). These, ideally, are under the control of the reason and will and manifest themselves in various good or bad passions. Agrippa, I.lxii,140, explains: '. . . when the concupiscible power respects good, and evil absolutely; Love or Lust, or on the contrary, hatred is caused: When it respects good, as absent, so desire is caused; or evill, as absent, or at hand, and so is caused horror, flying from, or loathing: or if it respect good, as present, then there is caused delight, mirth, or pleasure; but if evill, as present, then sadness, anxiety, grief. But the irascible power respects good or bad, under the notion of some difficulty; to obtain the one, or avoid the other, and this sometimes with confidence: and so there is caused Hope or Boldness; but when with some diffidency, then Despair, and Fear. But when that irascible power riseth into revenge, and this be onely about some evill past, as it were of injury or hurt offered, there is caused Anger.' Moreover – and this is a notion that again goes back to Plato – temperance is at the root of cosmic and political as well as microcosmic order: 'this word World signifieth as much as Ornament, or a well disposed order of things. Now as a constant and temperate order is the foundation thereof, so the groundeworke and preservation of mans happy life, for whom all things were made, is the virtue of Temperance' (Peter de la Primaudaye, *The French Academie* (1618), 74). Not surprisingly, then, temperance was the virtue that governed the ethic of chivalry as it was revived in the sixteenth century under the Tudors. In Ramon Lull's *Book of the Ordre of Chyvalry*, which Caxton translated and printed in the early 1480s, we read that kinghts must attain virtue by 'right measure' because 'Virtue and measure abide in the middle between two extremes' (Yates, 107–8). The revival of chivalry was intimately bound up with the Arthurian legend which the Tudors exploited to the full. The contemporary courtly reader would therefore have found in Book II an elaborate unfolding of the central virtue which contributed to the making of the chivalric gentleman – himself a walking embodiment of the cosmic temperance exemplified in a larger way in the court itself.

From the Platonic idea of temperance as the health of the soul and body it is just a short step to the ancient, pre-Galenic medical term *krasis*, which means the mixing or balancing of the four bodily humours which are under the power of the vegetable soul: blood, yellow bile, black bile, phlegm. (These in turn, depending upon which one dominates, give the following physiological and moral temperaments: sanguinic, choleric, melancholic, phlegmatic.) *Krasis* means combination, blending, mixing; its opposites are *akrateia* (powerlessness, incontinence), *akratos* (intemperance, violence), and *akrasia* (bad mixture). Guyon's opponent in the book – she is the cause of the deaths of Amavia and Mordant in canto i, and is seen in her Bower of Bliss in canto xii – is Acrasia. On one level she is a bad version of the worldly Venus, representing *libido*, sensuality. But she is also literally unmixed, dis-tempered, and so she embodies excess of desire leading to bodily and moral disintegration. Guyon overcomes her, but only after encountering in his quest projections of the various excessive humoral tendencies within him: aided by prudence and reason (the Palmer who accompanies him) he tries to achieve *krasis* as he battles with choler (Pyrochles), phlegm (Cymochles), melancholy (Mammon) and the sanguinic (Phaedria, and Acrasia herself in some respects) as they attempt to assert mastery over him.

Aristotle's definition of virtue as the mean between extremes, combined with the division of the sensitive soul into concupiscible and irascible, governed by the rational soul, together with the four humours, gave the Middle Ages and Renaissance a good working basis for psychological and moral analysis. To these Spenser adds the discriminating and wide-ranging vocabulary of the Italian Neoplatonists that includes important astrological elements. Planetary influences and the attributes of the planetary deities are many and varied, and to someone like Ficino or Spenser a belief in actual astrological influences on character formation was complemented by a belief in the value of astrological lore as a metaphor for psychological and moral states. So that for Spenser in Book II (and of course elsewhere) there is rarely such a thing as a simple character. Cymochles is not just phlegmatic: his name, description, and actions expand and qualify the humoral label which is then seen to be inadequate shorthand for a very complex set of tendencies within the psyche.

Astrologically, Cymochles is under the opposing influences of both Mars and Venus; and in fact all the characters in Book II are portrayed in planetary terms, and the burden of Spenser's argument is that the ideal is expressed as a combination of influences and qualities. Here his view of temperance, influenced by his Neoplatonism, broadens to become a vision. True temperance achieves in the individual soul the cosmos achieved by God through the act of creation: a *discordia concors*, the reconciliation of opposites that in the end means self-transcendence.

Book I, as A. S. P. Woodhouse has argued ('Nature and Grace in *The Faerie Queene*', *E.L.H.*, XVI (1949)), takes place in the realm of grace. Its concern is man's salvation; its psychological domain is the intellect or understanding, the mind as it contemplates the divine. Book II, he suggests, is concerned with the order of nature: man as an inhabitant of the physical world with its natural law, interpreted by the reason, upon which Plato and Aristotle had erected their ethical systems. To a large extent Woodhouse was right. Temperance is a natural virtue, and Book II is concerned with reason, lower than intellect, the specific function of which is to control the passions. An important aspect of temperance, though, is the moderating of concupiscence. And as we saw in Book I, concupiscence is, according to Christian theologians, our inheritance from the old Adam; so that it is unthinkable that Book II, which opens with an image of the spiritual death that results from abandoning oneself to it (Mordant and Amavia) should be regarded as operating without constant, if often implied, reference to the order of grace.

Another implied component of Book II is the Platonic–Stoic definition of the main types of lives followed by human beings. They are three in number and are described, for example, in Dio Chrysostom's *Fourth Discourse on Kingship* as being, first, the luxurious, which is self-indulgent with regard to bodily pleasures; second, the acquisitive and avaricious; and third, the one dedicated to the pursuit of honour and glory, which 'manifests a more evident and violent disorder or frenzy [than the other two], deluding itself into believing that it is enamoured of some noble ideal' (*Works*, tr. J. W. Cohoon, Loeb edn (1932–51), I.207). Instances conforming to this scale of pleasure, wealth, and ambition (which was easily assimilated into the Flesh, World, Devil scheme) can be found everywhere in Book II: Pyrochles, Cymochles, and Braggadocchio pursue honour wrongly; Guyon and Arthur pursue true honour and glory. The luxurious life is followed by Amavia, Mordant, Cymochles, Phaedria, and Acrasia; the acquisitive is embodied in Mammon, in whose cave, incidentally, we find the most explicit embodiment of false honour and glory in Philotime.

Earlier on I mentioned the Tudor revival of chivalry; and it would be a mistake to conclude without a further reminder of the importance of political and historical symbolism and allegory in Book II. The castles of Medina and Alma in cantos ii and ix are, tropologically, the temperate body. In terms of historical allegory, though, they are the Elizabethan State, in each case governed by a woman who embodies the Venerean–Dianan ideal of chaste love (Elizabeth as Virgin Queen and expression of God's love as it permeates the microcosm of the State). But Spenser's historical concerns are nowhere more evident than in canto x, where Arthur reads a history of the kings of Britain and Guyon reads a history of fairyland. Although I have not annotated this fully, partly for reasons of space, and also because the modern student of the poem tends to find this canto boring and excessive annotation would not make him or her find it otherwise, it is crucial to Spenser's eulogy of Elizabeth–Gloriana as Arthur's successor: it is as crucial to the ultimate meaning of Book II as Aeneas's vision of his imperial descendants in Book VI of the *Aeneid* was to Vergil's epic design.

PROEM

1–5 Spenser alludes to *O.F.*, VII.1 ('He who has left his homeland sees strange things which, when recounted on his return, will seem like lies to the stay-at-homes'); but at the same time geographical exploration becomes an implicit metaphor for the exploration of man's moral being. As ancient fables are 'now found trew' (Francisco de Orellana had sailed down part of the Amazon in 1541 in search of El Dorado; Peru had been conquered by the Spaniards by the middle of the century) so, Spenser suggests, moral truth exists on earth in Elizabeth's court and is reflected in the fairyland of his epic. The veil of the allegory enables feeble eyes to see the queen's glory without being blinded. The hyperbole here does not run counter to the poem's overall Neoplatonic affirmation that the ideal lies beyond the earth (e.g., I.iii.4n.): the court is glorious in itself, and as such too bright for ordinary mortal eyes. But it is – like classical mythology itself as understood in the Renaissance – still an imperfect fragment or shadow of the truth or the ideal. On maritime exploration as a sign of a restored golden age of universal empire (compare and contrast El Dorado), see *O.F.*, XV.21ff.; Yates, 54–5; and II.ii.40–2n. (also I.ii.22n.). On the relationship of 'just memory' to the imagination, which produces 'painted forgery', see II.ix.49–58n.

2 'Fruitfullest *Virginia*' was named after the Virgin Queen in 1584 on Raleigh's return from his expedition to North America. Spenser implies that Virginia's fertility is a concrete emblem of one of the attributes of Elizabeth, *ubertas rerum* (the fertility of things): see the plate identifying the queen as the *primum mobile* embracing the planetary spheres, each sphere identified with a specific virtue or quality, in John Case's *Sphaera civitatis* (1588); reproduced in Yates, plate 9c. The power of *ubertas* is given to the sphere of the moon. This attribute derives in part from Elizabeth's identification with Astraea, goddess of justice in the golden age, who was in turn identified with the zodiacal sign Virgo, one of whose emblems was an ear of corn: see *Mutability Cantos*, vii.37, and Yates, 29–87, especially 34, 53ff., 65–7. The imagery of the golden age contrasts with Spenser's vision of Mammon's iron age cave and Philotime's corrupt court in canto vii.

4 The tracking hound is a common metaphor for the search for truth: Lucretius, *De rerum natura*, I.404ff.; Chew, 197. Spenser's reference to the 'antique Image of [Elizabeth's] great auncestry' is to the chronicle read by Guyon at II.x.70ff.

5 Guyon embodies the virtue of temperance; his name derives from the paradisal river Gihon (I.vii.43n.).

CANTO I

1 On Archimago–Satan's escape, see I.xii.36n.

6 In the thirteenth-century romance *Huon de Bordeaux*, Sir Huon is a favourite of Oberon, king of the fairies (see II.x.75–6n.). Rathborne, 180–1 suggests that Spenser intends a general compliment to the Norman–French element in Elizabeth's ancestry and that of her nobility. She remarks, 180n., that Guyon is a common name in French romances.

7 The Palmer (pilgrims to the Holy Land carried a palm branch as a token of their pilgrimage) represents Guyon's reason in general, or, more specifically, prudence, the first of the four classical cardinal virtues (Tuve, 69, 94; for the definition of prudence, see vii.1–2n.). His description recalls the Good Counsel figure (I.x.46–63n.); on his staff, see II.xii.39–41n. The palm itself is an emblem of temperance and moral victory because it continues growing upright even though excessive weight is put on it (Ripa, 480: just as the tree does not yield to the weight, so does the temperate person not succumb to stormy passion). Compare, too, Psalms 92:12: 'The righteous shal florish like a palme tre'. On the 'equall steps' see I.iv.18–20n. and I.x.12–13n. The knight controls the 'trampling steed' of the passions (I.i.1n.): cf. our Plate 8.

8–13 Archimago induces in Guyon a just anger, but sows the seeds for his many temptations to excessive wrath in Book II. Note the progression 'sonne of *Mars*' (the appeal to his warrior qualities) – 'halfe wroth' (st. 11) – 'amoved from his sober mood' (12) – 'fierce ire' (13); at which point, significantly, Guyon rushes away from the Palmer. At st. 25 he is 'inflam'd with wrathfulnesse'.

14–15 The maid who parodies the downward gaze of true modesty or shamefastness (ix.40ff.) is identified in st. 21 as Duessa. As Fidessa, she has already deceived Redcrosse in similar fashion at I.ii.27.

22 Compare I.viii.46–8n. on the stripping of Duessa.

24 The scene recalls the entry into Error's wood and I.ii.28ff. and I.vii.2ff. It is a topographical emblem of temperance defined as a mean between extremes (see Introduction above): the two hills represent extremes, the valley with its 'little river' in the 'midst' represents the mean at which the virtuous Redcrosse sits. But Guyon, misled by Archimago and anger, is unable to read the emblem. Compare ii.12–20n. and xii.3–9n.

27–8 The cross, reminder of Christ's redeeming grace, calls to Guyon in spite of himself: he and Redcrosse are united here since reason and the order of nature complement faith and the order of grace – a point which Redcrosse himself almost underestimated and failed to recognise. Guyon's emblem is an image of Gloriana, with hints of the Virgin Mary: see I.vii.30n.; II.ii.40–2n. and ix.3–4. With 'wise temperance' reasserted, the Palmer reappears (st. 31).

32 Redcrosse, the solar knight (I.iii.5–9n.), is contrasted with

Temeritas.

THE waggoner, behoulde, is hedlonge throwen,
  And all in vaine doth take the raine in hande,
If he be dwrawen by horfes fierce vnknowen,
Whofe ftomacks ftowte, no taming vnderftande,
    They praunce, and yerke, and out of order flinge,
    Till all they breake, and vnto hauocke bringe.

That man, whoe hath affections fowle vntam'de,
And forwarde runnes neglecting reafons race,
Deferues by right, of all men to bee blam'de,
And headlonge falles at lengthe to his deface,
    Then bridle will, and reafon make thy guide,
    So maifte thow ftande, when others doune doe flide.

Guyon: his 'glorious name' is a symbol of glory shining down on those whose journey is just beginning (and see I.vii.46n. and I.x.59–63n.). The phrase 'like race to runne' recalls the Biblical idea of the race of life (1 Corinthians 9:24) as well as the 'race' of a completed planetary cycle. The similarity of the 'races' of the two knights has already been suggested in st. 26. The implication is that as Redcrosse is the solar knight, so is Guyon the lunar knight (the moon is associated with temperance, earthly honour, and reason, among other things: see I.vii.46n.; Fowler, ch. IX, especially 83ff. The sun, on the contrary, is an image of the divine intellect, the ultimate subject of Book I: see Fowler, 86–7.) The lunar Guyon is parodied by Braggadocchio at iii.38n. The structural implications of the phrase 'like race' as suggesting a parallel relationship between Books I and II are discussed by Hamilton, ch. III, and Fowler, ch. IX.

35–56 With the first emblematic encounter over, the second begins. It introduces the threat of Acrasia, the overcoming of whom is the goal of Guyon's own quest, and it parallels I.ii.28ff.: the bloody babe recalls the bleeding tree; there are two lovers in both cases; Fradubio's lament at I.ii.31ff. is echoed by Amavia at II.i.50ff.; Fradubio and Fraelissa must 'be bathed in a living well', and the babe's hands cannot be washed clean in the well (II.ii.3). The episode follows Trissino's *L'Italia Liberata da Gotti*, IV, where Belisarius's knights come across a healing fountain, sprung in part from a woman's tears, on grass where, on the orders of the enchantress Acratia, a woman has died (C. W. Lemmi, 'The Influence of Trissino on *The Faerie Queene*', *P.Q.*, VII (1928)), and in it Spenser gives us an allegory of man's mortal state. Amavia (named in the Argument stanza) means 'her that loves to live' (st. 55), from Latin *amo + vita*, with a strong suggestion of *amavi*, I have loved. She has stabbed herself for love of Mordant (= death-giver, st. 55) and, as Upton noted (*Var. Sp.*, II.191–2), details of Spenser's description come from *Aeneid*, IV where Dido's excessive love for Aeneas (unlike Amavia's, unfulfilled) led to her stabbing herself. (Note that Dido gives one of her names to Elissa at II.ii.35.) St. 45–6 recall Dido's struggle with her departing life after she has stabbed herself at *Aeneid*, IV. 688ff. ('Dido tried to raise her heavy eyes . . . Three times she rose . . . three times she fell back on the bed'); st. 61, with its cutting of the lock of hair, recalls the Graeco-

Roman sacrifice of a lock of hair at death to Proserpina, queen of the underworld, in accordance with which custom a lock of the dead Dido's hair is removed at the end of Book IV. Moreover, the suicide Dido was traditionally seen as an example of intemperance (Allen, 138, 151).

Mordant, Amavia's husband, is depicted in terms of youth and flowers (st. 41) and anticipates Acrasia's similarly described young lover Verdant at xii.79–80n. The flower suggests mortality (e.g., Job 14:2) and might also have pejorative moral implications: Mordant, like Fradubio in I.ii, has existed only at the level of his vegetable soul. He is a knight, and hence under the patronage of Mars; but we see him having succumbed to concupiscence, the tendency to bodily lust inherited from the fallen Adam (see ii.1–4n.) and under the patronage of the planetary goddess Venus (on the implications of the Venus–Mars theme see I Proem 3n. and references). His concupiscence exceeds Amavia's, as Spenser confirms by having him succumb to the 'vile *Acrasia*' (st. 51), symbol of Venerean intemperance (see Introduction to Book II above for the significance of her name; and for her Venerean–Circean attributes and the symbolism of her 'wandring Island' see xii.10–12n. and 42ff.nn.). Amavia adopts the Palmer's role and rescues Mordant by restoring in him sufficient reason for him to see his folly (st. 52–4; and cf. xii.39–41n.). But concupiscence (the influence of Acrasia through her symbolic curse) has the last word, proving more powerful than Amavia's call to 'faire governance': she is, after all, only disguised as a Palmer, and in listening to her Mordant is still following his sexual appetite. Amavia herself recognises her mortal limitations and unsuitability for the task in calling herself 'weake wretch' at st. 52; and the reversal of sexual roles directly contradicts Ephesians 5:22, quoted at I.v.50n., and so implies an up-ending of the moral hierarchy, man in the person of Adam supposedly embracing intellectual and rational powers, woman embodying the lower appetites: cf. *Paradise Lost*, IV.295ff. As a result of the curse Mordant, identified explicitly with Bacchus the wine god (for the symbolism see xii.46–9n., 55–7n., and 79–80n.), dies as soon as he drinks from the pure fountain of Diana's nymph (see ii.6ff.). That is, there is a shock confrontation of two antithetical elements (Mordant is extremely concupiscent, the nymph is excessively chaste) rather than a temperate mingling, which brings about physical disintegration: cf. Hankins, 82–3. The *mixing* of wine and water, on the other hand, is an emblem of temperance: Tervarent, cols. 8–9, 394; A. D. S. Fowler, 'Emblems of Temperance in *The Faerie Queene*, Book II', *R.E.S.*, n.s. XI (1960).

The well/fountain probably derives from Pierre Bersuire's reading of Solinus's account of a river called Diana, the waters of which, if drawn by anyone unchaste, would not mix with the wine he had drunk. For Bersuire, the water is doctrine, which reveals the wine of the concupiscent human will (Fowler, 'The Image of Mortality: *The Faerie Queene*, II.i-ii', *H.L.Q.*, XXIV (1961), citing Bersuire's *Morale reductorium super totam Bibliam*, VIII.iii.33). In addition, the death of the parents by the well leaving a baby behind them alludes to the Pauline notion of baptism into Christ's death leading to new life in Romans 6:3–4. The Geneva gloss says: 'we . . . receive vertue to kill sinne, and raise up our new man'.

53 Lucina = the goddess that 'brings to light'; hence goddess of childbirth, an epithet applied to Juno and Diana.

57–8 Guyon's explanation of intemperance anticipates in essentials the meaning of Elissa and Perissa in canto ii; Pyrochles and Cymochles in iv, v, vi, and viii; and the opposition of Phaedria–Acrasia and Mammon. He offers an Aristotelian reading of Amavia's and Mordant's story: excessive passion (appetite) has overriden the controlling power of reason (cf. Milton's description of the effects of the Fall, *Paradise Lost*, IX.1127–31), and it is the function of temperance to assert rational control, maintaining a mean between extremes (see Introduction to Book II above, and for its structural enactment, ix.22n.). The 'squire' is the mason's or carpenter's set-square; 'golden' because gold is the temperate metal (I.vii.43n.), and also anticipating the architectural symbolism of Book II, specifically Medina's castle (canto ii) and Alma's (canto ix): see Fowler, 'Emblems of Temperance'. Spenser implies in addition the notion of the square of virtue (see I.iv.4n.; to the references there should be added Pietro Bongo, *Numerorum mysteria*, 195, identifying the right angle with 'right reason'). Intemperance's excesses are described in terms of the irascible and concupiscible powers ('bold furie', 'pleasure', st. 57) and in st. 58, referring directly to Mordant and Amavia, Guyon sees the former as melting 'in pleasures whot desire' and the latter as having succumbed to 'hartlesse griefe and dolefull teene'. Mordant died through excess of concupiscence, under the patronage of Venus; Amavia, like Dido, died through grief and woe – possibly irascible (see III.iv.13 on the closeness of grief and wrath, also Phedon at II.iv.33, who combines 'griefe and furie') but more likely again a manifestation of uncontrolled concupiscence (see Agrippa, I.lxii,140 cited in Introduction to Book II).

59–60 Guyon refers to the Day of Judgement (e.g., Matthew 25:31ff.). On the burial of the dead, see I.x.36–43n.; and on the cypress as an emblem of death, see I.i.7–9n.

CANTO II

1–4 The baby is baptised in the well, but the blood remains: i.e., we are all born with original sin (cf. Augustine, *City of God*, XX.xxvi), the effects of which are not effaced even by baptism: 'Original Sin . . . is the fault and corruption of the Nature of every man, that naturally is engendered of the offspring of *Adam*. . . . And this infection of nature doth remain, yea in them that are regenerated; whereby the lust of the flesh, called in Greek *phronema sarkos*, which some do expound the wisdom, some sensuality, some the affection, some the desire, of the flesh, is not subject to the Law of God. And although there is no condemnation for them that believe and are baptized, yet the Apostle doth confess, that concupiscence and lust hath of itself the nature of sin' (Article IX of the Thirty-nine Articles). Baptism regenerates; temperance controls the concupiscence left within us. Ruddymane, named at iii.2, is the new man rising phoenix-like from the ashes of the old (st. 2; on the phoenix as an emblem of resurrection, see Ansell Robin, 38–9).

5–6 See I.xi.29–30n. on rivers, etc.; and xii.21–3n. on Flora.

7–10 Compare and contrast the Ovidian fable at I.vii.5n.; there are probably suggestions of the stories of Daphne (xii.52n., 63–9n.) and of Arethusa (who bathed in the river Alpheus, was pursued by the river-god and was herself changed into a river: *Met.*, V.572ff.). The well represents virginal purity in contrast to the lustful Faunus (see I.vi.7–10n.) who was particularly fond of nymphs (Horace, *Odes*, III.xviii): it is Faunus who gazes on the naked Diana in Spenser's version of the Actaeon myth at VII.vi.42ff. The structural and symbolic opposition of this well and Acrasia's fountain (xii.60ff.) is based on the juxtaposed fountains of Sinesia and Acratia in Trissino's *L'Italia Liberata*, IV and V. 'Virginal purity' is too simple a phrase, though: the Dianan maiden is metamorphosed into a permanent emblem of virginity retaining her original fears (st. 9). She therefore embodies an extreme state not only opposed to 'filth' (concupiscence) but to everything Venerean. The ideal of this book as of Book I is a just mingling of Diana and Venus (e.g., Belphoebe in canto iii). On the other hand, the well inevitably suggests Christ as the rock and the fountain of life (I.viii.10n. and also I.ii.40–1n., with which there is a direct parallel).

11   Guyon takes upon himself the burden of Mordant's fleshly guilt. His horse of the passions with its golden saddle has been stolen by Braggadocchio (II.iii.4) who cannot control it (iv.1–2n.). The horse's name is revealed as Brigador at V.iii.34, modelled on Orlando's steed Brigliadoro in *O.F.* The name = golden bridle: on gold as temperance see I.vii.43n., and for the bridle as an emblem of temperance, see Ripa, 480–1, and Fowler, 'Emblems of Temperance'.

12–20   Another emblematic description (cf. II.i.24n.) embodying three elements: castle, rock, water. On 'frame' see ix.22n. and xii.1n. Medina is the 'golden Meane' of the prefatory Argument stanza. Her braided hair (st. 15) is emblematic of chastity (Wind, 117), and it is 'golden' to emphasise her Venerean qualities (see I.x.29–31n.): Venus as a goddess of moderation is discussed by Wind, 86ff. and 119. Medina thus contrasts with the intemperately Venerean Phaedria and Acrasia. She is flanked by her two sisters, the eldest of whom is Elissa (named at st. 35 and discontented), and the youngest of whom is Perissa (st. 36, wanton and pleasure-seeking). Together they are an allegory of the difficulty of controlling the irascible and concupiscible powers. Elissa is an alternative name for Dido (love turned to anger and despair: see II.i.35–56n.), an identification which connects her at once with Mars (anger) and Saturn (despair: see I.ix.33–4n.). These qualities are confirmed by the 'sterne melancholy' of her knight, Huddibras (st. 17), whose Saturnian melancholy is complicated by the influence of Mars to produce irascible rashness (Ptolemy, *Tetrabiblos*, II.xiii, 343, where rashness is a result of the alliance of Saturn and Mars; also Fowler, 112). The brass of his armour is

Martian (I.xi.8–15n.). These two are opposed by the concupiscible Perissa and Sansloy, representing intemperate Venus. Upton, *Var. Sp.*, II.200–1 identified Elissa with Aristotle's *elleipsis* (deficiency in moral virtue) in the *Ethics* (e.g., II.viii): Greek *elasson* = too little; while Perissa is excess, from Greek *perissos* (excessive). In terms of ecclesiastical allegory, Medina is usually regarded as symbolising the Elizabethan *via media* between puritan reformism and catholic ritualistic excess (e.g., *Var. Sp.*, II.440): Elissa and Huddibras have something in common with the puritan kill-joy: see Phillip Stubbes's *Anatomie of Abuses* (1583), cit. C. L. Barber, *Shakespeare's Festive Comedy* (Cleveland, 1968), 21ff. Medina's castle offers a simple view of the problem of temperate self-control; a more elaborate Christian view is presented in Alma's castle in canto ix, with its awareness in Maleger of original sin.

21   On Guyon's 'sunbroad shield', see I.xi.40–3n.

22   'lybicke Ocean' = Libyan desert: see Starnes and Talbert, 73–4. The bear is choleric and Martian (Klibansky, 378; Tervarent, col. 292) as well as Saturnian (Agrippa, I.xxv,56) and therefore represents Huddibras; the tiger is Bacchic (I.vi.20–6n.) and so appropriate to the wanton Sansloy.

24   The ship simile recalls that in *O.F.*, XXI.53 (Filandro like a ship tossed to and fro by two winds) and the image of the mean flanked by extremes.

27   Medina's gestures are those traditionally symbolic of grief: compare *Met.*, V.472–3, where Ceres tears her hair and beats her breast in her grief over the loss of Proserpina.

29   The Erinnyes were goddesses of vengeance and one of their attributes was a torch (Smith, II.91–2). They are invoked here as a symbol of rage.

31   Compare Dame Concord's reconciliation of Love and Hate at IV.x.31–5 (the Temple of Venus), where she is also responsible for maintaining the world order, and see Spenser's *Hymne of Love*, 78ff. on love binding the four elements together, which ultimately follows Plato, *Timaeus*, 32B–C. The olive has here its traditional meaning of peace and reconciliation: I.vi.13–14n.; Tervarent, cols. 131, 290. Elizabeth was predictably depicted holding an olive branch: Yates, 58, 72.

35–8   On the characters of the sisters, see st. 12–20n. above. The 'Malecontent' was a conventional Elizabethan–Jacobean melancholic character: e.g., Jaques in *As You Like It*.

40–2   Medina, who has just voiced and embodied the cosmic principle of concord (st. 31n.), is now seen to be an aspect of Elizabeth–Gloriana, herself an image of the divine sun (see I Proem 4n.; VI.x.28; and Yates, 62). Gloriana's combination of 'faire peace, and mercy' alludes to Psalms 85:10 ('Mercie and trueth shal mete: righteousnes and peace shal kisse one another'). Gloriana, like the Aristotelian Medina, is the reconciler of opposites – here the syntactically opposite peace and mercy of the psalmist's verse. Contemporaries would have recognised an allusion to the mythologisation of Elizabeth as Astraea, restoring the peace and concord of the golden age as the Roman Augustus had done before her: see V Proem 9; Merlin's prophecy in III.iii.49; and Yates, 33ff., 47ff., 59ff. Ariosto praises Charles V in similar terms at *O.F.*, XV.24ff. Elizabeth as Astraea, restoring peace, concord, justice, and mercy was a favourite pageant topic (Yates, 59ff.; Fowler, 129–30; *clementia*, or mercy, is the imperial virtue that traditionally complements justice: e.g., Yates, 65, 71). This is Elizabeth in her public character as a prince. In the next canto she will be introduced in her private character as a chaste woman (see iii.21–30n.). St. 41 states explicitly that Gloriana herself is only an idol or sign of divine power and beauty; while the reference to the annual feast day (cf. the prefatory letter to Raleigh) in st. 42 is to Elizabeth's Accession Day tilts, held on 17 November, at which the Astraea theme was predominant: Yates, 61, 88ff., and especially 101; cf. I.v.3–4n. Yates, 90 confirms that the Accession Day was seen as announcing a new creation or a new year. Moreover, Medina imposing concord on the jousting knights at st. 31 might allude to Elizabeth's apparently similar pacifying role, an example of which has come down to us in the Woodstock entertainment of 1575 (Yates,97). Medina's castle is, therefore, not only the castle of the body but of the body politic: on the metaphor, see Leonard Barkan, *Nature's Work of Art*, ch. II.

46   Orion was a hunter killed by a scorpion sent by Diana. He was stellified (Ovid, *Fasti*, V.543), as was the scorpion (*Var. Sp.*, II.204–5; Starnes and Talbert, 70–1). The 'hissing snake' is an allusion to the constellation *Anguis* (the Serpent) held by Ophiucus which spreads over Scorpio: see, e.g., Dürer's star map (*Complete Woodcuts of Albrecht Dürer*, ed. Willi Kurth (New York, 1946), 295). Orion sets as Scorpio rises. Spenser implies an identification of Guyon with Orion (who symbolises God's judgement – see I.iii.31n. – and as a hunter of wild animals symbolises the taming of the passions: cf. I.vi.20–6n. As a constellation, Orion bestows victory: Agrippa, II.xxxvii,297). The snake suggests the Satanic serpent and hence the concupiscence of original sin: i.e., Acrasia and the effects she has had on Mordant and Amavia, whose tale has just been told. By sleeping, Guyon and his temperate listeners reject Acrasia, the serpent in the false paradise of the Bower of Bliss in canto xii on whom Guyon–Orion will wreak vengeance.

CANTO III

3 Compare ii.11n. Spenser emphasises the pedestrian nature of Guyon's journey to affirm its spiritual implications, since pilgrims, like the Palmer, travel on foot, and to withhold from Guyon any possible accusations of pride, since Pride traditionally rides a horse (Katzenellenbogen, 5, 76, 83n.). 'Patience perforce' is proverbial.

4–6 Guyon, horseless, contrasts with Braggadocchio, embodiment of all that is unknightly and intemperate: vainglory, pride, lust, cunning, cowardice, etc. He derives from the boasting soldier (*miles gloriosus*) of Roman comedy (cf. Falstaff in *1 Henry IV* and Pistol in *Henry V*) and exemplifies Aristotle's rash man, the pretender to courage who is a coward at heart (*Nicomachean Ethics*, III.vii); and compare Whitney's emblem 38 (our Plate 9). The kestrel, as a hawk, is dedicated to Mars (I.xi.8–15n.), and the peacock is an emblem of pride (I.iv.16–17n.).

9–12 The two similar characters come together in a parody of concord. On the connection between wind and pride, see I.vii.8–10n. Trompart is the trumpet of vanity (Tervarent, col. 388), parody of the trumpet of Clio, Muse of fame (I Proem 2n.), with a pun on French *tromper* = deceive, cheat. On the 'golden sell' see II.ii.11n., and Fowler, 'Emblems of Temperance' for the saddle as an emblem of authority and responsibility.

14 Parodying Guyon and Archimago at II.i.8ff.

Non locus virum, sed vir locum ornat.

To the Honorable Sir PHILLIP SIDNEY Knight, Gouernour
of the Garrison and towne of Vlissing.

THE trampinge steede, that champes the burnish'd bitte,
Is mannag'd braue, with ryders for the nones:
But, when the foole vppon his backe doth sette,
He throwes him downe, and ofte doth bruse his bones:
  His corage feirce, dothe craue a better guide,
  And eke such horse, the foole shoulde not bestride.

By which is ment, that men of iudgement graue,
Of learning, witte, and eeke of conscience cleare,
In highe estate, are fitte theire seates to haue,
And to be stall'd, in sacred iustice cheare:
  Wherein they rule, vnto theire endlesse fame,
  But fooles are foil'd, and throwne out of the same.

————*magnum hoc ego duco,*
Quòd placuit tibi, qui turpi secernis honestum.

18 On Arthur's sword, see II.viii.20–1.

19 Archimago uses the north wind because of its association with evil: see I.ii.33n. and Jeremiah 1:14 ('Out of the North shal a plague be spred upon all the inhabitans of the land').

21–30 Belphoebe (named in the Argument stanza) = Italian *bella* (beautiful) + Phoebe (the moon goddess), in allusion to the cult of Elizabeth as Diana–Phoebe–Cynthia. Gloriana is Elizabeth in her public character of 'a most royall Queene or Empress' (Spenser's prefatory *Letter of the Authors*); Belphoebe is the queen in her private character 'of a most vertuous and beautifull Lady', her primary private virtue being chastity. Her sudden stepping forth, dressed as a hunter, with bow and quiver (st. 29) – attributes of Diana, to whom she is compared at st. 31 – recall Venus's appearance to her son Aeneas at *Aeneid*, I.314ff. Aeneas's reaction – '*O Dea, certe*' – is echoed by Trompart at st. 33. There is an exact parallel with Una at I.vi.16n. Belphoebe, too, has Venerean attributes, thereby illustrating Elizabeth's capacity to make 'her ladies by love chaste' (Sidney, *Arcadia* (1590), II.xxi).

The mystery embodied in her reconciliation of Dianan and Venerean opposites is the same as that achieved by Una because Una and Belphoebe (and Medina and Alma) are the same person seen in different roles and under different aspects. In the book of temperance Belphoebe has the specific role of being an elaborate mythical statement of transcendence. Temperance is the workaday, albeit difficult, task of balancing extremes. Belphoebe is included as a reminder that transcendence is temperance's goal – the self-transcendence that emerges from the combination of opposites when the opposites take on the identities of each other and become a new whole (Wind, 97ff., 204ff.). At the same time, she is an almost inexplicable irruption of the mythological and divine (comparable to the descent of divinities in a masque) into Spenser's more mundane poetic world, equivalent to the other Venus epiphanies in the *F.Q.* at IV.x and VI.x.

Although conventional (e.g., Ovid, *Amores*, II.v,37, and the description of Alcina in *O.F.*, VII.11ff.), the roses and lilies are precisely emblematic: the rose belongs to Venus (Tervarent, cols. 323–4; at III.v.51 Belphoebe tends a rose that is the symbol of her honour), and the lily represents purity and modesty (Tervarent, col. 248) and beauty (ix.18–19n.). Spenser emphasises, by the phrase 'goodly mixture', not only that she has the best temperament according to the doctrine of humoral pathology (hence the reference to 'complexions'), but also that she reconciles opposites: cf. *Shepheardes Calender*, 'February', 129–32 where 'Lilly white, and Cremsin redde' are 'Colours meete to clothe a mayden Queene'. Further considerations are Elizabeth as the Tudor rose reconciling the red and white roses of York and Lancaster (Yates, 50–1, plates 4a, 8c) and the lily as an attribute of Juno, goddess of marriage, when it was known as the *rose* of Juno (Gilbert, *Symbolic Persons*, 151 with sources). Compare, too, Song of Solomon 2:1 ('I am the rose of the field, & the lilie of the valleis') and 5:10 ('My welbeloved is white and ruddy'; this is the Church's description of Christ, who, like Belphoebe, also has 'leggs ... as pillers of marble': *ibid.*, verse 15; cf. st. 28).

Upton, *Var. Sp.*, II.213 noted an additional echo in st. 22, l.3 of Song of Solomon 4:7 ('Thou art all faire, my love, and there is no spot in thee'); and in her Christlike ability to 'heale the sicke, and to revive the dead' Belphoebe contrasts with Mordant at i.41 (to whom, and Verdant in canto xii, she is a moral antitype). The connection of her with angels and light is in characteristic Christian Platonising vein (cf. Spenser's *Amoretti*, LXI), while her quenching of Cupid's fire confirms her as Diana in her role of militant goddess of chastity (see the debate between Venus and Diana in III.vi., especially st. 24, and I.x.29–31n. for a parallel with Charissa as Venus Urania in opposition to Venus Pandemos).

The details of st. 24 are conventional Petrarchan ones: the ivory forehead (perhaps with a suggestion of the ivory of Song of Solomon 7:4) is in *Epithalamion*, 172 and *Amoretti*, XV, where also are ruby lips and pearl teeth, as here. For the honey, cf. Song of Solomon 4:11 ('Thy lippes, my spouse, droppe as honie combes: honie and milke are under thy tongue'); while the 'many Graces' of st. 25 hint at Venus's companion Graces who are invoked to adorn the bride in *Epithalamion*, 103ff. (cf. I.i.48n. and I.x.4n.). In st.26 the gold of temperance (I.vii.43n.) combines with the lilywhite of purity (I.xii.21–3n.) on a 'silken Camus' (= loose robe or chemise, from Latin *camisia*) which puns on Latin *camus*, meaning muzzle or collar and hence an emblem of temperate restraint, carrying with it the common notion of the bridling of the passions. The legs as pillars, from Song of Solomon 5 (see above), relate to the book's architectural symbolism; to the familiar classical and Biblical notion of the body as a temple or building reflecting the harmonies of the cosmos (see ii.40–2n. and headnote to ix); and to the association of the Corinthian column with the slender form of a maiden (Vitruvius, *De architectura*, IV.i), as well as the identification of the pillar or column with virtue, constancy, and chastity (Tervarent, cols. 106–7). The phrase 'temple of the Gods' (st. 28) in this connection suggests the Roman Pantheon as an example of pagan virtue (see I.x.58n.). As a hunter of leopards Belphoebe banishes an emblem of Bacchus and of lust (I.vi.20–6n.), and she hunts the boar for the same reason (*ibid.*). But the Dianan hunter in her is complemented by her Venerean 'yellow lockes' (I.x.29–31n.; cf. II.ii.12–20n. and xii.65) which stream in the wind like Venus–Diana's at *Aeneid*, I.323; and the flowers turn her into a Flora (I.xii.21–3n.) as well as recalling the flower garlands of the Graces (Ovid, *Fasti*, V.219–20). It is either art or chance ('heedlesse hap') that has bedecked her with flowers and leaves. The moral point of this is that, if it is art, it is an art not in conflict with nature: contrast Acrasia's Bower at xii.50n. where, significantly, Flora reappears.

31 Compare *Aeneid*, I.502–3 (Dido compared to Diana with her nymphs on the banks of the Eurotas or on the slopes of Cynthus: Belphoebe here subsumes and transcends the self-destructive Dido of i.35–56n.) and 494ff., where Aeneas, viewing scenes of the Trojan war depicted in the temple of Juno that Dido is having built, sees the 'furious Penthesilea leading her Amazons with their crescent shields, burning amid thousands, her breasts bare with a gold belt tied underneath' (cf. Belphoebe's 'golden bauldricke' at st. 29). The Amazons fought on Priam's side against the Greeks during the war. In some traditions she is killed by Pyrrhus, but more commonly is supposed to have been killed by his father, Achilles (Smith, III.184–5); she was celebrated for her virtue and beauty (see Jonson's note on *Masque of Queens*, 449 with sources; *Masques*, ed. Orgel, 542).

38 Braggadocchio is bound to the sphere of the moon and earthly honour (cf. i.32n. and I.vii.46n.), a parody of Guyon and also of Aeneas (*Aeneid*, I.383, where he tells Venus 'My fame is known beyond the heavens'). On Fame's trumpet, see Tervarent, cols. 387–8; and on the laurel garland of victory, *ibid.*, 233.

39–41 Belphoebe offers an ideal of rigorous honour, the opposite of Braggadocchio's and Philotime's (vii.43ff.), but corresponding to that of Arthur, Redcrosse, Guyon, etc. The satire is aimed at the degenerate reality of Elizabeth's court as opposed to the ideal that it could aspire to, and the imagery of swimming and bathing in bliss anticipates Phaedria's lake in canto vi, the meaning of Cymochles (e.g., v.35), and Acrasia's fountain of concupiscence (xii.60–2), as well as the sea of xii.1n. The terms of Belphoebe's statement recall the opposition of Pleasure (Venus) and Virtue (Diana) in the 'Choice of Hercules' (I.ii.36–8n.) with a further echo of Hesiod, *Works and Days*, 287–92: 'Badness can be caught / In great abundance, easily; the road/To her is level, and she lives near by./But Good is harder, for the gods have placed/In front of her much sweat; the road is steep / And long and rocky' (tr. Dorothea Wender (Harmondsworth, 1973), 67–8). Compare the Biblical imagery of narrow and wide paths at I.iv.2n. and I.x.10.

42 As a Venus figure, Belphoebe represents the sum of the component parts embodied in her three Graces (see st. 25): *Pulchritudo, Amor, Voluptas* (Beauty leading to Love leading to ultimate Pleasure, that Pleasure, to the Neoplatonists, being the joy of mystical exaltation: Wind, 55 and ch. III; and Panofsky, *Studies in Iconology*, 168–9 for the Graces as the threefold aspect of Venus, the trinity of which she is the unity). Braggadocchio mistakes physical beauty as an incitement to direct lustful pleasure instead of to contemplation of ideal beauty and the achieving of pleasure in its mystical sense: compare Sansloy's abuse of Una at I.vi.4n. Both parody Arthur's quest for Gloriana.

CANTO IV

1–2 Compare II.iii.3n. Braggadocchio's inability to manage the horse is a pointer to his social baseness, since skill in riding is a sign of noble blood: e.g., the opening paragraph of Sidney's *Apology for Poetry*: 'He said soldiers were the noblest estate of mankind, and horsemen the noblest of soldiers . . . [and] that no earthly thing bred such wonder to a prince as to be a good horseman'.

3 Spenser's concern here and in canto v is with the uncontrolled irascible faculty. The encounter with Phedon, Furor, and Occasion leads to the more extended and internalised struggle with Pyrochles in the next canto. After this Guyon encounters Venerean temptations because, on Aristotle's authority (*Nicomachean Ethics*, II.iii.10) it is hard to fight against anger, but harder still to fight against pleasure: see vi.1n. The opening lines of the stanza ('saw . . . or seemed for to see') echo *Aeneid*, VI.454: Aeneas glimpses Dido in the shadows 'like one who . . . sees or thinks he sees the moon through the clouds'. This is not a chance allusion. The hag of st. 4ff. is eventually identified by the Palmer as the well-known figure of *Occasio* (st. 10) and, at st. 44, more precisely as '*Occasion* to wrath, and cause of strife': i.e., the objectification of the impulse within us that takes any opportunity to behave excessively. So that the *Aeneid* echo recalls Dido's love that found occasion to turn to anger and hate and also Aeneas's question to her at l. 458, 'Could I have been the cause of your death?' – with the inference on Spenser's part that the cause was both external and internal. For other Dido references in Book II, see i.35–56n.; ii. 12–20n.; and iii.31n.

4–5 The hag, old, lame, and supporting herself 'on a staffe', contrasts with the Palmer. Her hair, growing 'all afore', together with the bald back of her head, are details from emblematic descriptions of *Occasio–Fortuna*: e.g., Whitney, *Emblemes*, 181: 'What meanes long lockes before? *that such as meete, / Maye houlde at firste, when they occasion finde.* / Thy head behinde all balde, what telles it more? / *That none shoulde houlde, that let me slippe before*'. On the conflation of *Fortuna* and *Occasio*, see H. R. Patch, *The Goddess Fortuna in Medieval Literature* (Cambridge, Mass., 1927), and Chew, 59–60. The similarity with Impotence, companion of Maleger at xi.20–3n., is deliberate (both are aspects of Spenser's concern with temperance in relation to time), though apart from her *Occasio* aspects, her general appearance, together with her evil tongue, recall descriptions of Envy (but without Envy's characteristic serpents): Ripa, 242 ('An old woman, ugly, pale, dried up body, squinting eyes, dressed in a blighted, mildewy colour') and Whitney, 94: 'What hideous hagge with visage sterne appeares? / Whose feeble limmes, can scarce the bodie staie: / This, Envie is: leane, pale, and full of yeares'. She is depicted leaning on a staff. Envy and Slander are traditional enemies of

Truth, who vanquishes them when she is revealed by time (see I.i.13–16n. and Plate 1).

6–15 Guyon has to learn that the unreasonable occasion to wrath must be suppressed (st. 10–11) before Furor can be bound. Furor is a compound of characteristics associated with choler–wrath–Mars; and Burton, *Anatomy*, I.ii.3.9 (*ed.cit.*, 234) refers to the traditional identification of anger with madness and to the way anger makes men 'void of reason, inexorable, blind, like beasts & monsters'. The bull (st. 7) is usually wrathful (see I.vi.20–6n.); and the binding of Furor (st. 14–15) recalls the binding of Mars in a vessel of bronze in *Iliad*, V.385ff. and of 'godless Furor' at *Aeneid*, I.298–300 ('within the terrible iron-bound gates of war will safely stay godless Furor, sitting on his barbarous armoury, bound by a hundred bronze chains knotted behind his back, bellowing from his bloody mouth'). The iron that predominates in Spenser's description is attributed to Mars (Agrippa, I.xxvii,58); the blood-streaked eyes are Martian (Curry, *Chaucer and the Mediaeval Sciences*, 132), and the burning and fire are typical of the choleric (I.iii.33–6n.). Copper (st. 15) does not seem to be specifically Martian, but its colour suggests Mars (Agrippa, *ibid.*, gives Mars 'Iron, and red Brass; and all fiery, red, and sulphureous things'); and the 'tawny beard' is also Martian (Curry, *op.cit.*, 133). The description should be compared with that of the dragon at I.xi.8–15n.: the difference is that Guyon is encountering irrational, blind, wrath at the mundane level of its fundamental control; Redcrosse confronts it as a continuing threat at a much higher level to Christian fortitude and patience.

16–17 The blood and mire are symbols of the squire's moral state. His wrathful intemperance is a consequence of original sin, and the paradigm for this episode is Mordant and Amavia's tale of love and death (i.35–56n.) with hints of Dido's love turned to hatred and death (see st. 3n. above). The mire is a recurring symbol in this book as in Book I (e.g., I.x.52n. and 64–6n; II.xi.35–45n.), and has a Biblical base in Psalms 69:2 ('I sticke fast in the depe myre, where no staie is') and 2 Peter 2:22 ('The sowe [is returned] to the wallowing in the myer'). The squire's name is Phaon in the 1590 edition, changed to Phedon in 1596. Both have appropriate connotations, since Phaon was a beautiful youth with whom the poet Sappho was supposed to have fallen in love (Smith, III.238);

and Phedon suggests the young and beautiful Phaethon, son of
Cephalus and Eos, whom Aphrodite loved and whom she made
keeper of her temple (Hesiod, *Theogony*, 986ff.). The tale that
follows of love perverted to hate parodies the ideal union of Venus
and Mars which produced the daughter Harmonia, because
harmony is *discordia concors* (Wind, 86ff. citing, among others,
Plutarch, *De Iside et Osiride*, 370C–D: 'Concord is sprung from
[Venus and Mars], the one of whom is harsh and contentious, and
the other mild and tutelary' (*Moralia*, tr. F. C. Babbitt, Loeb edn, V
(1936), 117; and cf. vi.29–37n.). The psychological implications of
love and hate, attraction and repulsion, are raised by Spenser at
IV.x.32ff., where Dame Concord reconciles the two principles.
Compare II.ii.31n.

18–33   Phedon's story derives from *O.F.*, IV, V, and VI, the tale
of Ariodante and Ginevra; it is also the main plot of *Much Ado
About Nothing*. Alpers, 55ff. discusses it in detail. Philemon is from
Greek *philema* = kiss (and *philos* = friend). The subject of
Spenser's story is the uncontrolled emotions and actions resulting
from them; and it is related closely to the tradition of tales about
two friends: Palamon and Arcite in Chaucer's *Knight's Tale*; 'The
wonderful history of Titus and Gisippus' in Sir Thomas Elyot's
Governor, II.xii; Anselmo and Lothario in 'The Novel of the
Curious Impertinent' in *1 Don Quixote*, IV.vi–viii, to name three of
many possible mythological and later examples (see, e.g., *F.Q.*,
IV.x.27). As in *The Knight's Tale* and other two-friends stories, the
woman is the cause of strife. In Spenser's tale of Phedon, as with
Dido and Aeneas, lack of moral and psychological self-awareness
leads to destruction and, nearly, self-destruction.

37–42   Guyon, through the Palmer's advice, has overcome
Occasion and Furor as they relate to Phedon; he is now
confronted, in the person of Pyrochles, with his own tendency to
wrath. The 'varlet' is Pyrochles's squire, Atin (named at st. 42),
who recalls the classical Ate, goddess of rash and inconsiderate
actions. She appears in *F.Q.*, IV.i.19ff. as the 'mother of debate',
hellish, slanderous, and dedicated to the overthrow of 'that great
golden chaine' which holds the cosmos together (st. 30). Hence
Atin's two darts 'of malice and despight' at st. 38 (where two
signifies evil and discord: see I.ii, headnote, and IV.i.27–8 for Ate's
doubleness). 'Atin' also suggests the Old French word for

'challenge' or 'incitement to battle' (A. Kent Hieatt, 'Spenser's
Atin from *Atine*?', *M.L.N.*, LXXII (1957)).

Pyrochles derives from Greek *pur* = fire, and *ochleo* = move
(i.e., inspired, motivated, by choler), together with a suggestion of
kleos (fame, glory); so that he represents not just irascibility but
raises the question of the correct proportion of wrath needed by a
knight in his heroic pursuit of honour (see I.i.1n. and G. R.
Crampton, *The Condition of Creatures* (New Haven and London,
1974), 152ff.). The shield of brass with flames depicted on it
suggests Mars and choler (see st. 6–15n. above), and Pyrochles and
his brother Cymochles (see v.25–8n.) have an infernal genealogy
not dissimilar to that of the Sans-brothers (cf. I.v.22–3n.).
Lotspeich, 34 suggests that it derives from Boccaccio's *De
Genealogia Deorum*, I.i, where 'Aeternitie' is named as a divinity
and is the partner of Demogorgon who is the father of Herebus and
Litigium (Strife) and grandfather of Night. Spenser also follows
Hesiod, *Theogony*, 123ff., where Chaos brings forth Night and
Erebus (a personification of the underworld): compare III.iv.55.
The rest is basically Spenser's own: Phlegethon is the infernal fiery
river (I.v.31–4n., II.vi.50) associated with Fury (Lotspeich, 100,
citing Boccaccio, I.xiv and III.xvi); and Acrates is from Greek
akratos (intemperance, violence): see Introduction to Book II.
Spenser thus traces the tendency to choler back to ultimate cosmic
strife.

CANTO V

1   In the last line Spenser raises the essential problem, in a
Christianised view of the relationship between reason and the
passions, of the role of the will. As fallen beings we inherit a
predisposition to sin, and Spenser is concerned here with willed sin,
the tendency of the will to act against the evidence of the
understanding and reason: see II.ix.27n., and Burton, *Anatomy*,
I.i.2.11 (*ed.cit.*, 146–7): '*Will* is the other power of the *rational soul*
[the first being understanding], *which covets or avoids such things
as have been before judged and apprehended by the understanding*.
If good, it approves; if evil, it abhors it . . . [But] we know many
times what is good, but will not do it'. Hence, as Guyon spells out
at st. 15–16, Pyrochles has willed his own destruction, like Amavia

and Mordant in canto i and Grille at xii.86–7. In st. 17 it is made plain that Guyon has willed the binding of Furor and Occasion.

2–14 Pyrochles's choleric nature is confirmed by his red horse: red is Mars's colour, and the horse was dedicated to him (Agrippa, I.xxvii,58; William Lilly, *Christian Astrology* (1647), I.x,68). The fact that the horse signifies uncontrolled passion (Pyrochles spurs it in st. 2 rather than bridling it: see ii.11n.) indicates that for Guyon to kill it, albeit accidentally as he does in st. 4, is to win at least half of the moral battle against Pyrochles right at the beginning. The comparison of Pyrochles to sunbeams glinting on water (also st. 2) suggests his affinities with his watery brother Cymochles (see st. 25–8n.) and, ironically, a traditional emblem of temperance (the tempering of fiery iron in water: Ripa, 482. This is parodied when Pyrochles burns in the lake at vi.42ff.) The juxtaposition of fire and water also symbolises discord (Tervarent, cols. 183, 195–6) and deceit, because the two elements are incompatible like deceit and virtue (Ripa, 228). Pyrochles's 'sandy lockes' are again Martian in colour (Lilly, *op.cit.*, 67: those under Mars have 'their haire red or sandy flaxen'); and note the 'bloud and dust' here and at st. 22 (see iv.16–17n.).

6 The 'sevenfolded shield' is a commonplace: e.g., *Aeneid*, XII.925.

10 Guyon is the lion, whose enemy is the unicorn. Spenser tells the story in its traditional form (*Var. Sp.*, II.235–6), also evoking the associations of the lion with both moral strength and the imperial virtue, clemency (Tervarent, cols. 243, 245–6), and the unicorn with untamableness (Job 39:12ff.).

18–24 The temperate (st. 13) Guyon, having defeated Pyrochles, releases Furor and Occasion at Pyrochles's request and stands back to observe the ensuing destruction as an emblematic tableau. The request was an act of the infected will (see st. 1n.); hence the austere Palmer recommends that he should be left to the results of his folly. On the Styx (st. 22) see I.i.37n.: Furor's 'fire brond', attribute of choler and Mars (Tervarent, col. 382) has been kindled from hate (the Styx's hateful waters). There is a hint, too, of fire and water as an emblem of discord (see st. 2–14n.).

25–8 Cymochles is discovered in a *locus amoenus* that recalls

I.vii.2–4 and n. The sensuous appeal of the 'pleasant place' is made explicit here. For a detailed description of Acrasia's Bower, see xii.42ff. Literary sources and analogues for this episode include Odysseus's stay with Calypso in *Odyssey*, V; Aeneas's dalliance with Dido in *Aeneid*, IV; and Rinaldo in Armida's paradisal garden in *Ger. Lib.*, XV–XVI. *Cymochles* derives from Greek *kuma* = wave, with a hint of *kauma* = burning (to symbolise his lust – the 'close fire' of st. 34 – as well as his tendency to choler which he shares with his brother: cf. st. 37). On the meaning of the last syllable of his name, see iv.37–42n. above. In a general sense he represents the concupiscible power, as Pyrochles embodies the irascible. He also symbolises instability, or flux: he is a version of the *humidus homo* (moist, watery man) discussed by George de F. Lord, *Homeric Renaissance*, 94, where the adjective implies instability of moral character, demonstrated by Cymochles in his wavering between Martian irascible and Venerean concupiscible extremes (Mars and Venus should unite to produce harmony: iv.16–17n.). He is 'watery' also in the sense of being lustful (a traditional meaning of water given by Hankins, 80–1 and exploited in Phaedria's lake in canto vi; cf. iii.39–41n.). Finally, he suggests aspects of the phlegmatic temperament, the corresponding element to which is water, as fire is to choler (S. K. Heninger, *Handbook of Renaissance Meteorology*, 110–12). The phlegmatic could be depicted as a fisherman or river god (Klibansky, 399) and, like the melancholic with whom he was often confused, as slothful and sleepy (*ibid.*, 299–300 and n.66). Berger, 60–1 makes the passing identification of Cymochles with the phlegmatic. In schemes correlating the temperaments with the four winds, the west wind, Zephyrus, was associated with the phlegmatic (Heninger, *ibid.*); though his presence in st. 29 is explained also by his amorousness (Ovid, *Fasti*, V.201ff., his rape of Flora) and by the fact that he is the wind of spring (Catullus, XLVI; Wind, 115ff.), which is the season of lovers (Lucretius, *De rerum natura*, I.1ff.; Klibansky, 294 and n.).

29 On the common theme of Art and Nature, see xii.50n. The ivy is Bacchic (Tervarent, cols. 240–1); the 'Eglantine' or sweet-brier (wild rose) is Venerean (iii.21–30n.), while the emphasis on its 'pricking armes' affirms that this is a fallen false paradise, since the rose's thorns were regarded as a consequence of the Fall (deriving from Genesis 3:18: 'Thornes also . . . shal it bring forthe to thee').

30 In view of Cymochles's phlegmatic sloth, it should be recalled that in the gifts–vices–virtues schemes (e.g., I.viii.30–4n., x.5n.), the Holy Ghost's gift of *fortitudo* displaces sloth and bestows the virtue prowess – a chivalric virtue known also as 'doughtyness' (Tuve, 84, 97). Like Braggadocchio in his different way, Cymochles is the antithesis of true knighthood. Compare Verdant at xii.79–80.

31 The oak is Jupiter's tree (Agrippa, I.xxvi,57) and it is the poplar that is usually dedicated to Hercules–Alcides (Vergil, *Eclogues*, VII.61); but Alcides incorporates Greek *alkē* (oak), after which he was named 'from his extraordinary strength' (Tooke, *Pantheon*, 257). The oak symbolises fortitude (Tervarent, col. 91) and is appropriate to Hercules as exemplar of heroic virtue and fortitude (I.xi.26–8n.; Tervarent, col. 210): an ironic reminder to the oblivious Cymochles. Spenser refers to Hercules's victory over the Nemean lion, the first of his twelve labours, in memory of which the Nemean wood was planted.

32–3 On the lily, see iii.21–30n. and vi.15–17n. The garden, with its roses (st. 29), lilies, and Bacchic ivy is a parody of the temperate anti-Bacchic Belphoebe (described in terms of roses and lilies at iii.22). Contrast the true earthly paradise that is Belphoebe's home at III.v.39ff. (note the structural parallel). The 'words, dropping like honny dew' again parody Belphoebe at iii.24.

34 For the adder, see I.ix.28n.

35–7 Cymochles's excessive sloth is about to yield to equally excessive wrath. Atin (discord) reminds us of his intemperate parent (see iv.37–42n.) to drive the point home. His speech recalls that of Mercury to Aeneas at *Aeneid*, IV.265ff., reprimanding Aeneas for living in idleness with Dido (271), forgetful of glory and his destiny. Atin brings the traditional accusation of effeminacy – the abandonment of the heroic because of love – against Cymochles: earlier defaulters were Hercules abandoning himself to Omphale, and Antony succumbing to Cleopatra: Hamilton, 118; A. Kent Hieatt, *Chaucer, Spenser, Milton*, 192. Spenser also recalls the rousing of Rinaldo by Ubaldo at *Ger. Lib.*, XVI.32ff. Cf. Verdant at xii.79–80 and n., and note that the Genius at the porch to Acrasia's Bower is also effeminate (xii.46). Cymochles's reaction to Atin's words recalls Aeneas's reaction to his vision of Mercury at *Aeneid*, IV.279–80 (his hair bristles with fear, etc.).

CANTO VI

1 Apparently echoing Aristotle, *Nicomachean Ethics*, II.iii.10, cited at iv.3n. The theme of the opposition and false reconciliation of Mars and Venus continues in this canto.

2–10 The boat is decorated so as to become a *locus amoenus* (cf. v.25–8n.) with, as its attendant deity, another Venus who represents mocking and 'immodest Merth' (see Argument stanza). Guyon encounters true modesty, one of the parts of temperance, at ix.40–3n. Venus is traditionally associated with laughter and cheerfulness (Hesiod, *Theogony*, 989; Ptolemy, *Tetrabiblos*, III.xiii,357); taken to extremes this produces a Phaedria. She is close to the Venus figure (complete with yellow hair, rose garland, and mirror) who is in fact not a Venus but *Oiseuse* (idleness, leisure leading to amorous play) and who introduces the dreamer to the paradisal garden of Mirth, her 'dearest friend', in the *Romance of the Rose*, 521ff. In the 1590 edn, l. 4 of st. 3 reads 'as merry as Pope Jone', changed to 'that nigh her breth was gone' in 1596. The medieval legend of Pope Joan says that she succeeded Leo IV and became pregnant and gave birth while in office. She was known for her lust, and the story was a favourite anti-papal one in the sixteenth century (Boccaccio, *Concerning Famous Women*, XCIX; Baring Gould, *Curious Myths of the Middle Ages*, 171ff.). Phaedria's name (st. 9) is from Greek *phaidros* = joyful, smiling, with a hint of the mythological Phaedra, lustful stepmother of Hippolytus (see I.v.36–44n.). The boat – called a 'Gondelay' to suggest Italian moral depravity (Craig, 'The Secret Wit of Spenser's Language', in Alpers, ed., *Elizabethan Poetry*, 464) – perhaps recalls *Odyssey*, VIII.557ff., the self-steering ships of the Phaeacians; or the similar vessel that moves without sail or oar in *Ger. Lib.*, XV.3; or *O.F.*, XXX.11. In st. 8 the Venus–Mars opposition is underlined by the elemental opposition of water and fire (see v.2–14n.): Venus is traditionally associated with water (and air: see st. 3, l. 3, and Agrippa, I.xxviii,59) and Mars with fire (*ibid.*, I.xxvii,57). The 'Idle lake', another watery contrast, like fiery Phlegethon (iv.37–42n.), to the cold, chaste well of ii.7ff., is related to the sloth-inducing fountain encountered by Redcrosse at I.vii.4–6: compare Mantegna's late–fifteenth–century painting *Triumph of Wisdom over Vice*, in which Wisdom–Minerva, with Diana and Chastity, puts Venus, mother of vices, to flight. The vices are shown in a stagnant pool along the bank of which is written 'Otia si tollis, periere Cupidinis arcus' ('If you abolish sloth, Cupid's bows perish': Ovid, *Remedia Amoris*, 139): see Seznec, *Survival of the Pagan Gods*, 109 and n., and fig. 37; Hankins, 83; and, on Venus–Oiseuse in general, Twycross, *Medieval Anadyomene*, 86–7.

15–17 Phaedria's invitation to ease parallels Despair's at I.ix.38ff. and anticipates the *carpe diem* song at II.xii.74–5n. It has its roots in Odysseus's encounter with the Lotus-eaters in *Odyssey*, IX, and recalls the song sung to Rinaldo by the Siren on an island, inviting him to reject glory and to succumb to present enjoyments and idleness, since this is what nature requires of him, in *Ger. Lib.*, XIV.62–4. Phaedria specifically ignores Genesis 3:19, God's sentence of toil on Adam after the Fall, and misapplies Matthew 6:28 ('Learne, how the lilies of the field do growe: they labour not, nether spinne'; Geneva gloss on 'labour': 'The worde signifieth, they weary not themselves'). The Matthew verse is a reminder of God's providential power and not an invitation to sloth: its corollary is 'But seke ye first the kingdome of God, and his righteousnes, & all these things shalbe ministred unto you'. Phaedria emphasises the purely physical: she personifies nature and ignores the creating God whose visible expression it is. As Berger, 25 notes, she tempts Cymochles to become a vegetable – the fate of Fradubio at I.ii.30ff. and the sleeping Verdant at II.xii.79–80.

19 The Palmer's sadness is a reminder that prudence (or wisdom) was traditionally dedicated to Saturn, planetary god of contemplation and melancholy (I.x.46–63n.; II.ix.49–58n.). For the definition of prudence, see vii.1–2n.

23 Echoing Despair again at I.ix.40 and ignoring the traditional metaphor of the pilot of reason governing the ship of the body through the sea of passion: see II.xii.1n.

24 The budding trees etc. are a reminder that Phaedria is not all bad. She is in part a good Venus Pandemos or Venus Genetrix, the natural, creating Venus who is invoked, e.g., at the beginning of Lucretius's *De rerum natura*, I.1ff.: 'life-giving Venus . . . For you the inventive earth flings up sweet flowers. For you the ocean levels laugh' (tr. R. E. Latham, 27). On the Platonic view of Venus Pandemos, see General Introduction. Phaedria, like Acrasia, offers temptation to 'bestial love' and ignores the fact that man is a rational and spiritual being (Panofsky, *Studies in Iconology*, 141ff.)

29–37 Guyon confronts his own Cymochlean tendencies in the battle just as, earlier, he had generated the parody of his aspirations in Braggadocchio. Phaedria overcomes their wrath by an appeal to the Mars–Venus legend. Guyon listens to her because he acknowledges the implications of the well-known cosmogonic myth – that harmony is expressed in the concordant coming-together of opposites: Venus overcomes Mars who is, however, necessary to her. She cannot exist without his opposing power (Wind, 88–9, quoting Pico della Mirandola; and see iv.16–17n.). The logical objections to Phaedria's argument are that she misrepresents the end of knighthood (st. 35: its true end is glory, to obtain which involves the knight's victory over the passions) and exalts the wrong kind of love. The ideals of knighthood and love are embodied in Arthur and his quest for Gloriana. So Guyon, unlike Mars, does not yield to the Venerean Phaedria. And yet she rejects him as much as he rejects her, and there is truth in her accusation that he brings 'unquiet jarre' to annoy her 'pleasures', and that he manifests 'solemne sadness' and 'disdain' (st. 37): if Cymochles wavers too extremely between Mars on the one hand and Venus on the other (v.25–8n.), then Guyon perhaps has a tendency to ignore Venus altogether. His 'solemne sadness', recalling the prudent Palmer (st. 19n. above), also suggests the Saturnian joylessness of Elissa and Huddibras (ii.12–20n.), while Phaedria herself is reminiscent of Perissa ('full of disport, still laughing, loosely light'; ii.36), as well as being at the same time a parody of Medina in her role of pacifier of the fighting knights. There is a direct parallel between ii.30–1 and vi.34–5, the crucial difference being that the Venerean Medina does understand the true goal of knighthood: 'Brave . . . warres, and honorable deeds' leading to concord, peace, and virtue. Guyon will know how to accommodate the Venerean-concupiscible side of his nature only when he has explored the terrifying depths of his Saturnian tendencies in the Cave of Mammon in the next canto and overcome, through Arthur, the warring Pyrochles and Cymochles in canto viii. Then he achieves temperance, embodied in the castle of the Venerean Alma, in canto ix.

42–5 On the 'bloud and filth', see iv.16–17n. The waters of idleness (st. 2–10n.) can be no antidote to the inward flames of irascibility. What we have here is a coming-together of two antithetical extremes and a parody of a traditional emblem of temperance (v.2–14n.). Spenser recalls the shock confrontation of pure water and wine that kills Mordant (i.35–56n.). The extremes of concupiscence (as in Amavia's case) and irascibility are alike, too, in that they both lead to a Dido-like impatience with life and desire for death. Note that the lake washes the 'bloud and filth' from Pyrochles's armour to replace them, presumably, with its own filth; but it cannot quench his fire: there is a parallel and contrast with the pure well which cannot wash away the blood from Ruddymane's hands but does regenerate him (ii.1–4n.).

47–51 For Phlegethon, see iv.37–42n. Archimago arrives as a parody Palmer. Significantly, at first he does not understand the problem, but he then effects a cure by the external application of herbs (cf. I.ii.40–1n. and I.v.36–44n.). In other words, Archimago and the excessive Pyrochles cannot achieve a moral healing because they lack the rational means for attaining temperate self-control and the realisation that, in any case, more than reason is needed. Contrast Guyon's restoration through the Palmer and Arthur in canto viii.

CANTO VII

1–2 Guyon, still without the Palmer (see vi.19), has to be self-sufficient. For the symbolic mists, see xii.33–4n. The 'stedfast starre' is the pole-star (see I.ii.1n. and II.x.1–4n.). Left alone, Guyon has to rely specifically on his memory of past virtuous actions. Memory is, traditionally, one of the three parts of prudence (the probable inclusive meaning of the Palmer: i.7n.) which had been authoritatively defined by Cicero: '[Prudence] is the knowledge of what is good, what is bad and what is neither good nor bad. Its parts are memory, intelligence, foresight. Memory is the faculty by which the mind recalls what has happened. Intelligence is the faculty by which it ascertains what it is. Foresight is the faculty by which it is seen that something is going to occur before it occurs' (*De inventione*, II.liii; Loeb edn, tr. H. M. Hubbell (1949), 327). That is, prudence is a rational virtue which enables us, through the exercise of its parts, to distinguish between good and evil and discriminate between false and true. By itself memory is merely a record of past events and images. It takes on a moral function only in conjunction with intelligence and foresight (Yates, *The Art of Memory* (1966), 62, citing Albertus Magnus). So that, without the Palmer, Guyon is not fully prudent: his prudence is symbolically attained when he encounters the three faculties working together in Alma's castle at ix.47ff.; though in practice he finds little difficulty in rejecting Mammon's temptations anyway. Guyon's three-day descent into the cave is a re-enactment of Christ's harrowing of hell (I.x.36–43n.) and of the epic hero's descent into the underworld. It is also a descent into the depths of the concupiscent self, where he encounters desire in all its common aspects except the sexual, which is separately embodied in Acrasia and Phaedria. There are hints of sexual temptation in the myths of st. 55, but they are unimportant. Mammon himself has a Biblical origin, his name originally merely meaning 'wealth' as at, e.g., Matthew 6:24: 'No man can serve two masters. ... Ye can not serve God and riches' (Authorised Version: 'God and mammon'). Burton, *Anatomy*, I.ii.1.2 (*ed.cit.*, 164) follows one tradition in naming Mammon as the prince of the last (ninth) order of devils, which are 'tempters in several kinds'. Mammon thus personified was frequently identified with the Greek personification of wealth, Plutus, who was often confused in the Middle Ages and Renaissance with Pluto, god of the underworld (Lotspeich, 102); and, too, he was the opposite of the Senecan contemplative who gazed at the heavens, despising worldly possessions (John M. Steadman in *Notes and Queries*, CCV (1960), 220). In astrological terms, Mammon is largely Saturnian: not the benevolent Saturn of prudence, wisdom, and contemplation; but Saturn as a malign planetary influence, making his children avaricious and amassers of treasure (Ptolemy, *Tetrabiblos*, III.xiii, 341). This is yet another side of the malign Saturn encountered in Despair in I.ix.33–4n. and 35–6n. The link between melancholy, wealth, and the underworld is a simple one: as Tooke, *Pantheon*, 220 explains, Plutus/Pluto

'signifies wealth ... because all our wealth comes from the lowest
and most inward bowels of the earth. ... The name *Hades*, by
which he is called among the Greeks, signifies dark, gloomy, and
melancholy'. Saturn is traditionally antithetical to Venus, as is
Mars. The main argument of Book II – beginning with Mordant
and Amavia and ending with Acrasia's Bower, with the Venerean
Phaedria in the middle – is the overcoming of sexual
concupiscence. Guyon, as we have seen, has not quite learned how
Mars and Venus can be reconciled (vi.29–37n.). In canto ix, in the
castle of Alma, he will find the answer to the problem of controlling
Venus. In the meantime he now explores how Saturn can offset her:
this is an extreme planetary antithesis, however, and Spenser's
point (it was the Neoplatonist Ficino's before him) is that, being so
extreme, it offers a very unstable solution to the problem and is
therefore not recommended (Klibansky, 271–2, n.101, citing
Ficino's *De vita*, II.xvi; and Fowler, 110–11). It is the astrological
equivalent of the bringing together of pure water and wine in
Mordant's body at i.35–56n. And it has its own dangers, those of
Saturnian concupiscence. The correct method is to moderate the
influence of the two planets by another, mediating, planet. Such
mediating planets include Jupiter and the moon (Fowler, *ibid.*):
hence the mixture of Venus and Diana (moon) in Alma's castle in
the figure of Alma herself (ix.18–19n.) and the appearance of
Jupiter together with Saturn at ix.49–58n. But Guyon has still to
learn this; so, using only Saturnian memory as a guide (see Yates,
Art of Memory, 162) and led also by his Saturnian kill-joy
tendencies (vi.29–37n.), and ignorant of the full dangers of Saturn,
he mistakenly reacts to the too light-hearted Phaedria–Venus at the
end of the first half of the book by espousing the too joyless
extreme of Saturnian Mammon at the beginning of the second half.
The exploration of Saturn occurs in canto vii because seven is
Saturn's number, since it is the seventh planet counting outward
from earth in the Ptolemaic system, and since as god of time Saturn
governs mortality and mutability, both of which are among the
meanings of seven (see headnote to I.vii).

3–6 Many of Mammon's Saturnian–melancholic characteristics
are illustrated by the Peacham emblem (our Plate 10): the owl
appears at st. 23 (and see I.v.30n.). Ptolemy, *Tetrabiblos*,
III.xiii,341, notes that under Saturn's malign influence one becomes

Melancholia.

HEERE *Melancholly* muſing in his fits,
  Pale viſag'd, of complexion cold and drie,
Allſolitarie, at his ſtudie ſits,
Within a wood, deuoid of companie :
    Saue Madge the Owle, and melancholly Puſſe,
    Light-loathing Creatures, hatefull, ominous.

His mouth, in ſigne of ſilence, vp is bound,
For *Melancholly* loues not many wordes :
One foote on Cube is fixt vpon the ground,
The which him plodding *Conſtancie* affordes :
    A ſealed Purſe he beares, to ſhew no vice,
    So proper is to him, as *Avarice*.

solitary, gloomy, careless of the body, and fond of toil (on the toil in Mammon's hell, see st. 35–6). On the infernal associations of iron (st. 4, 23), see I.v.20n. The 'wild Imagery' of st. 4 might recall I.viii.36, the 'cunning imagery' on Orgoglio's altar (see, too, II.xii.50n.). Mulciber (st. 5) is a surname of Vulcan, metal-worker of the gods and lord of fire. Note that Mammon's wealth cannot be spent: metal shines only if it is used (Horace, *Odes*, II.ii.). Mammon is scared because Saturn can make his subjects cowardly and easily frightened (Ptolemy, *Tetrabiblos, ibid.*).

7   The emphasis here and in st. 2 on 'desert' suggests Saturnian solitude and that the temptation Guyon is to undergo will parallel that of Christ by Satan in the wilderness (Matthew 4, Luke 4): see Cullen, ch. II, and Kermode, 69–70.

8–11   Christ's last temptation (Matthew) or second (Luke) was to 'all the kingdomes of the worlde, and the glorie of them' (Matthew 4:8). Mammon tempts Guyon similarly. The temptation is continued in Philotime at st. 43ff. Mammon is 'greatest god below the skye' because devils rule only the sublunary world (Burton, *Anatomy*, I.ii.1.2, *ed.cit.*, 165; on Mammon as devil, see st. 1–2n. above).

12–13   Echoing 1 Timothy 6:9–10: 'For they that wil be riche, fall into temptation and snares, and into many foolish & noysome lustes, which drowne men in perdition and destruction. For the desire of money is the roote of all evil'. Mammon has called himself 'god of the world' in st. 8 (cf. John 12:31: 'now shal the prince of this worlde be cast out'): like Lucifera, he is a usurper (cf. I.iv.12).

14   Both seas were well known for their storms: e.g., Horace, *Odes*, II.ix.2–3 (rough winds in the Caspian) and III.iii.4–5 (restless Adriatic). Mammon 'wex[es] wroth' here as also at st. 51: he is Saturnian but, like Huddibras at ii.12–20n., has more than an element of wrathful Mars in his character – the Mars whom Guyon has already confronted in Pyrochles, but who is defeated ultimately only in canto viii. Astrologically, Saturn allied with Mars produces characters who are harsh in their conduct and pitiless (cf. Mammon's roughness at st. 63), generally evil, and 'eaters of forbidden foods' (Ptolemy, *Tetrabiblos*, III.xiii,343): important in relation to the interpretation of the Garden of Proserpina at st. 51ff.

The giant Disdayne of st. 40–3, stern, fierce, and disdainful, is again Saturnian–Martian: Ptolemy, *ibid.*, lists those who are contemptuous as being a product of both planets. Mammon himself is disdainful in st. 7. Cullen, 79n. draws attention to the emphasis on irascibility in the cave. As Burton, I.i.2.8 (p. 141) reminds us: '*Concupiscible* covets always pleasant and delightsome things. ... *Irascible* ... [avoids the unpleasant] with anger and indignation'. Mammon's irascibility and disdain are probably a projection of Guyon's own initial inner reactions to the temptations he is being offered, though his actual spoken responses are temperate and courteous. See also st. 35–9n.

15–17 Guyon looks back to the golden age when Saturn (a very different Saturn from the avaricious Mammon) traditionally ruled the earth. Compare Boethius, *Consolation of Philosophy*, II, prose and metre v, on the vanity of riches and the temperate frugality of the former age: now 'the desire of having gold / Doth like the flaming fires of Aetna burn. / Ah, who was he that first did show / The heaps of treasure which the earth did hide . . .?' (Loeb edn, tr. 'I.T.' (1609), rev. H. F. Stewart (1953), 205–7). But above all Guyon echoes *Met.*, I.89ff. on the decline from the golden to the silver, bronze, and finally iron age (127ff.): 'Straightway all evil burst forth into this age of baser vein: modesty and truth and faith fled the earth [and men] delved . . . into the very bowels of the earth. . . . And now baneful iron had come, and gold more baneful than iron; war came, which fights with both' (Loeb edn, tr. F. J. Miller (1929), I.11–13). The action of wounding the earth recalls Orgoglio at I.vii.10; and note in st. 15 the opposition of pure and polluted water: compare the fountain of ii.7–10n. and the 'Idle lake' of vi.2–10n.

18–19 Mammon's temptation to abuse nature parallels Phaedria's (vi.15–17n.). The temperate answer is that of the Lady in Milton's *Comus*, 761ff. and, movingly, of Gloucester in *King Lear*, IV.i: 'that I am wretched / Makes thee the happier: heavens, deal so still! / Let the superfluous and lust-dieted man, / That slaves your ordinance, that will not see / Because he doth not feel, feel your power quickly: / So distribution should undo excess, / And each man have enough'. Unjust division is a characteristic of the iron age when, finally, Astraea, goddess of justice, left the earth (*Met.*, I.150).

20 Mammon grotesquely echoes John 1:38–9: 'Then Jesus turned about, and sawe them followe, & said unto them, What seke ye? And they said unto him, Rabbi ... where dwellest thou? He said unto them, Come, and se.'

21–5 On the 'broad high way' see I.iv.2n. The descent echoes *Aeneid*, VI.262ff., Aeneas's entrance into Hades with the Sibyl through a cavern. In front of the entry to Hades itself are Grief, Care, Diseases, Old Age, Fear, Hunger, Poverty, Death, Pain, Sleep which is kin to death, the Furies, Strife, etc. Many of the traits embodied by Spenser are produced by Saturn allied with one or other of the planets: revenge, treachery, hatred, jealousy, and fear (Ptolemy, *Tetrabiblos*, III.xiii, 341–7). Lotspeich, 65–6 suggests additional influences: the personifications in the temple of Mars in Chaucer's *Knight's Tale*, 1995ff., where Strife appears 'with blody knyf', and Sackvile's Induction (see I.ix.22–4n. and 33–4n.). Celeno (st. 23) is chief of the Harpies, who are traditionally rapacious and bird-shaped with girls' faces and talons on their hands (*Aeneid*, III.211ff. and 245–6). On the night-raven, see xii.35–6n. Guyon's descent has parallels with Aeneas's as it was interpreted by medieval and Renaissance commentators, according to whom it began with the rejection of vainglory (the burial of Misenus) and consisted of an allegorical Platonic descent, under the guidance of wisdom (the Sibyl), of the mind into the body and its cares. After the confrontation and contemplation of past errors Aeneas acquires divine knowledge from his father, Anchises, armed with which he can return to the upper world and fulfil his destiny (Allen, ch. VI, 152ff.).

26–7 The fiend that follows Guyon has a psychological meaning, and probably embodies, like Mammon himself (see st. 14n.), the destructive nature of Guyon's own potentiality for irascibility (for the psychological implications, cf. Coleridge's *Ancient Mariner*, part VI: 'Like one, that on a lonesome road / Doth walk in fear and dread, / And having once turned round walks on, / And turns no more his head; / Because he knows, a frightful fiend / Doth close behind him tread'). It also recalls Eurynomus, a daemon of the lower world which devoured human bodies (Pausanias, *Description of Greece*, X.xxviii.4–7, describing Polygnotus's picture of punishment in Hades for blasphemy: cf. st. 53–4n. and 57–60n.), and there may be a suggestion of the Eleusinian mysteries (see st.

53–4n.) in which the suppliant was followed by a fury and not permitted to turn around (Kermode, 75–6). Confirming the suggestion that there is at least an element of the mysteries in Guyon's experiences is the parallel with Plato's myth of Er (*Republic*, X.613–20), a descent to the underworld which tells in part how the despot Ardiaeus and other sinners thought that their punishment was ended and that they were at last to be admitted through the mouth reserved for the just. But as they approached, the mouth bellowed and fierce and fiery men seized them and flayed them before throwing them into Tartarus. This myth, like *Aeneid*, VI, was clearly influenced by the mysteries (*Republic of Plato*, tr. F. M. Cornford (1945), 348–50).

28–9 Spenser looks back to Lucifera's palace at I.iv and v and forward to Acrasia's Bower with its sterile gold. Arachne presumptuously challenged Athena to a weaving contest. The goddess could find no fault with her work and tore it to pieces in indignation. Arachne started to hang herself but at that moment Athena turned her into a spider (*Met.*, VI.1–145). Peacham, *Minerva Britanna*, 197 shows Athena/Minerva (Wisdom) entrapped in a net by Avarice and Fraud because 'The love of Money, and Dissimulation, / Hold thee MINERVA tangled in their snare: / For now the world, is growne to such a fashion, / That those the wisest, that the richest are, / And such by whome the simpler should be taught, / Are in the net, like PALLAS soonest caught'. Compare Archimago's web at i.8, and the net of xii.81–2. The last lines of st. 29 echo *Aeneid*, VI.268ff. (Aeneas and the Sibyl entering Hades 'as if walking through a wood under the grudging light of a fitful moon').

30 The avaricious Saturnian melancholic was traditionally associated with treasure chests (Klibansky, 284–6 and notes). The bones recall I.iv.36 and remind us of Saturn's connection with graveyards (Agrippa, I.xlviii, 96) and grave-robbers (Klibansky, *ibid.*).

31–4 Compare Acts 12:10 (Peter escaping with the help of an angel after being imprisoned by Herod): 'they came unto the yron gate, that leadeth unto the citie, which opened to them by it owne accorde'. The allusion equates Mammon and Herod, confirming Mammon's link with Orgoglio (see st. 3–6n. above, and

I.viii.35–6n.). Mammon, like Phaedria in her song (vi.15–17), ignores God. Guyon's answer recalls the reaction of Curius Dentatus, famous for his frugality, to the gold brought to him by the Samnites: 'it seems to me that the glory is not in having the gold, but in ruling those who have it' (Cicero, *De Senectute*, XVI.lvi, Loeb edn, tr. W. A. Falconer (1923), 69). The story became a common illustration of temperance: Barbara Lewalski, *Milton's Brief Epic*, 234. The dove, to which Guyon is compared in st. 34, was an emblem of temperance (Katzenellenbogen, 80n.); the fiend, appropriately in view of his irascible behaviour (see st. 26–7n.), is compared to the Martian falcon (I.xi.8–15n.).

35–9 The forges emphasise the laborious aspect of Saturn's influence (st. 3–6n.) and are based on the volcanic forges excavated by the Cyclopes in and around Etna, which are presided over by Vulcan: cf. I.xi.44, and *Aeneid*, VIII.416ff. Spenser implicitly invokes the chaotic rebellious power associated with volcanoes: I.vii.8–10n. The smiths are deformed in part because Vulcan himself was deformed (Hesiod, *Theogony*, 571, the limping god); and the bellows recall images of the devil with bellows fanning the flames of avarice (Chew, 329, n.19) as well as the bellows which fan the flames of discord or strife (*ibid.*). The sprinkling of water on fire (st. 36) parodies the emblem of temperance already encountered and is a further reminder of discord (v.2–14n.). The whole scene contrasts with the orderly kitchen in Alma's castle (ix.29–32n.); so that Mammon's forge is literally the belly or appetitive centre of the avaricious man. Guyon rejects this display with vigorous contempt or disdain (*mesprise*)) – a Saturnian–Martian action (st. 14n.) that is corrct here but as an habitual extreme characteristic is wrong, as the following embodiment of Disdayne warns him.

40–3 The giant Disdayne is described again at VI.vii.41–4, where he is 'sib to great *Orgoglio*', fierce, and carrying an iron club. On the battle of the Titans/Giants against the Olympian gods, see I.vii.8–10n.; and on the infernal and Martian iron, see I.v.20n. and Agrippa, I.xxvii, 58. His 'sterne . . . looke' links him with Huddibras's 'sterne melancholy' (ii.17). He guards the entrance to ambitious Philotime's palatial room: Guyon enters but abstains, rejecting Saturnian disdain and the false honour offered by Philotime (Greek, love of honour). Guyon's rejection symbolises his moral distance from the vainglorious Braggadocchio; and the episode as a whole contrasts with Belphoebe's praise of true honour at iii.40–1.

44–50 Philotime recalls Lucifera at I.iv.6ff.; and cf. Prays-desire at II.ix.36–9n. The reference to 'glory' in st. 44 together with Guyon's affirmation of his vow 'to other Lady' (st. 50) confirms her as a parody of Gloriana. Rathborne, 7–10 notes that Augustine, *City of God*, V.xii quotes Sallust to the effect that ambition is superior to greed because it is nearer to virtue (the pursuit of true honour): hence Guyon moves from the temptation to greed to that of ambition. Philotime has fallen (st. 45, 49), like Lucifer (I.iv.8–10n.), and now, like Acrasia, exerts her power through artifice (xii.50n.), deceiving the senses rather than being an earthly image of divine beauty. The crowds surrounding her perhaps recall the milling crowds in Dante, *Inferno*, III, and the souls waiting to be ferried across the Styx at *Aeneid*, VI.305ff. Spenser explains her golden chain as 'Ambition' at st. 46; inevitably suggesting the chain in *Iliad*, VIII (see I.v.25–6n.), usually interpreted as the chain of cosmic concord; though in, e.g., Comes, *Mythologiae*, II.iv, it is interpreted in part as avarice or ambition (Lemmi in *Var. Sp.*, II.261). Spenser gives us a horrifying vision of Elizabeth's own court, potentially an image of ideal order, as actually inhabited by self-seeking time-servers (compare the disillusioned reference in st. i of *Prothalamion*). The chain or scale of nature emanating from God through his love, each link or step bound to its neighbour again by love (cf. *Paradise Lost*, V.469ff.) is here grotesquely inverted. Instead of a movement from earth to heaven, flesh to spirit, these courtiers achieve an apparent ascent which is a spiritual and moral descent. The golden chain was traditionally conflated with Jacob's ladder (see I.x.5n.). Panofsky, *Studies in Iconology*, 143n. notes Pico della Mirandola's comparison of the stages of love to the rungs of Jacob's ladder. Finally, a ladder was sometimes associated with Fortune: if she smiled on you you climbed it with ease; if she frowned, you fell off (Chew, 52, citing Robert Allott, *Wits Theater of the Little World* (1599), fol. 219^v–220^r).

51–2 The Garden of Proserpina, queen of the underworld (cf. I.i.37n.), is a dark antithesis to Phaedria's island and Acrasia's Bower, and derives from the grove of Persephone (Proserpina's

Greek name) in *Odyssey*, X.508ff., and from the garden with a tree
which has gold-gleaming branches which Pluto offers Proserpina in
Claudian's *De raptu Proserpinae*, II.285ff. The deadly and
poisonous plants remind us of the identification of Proserpina with
Hecate, patroness of poisons (Lotspeich, 67); but the atmosphere is
also appropriately Saturnian, for to Saturn were dedicated the
cypress, hellebore, opium, 'and those things which stupifie, . . . and
those which bring forth berries of a dark colour, and black fruit'
(Agrippa, I.xxv,56). Individually, the plants offer a deceptive
combination of deadly poisons and antidotes to Saturnian
melancholy. Cypress is used by the witch Canidia in a spell
(Horace, *Epodes*, V.18); the 'sleep bringing poppy' (*Aeneid*,
IV.486, where it is given to the dragon guarding the golden apples
of the Hesperides: see st. 54) yields the Saturnian opium and is an
emblem of Night and Death (Wind, 165); the black hellebore is
Saturnian since 'it is good against all Diseases proceeding from
Melancholy': it is, however, 'a very dangerous purge' (Salmon,
London Dispensatory, I.i,8); coloquintida is 'cold' because 'it
purgeth all tough clammy humours, choler, flegm, melancholy'
(*ibid.*, I.vi,131); tetra is perhaps *tetrum solanum* (deadly
nightshade; Latin *taeter* = offensive, hideous): Upton in *Var. Sp.*,
II.262; 'mortal Samnitis' is, Upton suggests (*Var. Sp.*, II.263), the
Sabina or Savine, so called by Spenser perhaps in error, since the
Samnites were an offshoot tribe of the Sabines. It is 'mortal'
because it procures abortions (Salmon, *ibid.*, I.iv,98). Socrates died
by drinking cicuta, i.e. hemlock (Plato, *Phaedo*). Critias had been a
pupil of Socrates but was later his enemy (Smith, I.892–3) and
Spenser confuses him with Crito, the friend who was present at his
trial and death (see Plato's *Phaedo* and *Crito*). For a more
elaborate explanation, see A. Kent Hieatt, *Chaucer, Spenser,
Milton,* appendix D. Socrates was familiar in the Renaissance as a
type of Christ: his condemnation to death by fellow Athenians was
seen traditionally as a prefiguring of Christ's death (Lewalski,
Milton's Brief Epic, 240), a tradition Spenser takes advantage of
(see st. 62). In this Saturnian Garden Guyon is to undergo the
Saturnian temptation to forbidden knowledge.

53–4 The seat, which Guyon is invited to sit upon in st. 63 (it is
silver because this is a lunar metal, and Proserpina is an aspect of
the moon goddess: Agrippa, I.xxiv,54; Fowler, 82), is probably the

seat to which Theseus was bound for attempting to ravish
Proserpina (see I.v.35n.). In one tradition it was known as the chair
of forgetfulness, to which Theseus had been committed for
presuming to know occult matters (Pausanias, *Description of
Greece*, X.xxix.9; Kermode, 74–5). There is a link, too, as Upton
suggested (*Var. Sp.*, II.268–9), with the Eleusinian mysteries, the
ancient initiatory rites based on the Ceres–Proserpina myth (see st.
63n.), in which there was a forbidden seat which derived from the
stone on which the mourning Ceres sat as she wandered in search
of her lost daughter near Eleusis (Smith, II.509): the suppliant was
not permitted to sit on the seat for fear that he should seem to be
blasphemously imitating Ceres. In refusing to sit on the seat in st.
63, therefore, Guyon rejects sloth (cf. I.v.35), refuses to succumb to
a Phaedria-like moral laxity (canto vi), and rejects the Saturnian
temptation to forbidden knowledge, an extension and perversion of
the traditional Saturnian gifts of 'sublime contemplation &
profound understanding' (Agrippa, III.xxxviii, 466). Aeneas
acquired divine knowledge from Anchises, however: see st. 21–5n.
The golden apples are said by Spenser to be the origin of those
given by Earth to Juno when she married Jove and guarded by the
daughters of Atlas and Hesperis and a dragon. It was Hercules's
eleventh labour to obtain these apples. They were interpreted by,
e.g., Comes, *Mythologiae*, VII.vii as wealth; but in this context
their common identification with the alchemical Magnum Opus or
Great Work is appropriate as a symbol of arcane knowledge
verging on blasphemy (M. Caron and S. Hutin, *The Alchemists*
(1961), 135). Atalanta's apples were also Hesperidean. She
promised to marry the man who could defeat her in a foot-race.
Meilanion of Euboea (or, in some versions, Hippomenes) beat her
by dropping before her three Hesperidean apples which Venus had
given him and which Atalanta stopped to pick up. The couple were
metamorphosed into lions for Meilanion's failure to thank Venus
for the apples and for desecrating the shrine of Cybele (*Met.*,
X.560ff.). The notion of blasphemous transgression of the divine is
explicit here.

55–6 Acontius, in love with Cydippe, and in Diana's temple,
threw an apple before her on which he had written 'I swear by the
sanctuary of Diana to marry Acontius'. She read the words out
(thus pledging herself) but ignored the vow, though it had been

heard by Diana (Ovid, *Heroides*, XX, XXI). At XX.237–40
Acontius promised to offer up a *golden* image of the apple at their
marriage; and at XXI.123–4 Cydippe compares herself to
Atalanta. The tale again involves blasphemy. In the second tale,
Spenser has Ate (see iv.37–42n.) displace Eris, goddess of discord,
in the Judgement of Paris: in annoyance at not being invited to the
marriage of Peleus and Thetis, Eris threw down among the guests a
golden apple inscribed 'to the fairest'. The deities started squabbling
over who was meant and Paris was asked to judge on Mount Ida
between the three quarreling finalists, Juno, Minerva, and Venus.
Each goddess promised a bribe – Juno, riches and sovereignty in
Asia; Minerva, wisdom; Venus, the gift of the beautiful Helen,
betrothed to Menelaus of Sparta. Paris awarded the apple to
Venus, abducted Helen, and took her to Troy. From this the Trojan
War began. The traditional charge against Paris is that of lust
(Lotspeich, 97); but the myth probably relates to Spenser's
Neoplatonic conception of self-transcendence and the
reconciliation of opposites (iii.21–30n.), the point being in this
connection that one goddess alone should not have been preferred.
Instead, Paris should have aimed for the uniting of power, wisdom,
and beauty in an ultimate fusion (Wind, 82–3, 197–8, 270–1). A
well-known picture at Hampton Court of 1569 shows Elizabeth
receiving the apple as the goddess who does unite all these qualities
(*ibid.*, 83; Yates, 63, plate 9a). On Cocytus, see I.i.37n.

57–60 Tantalus's punishment was for revealing the divine secrets
entrusted to him by Jove; for stealing food from the table of the
gods; or for cutting his son Pelops into pieces and offering them to
the gods as a feast (Smith, III.974). Lotspeich, 110 notes a
reference to Jove being entertained by Tantalus in Comes,
Mythologiae, VI.xviii. The myth was often read as a simple emblem
of covetousness (e.g., Whitney, *Emblemes*, 74); but Guyon's
reference to his 'mind intemperate' and the fact that he contrives to
blaspheme (st. 60) confirm Spenser's reading of him here as a
further instance of blasphemous presumption.

61–2 Pilate is the ultimate unjust judge. The Biblical bases for
this passage are John 18:36–8, where Jesus tells Pilate that his
'kingdome is not of this worlde' and that he has come to earth 'that
I shulde beare witnes unto the trueth: everie one that is of the
trueth, heareth my voyce'. Pilate replies 'What is trueth?' (Geneva

gloss: 'This was a mocking and disdeineful question'); and
Matthew 27:24: Pilate 'toke water and wasshed his hands before
the multitude, saying, I am innocent of the blood of this just man'.
Guyon's temptations in the Garden which always implicitly, and at
least once explicitly, involve the problem of right judgement (Paris,
who also judges the gods, st. 55) culminate in a vision of the man
who decided against divine truth and is therefore also the ultimate
blasphemer. His ineffectual washing looks back to Ruddymane's
baptism at ii.3–4 and is a reminder that virtuous action must
complement baptism, which in itself does not efface original sin.
Murder, godlessness, perjury, and impiety are relevant
Saturnian–Martian characteristics embodied in Pilate and rejected
by Guyon (Ptolemy, *Tetrabiblos*, III.xiii,343).

63   On the seat, see st. 53–4n. The temptation to take 'that same
fruit of gold' alludes to the Ceres–Proserpina myth. Proserpina was
abducted by Pluto and taken to Hades. Jove promised to grant
Ceres's request that her daughter should be returned to her
provided that she had not tasted anything in hell. But she had
already wandered into the gardens there and eaten seven seeds
from a pomegranate [*pomum*] she had picked from a bough (*Met.*,
V.533ff.). Jove finally agreed, however, that she should spend half
the year with Ceres and half with Pluto. By refusing Mammon's
offer Guyon avoids Proserpina's underworld fate; or, in
astrological terms, he rejects the ultimate Saturnian–Martian
temptation of eating forbidden food (Ptolemy, *Tetrabiblos*,
III.xiii,343).

65–6   The three days allude to Jonah as well as Christ (Matthew
12:40: 'as Jonas was thre dayes, and thre nights in the whales
bellie: so shal the Sonne of man be thre dayes and thre nights in the
heart of the earth'), and also to the two nights and a day permitted
in the mysteries for the descent to the underworld (Plutarch, *De
genio Socratis*, 590A–B). This was generally agreed by
commentators to be the 'permitted time' granted to Aeneas
(*Aeneid*, VI.537). Guyon's 'deadly fit' is a demonstration of his
fallen nature, as the opening stanzas of canto viii indicate: he has
explored his subterranean, fallen, self, expressed symbolically in
Mammon and his cave as that tendency Saturn has to make a man
a 'daemon' or 'a fiend in hell, [his soul put] into a direfull hellish
purgatory by a cynicall meditation' (T. Walkington, *The Optick*

Glasse of Humors (1607), 64, cit. Klibansky, 250, n.23). He falls to the earth which is his and Adam's origin (and cf. iv.16–17n.) as a gesture of self-abasement, recognising the full extent of his fallen depravity. But recognition of spiritual deformity leaves one receptive to grace, which now comes to redeem him. Contrast the 'grace' already offered by the blasphemous Mammon at st. 18 (and cf. st. 32–3 and 50).

CANTO VIII

1–2 Man is matter but also spirit, and so an angel comes down, as angels came to Christ after his ordeal in the wilderness, 'to comforte him ' (Geneva gloss on Matthew 4:11). Guyon's angel signifies the free gift of grace: compare Hebrews 1:14: angels are 'all ministring spirits, sent forthe to minister, for their sakes which shalbe heires of salvation'. We recall that Guyon has refused forbidden food, and so Matthew 6 (the Biblical context of the Phaedria–Mammon temptations) comes to mind, especially verses 31–3: 'Therefore take no thoght, saying, What shal we eat? or what shal we drinke? ... (For after all these things seke the Gentiles) for your heavenlie Father knoweth, that ye have nede of all these things. But seke ye first the kingdome of God, and his righteousnes, & all these things shalbe ministred unto you'. The 'silver bowers' are the celestial answer to the infernal 'silver stoole' (vii.63), just as the 'golden pineons', bringing spiritual succour, are to the golden fruit.

3–6 The prudent and Saturnian Palmer (i.7n.) returns as a timely reminder of the benefits of a benign Saturn, who instead of making you a 'daemon' can make you an angel, your 'soule ... wrapt up into an Elysium and paradise of blesse by a heavenly contemplation' (Walkington, *Optick Glasse*, ref. in vii.65–6n.; and see I.x.46–63n.). Because the angel is a manifestation of divine love he is described as a celestial Cupid, son of Venus Urania (see I Proem 3 and 4n.; and Panofsky, *Studies in Iconology*, 101–2 for the tradition of the adolescent Cupid, sometimes identified with the Christian angels; he is the opposite of the wanton, blindfold Cupid: *ibid.*, 125ff., 142–3). Venus frequented Mount Ida (*Aeneid*, XII.411–12). The multicoloured wings are a detail from the profane Cupid as described in E.K.'s gloss to *Shepheardes Calender*, 'March', 79. On the Graces, see I.i.48n.; according to some traditions they were Venus's daughters (Starnes and Talbert, 89–90). The angel's 'tender bud' beginning 'to blossome' contrasts him with the flowering but corrupt Mordant at i.41 and Verdant at xii.79. Mordant died, leaving Ruddymane; Guyon will revive through redeeming grace; Verdant will be liberated by Guyon and the Palmer.

9 Compare and contrast the Palmer's reaction here with that of Braggadocchio and Trompart to Archimago's disappearance at iii.19.

10–15 As a pagan answer to the angel, Cymochles and Pyrochles return 'as bright as skie' (st. 10): the warring passions try to reassert themselves as the body slumbers. They were last seen in canto vi, where Archimago restored Pyrochles (st. 47–51n.): contrast Guyon, who will now reawaken with the assurance of divine grace to assist his understanding and reason in controlling his passions.

16 Pyrochles threatens Guyon's body with the ultimate indignity of being left to birds of prey: cf. 1 Samuel 17:44, 46 (David against Goliath).

17–18 Paralleling his delivery of Redcrosse in I.viii, Arthur arrives to rescue Guyon again in canto viii. On Arthur, see I.vii.29n. He rides on a Libyan steed probably as a reminder of crusades in Africa against the infidel (Chaucer's knight has undertaken these: *General Prologue*, 62–3): it is a North African (Barbary) horse.

20–1 'Medaewart' is, Upton suggests (*Var. Sp.*, II.274–5), the 'wort' (or herb) known as *medica* which, appropriately, 'heals wounds' (Salmon, *Dispensatory*, I.iv,76) and so presumably acts as a charm against injury on behalf of the user of the sword. On Etna, see vii.35–9n. Seven is a good number for use in purification: '*Apuleius* saith, and I put my self forthwith into the bath of the Sea, to be purified, and put my head seven times under the Waves' (Agrippa, II.x,196, also citing 2 Kings 5:10 on the purification of the leper); while the dipping in the Styx, which gives it mortal power (see I.i.37n.), echoes *Aeneid*, XII.90–1 ('Vulcan had made the sword for Turnus's father, Daunus, and dipped it white-hot into the Styx'). There is a parody of this at v.18–24n.; and see v.2–14n. for the tempering of metal as an emblem of temperance. See also I.vii.30n. on Arthur's sword.

22–3 Pyrochles rises as a pagan parody of a wrathful Guyon, armed with his shield, asserting himself with Arthur's sword against the grace that could save him. Arthur is met with Saturnian–Martian sternness and disdain; reactions that, when intended discourteously, Guyon has purged through entering Mammon's cave (vii.35–9n., 40–3n.).

28–9 'Dayes-man' = mediator (literally, one employed for duty on a particular day). Both stanzas follow Exodus 20:5: 'I am the Lord thy God, a jelouse God, visiting the iniquitie of the fathers upon the children'. 'Nephewes sonne' = great-grandson. The brothers, swearing pagan oaths ('by *Termagaunt*', st. 30; 'By *Mahoune*', st. 33: cf. VI.vii.47), embody the Old Testament ethic of revenge that had been characteristic of the Sans-brothers in Book I.

32 On the shield, see v.6n. As an external embodiment of Guyon's temperance it cannot protect intemperance.

33–53 The battle for Guyon's soul goes on within and above him. Obviously Arthur will win: the fundamental intemperate impulses can be overcome by understanding, reason, will, and grace. Guyon will awaken as the Christian temperate man, redeemed, as Cullen, 92 says, from the flesh (the earlier cantos of the book had tested the limits of the classical view of temperance. Grace steps in where man fails.) Arthur fights without obvious supernatural aid. His shield remains covered (st. 38), he uses Guyon's sword (st. 40); in the same way, Christ came as man to redeem mankind (Maurice Evans, 'The Fall of Guyon', *E.L.H.*, XXVIII (1961)). Arthur's side-wound, too (st. 38–9), recalls Christ's similar wound at the crucifixion (I.viii.10n.; Hamilton, 99). Arthur is compared to the solar lion (st. 40), also an emblem of mercy (Agrippa, I.xxiii, 53, who notes that all magnanimous and courageous animals are solar), and to the solar bull (st. 42) and eagle (st. 50): on both see Agrippa, *ibid.*; and on Arthur's solar role, see I.vii.29n. Pyrochles, at his final capture in st. 50, manifests Saturnian–Martian 'disdaine', 'rancour', and 'sad melancholy': extreme and out of place here, and to be contrasted with the morally justifiable wrath and disdain associated with Arthur in st. 42.

52 Pyrochles's 'use thy fortune' echoes Turnus's last speech to Aeneas (XII.932), 'enjoy your good fortune'. Arthur kills him as Aeneas killed Turnus; appropriately, since Turnus has just embodied the madness of anger (XII.101ff.). Allen, 139 cites Fulgentius's interpretation of Turnus as 'violent mind'.

CANTO IX

Guyon, fully temperate, explores the temperate body, traditionally seen as a temple or building. The tradition is Biblical (e.g., 1 Corinthians 6:19, 'your bodie is ye temple of the holie Gost') and classical, deriving from Plato (*Timaeus*, *Republic*); and it receives full treatment in Vitruvius's *Ten Books on Architecture* (*c.* 20 B.C.), III.i, which relates the proportions of the body to the proportions of ancient temples. The implications this had for Renaissance architectural theory are discussed by R. Wittkower, *Architectural Principles in the Age of Humanism* (1962). See also Panofsky, *Meaning in the Visual Arts*, ch. II, and Leonard Barkan, *Nature's Work of Art*. In the Renaissance, and following Pythagoras and Plato, the proportions governing the basic musical intervals were often regarded as governing the cosmos, the temperate human body, the soul, and, ideally and in certain instances, architecture. Hence the architectural imagery in Book II (e.g., i.57–8n., iii.28, xii.1). The idea of the *castle* of the body is a commonplace in medieval romance and religious works, though it too goes back to Plato (e.g., *Timaeus*, 70). Medina's castle embodied the basic problem of reason controlling the warring passions in Aristotelian terms (canto ii); Alma's castle exemplifies Christian temperance achieved in the face of original sin (the besieging forces of Maleger). It appears in canto ix because nine is the number of the soul (see st. 22n.), the meaning of Alma's name (st. 18–19n.).

3–4 Compare i.27–8n., and I.vii.30n. for the morning star.

6 Arthegall is important in Book III and is the titular knight of Book V. Sophy (Greek *sophia*, wisdom) is not mentioned again.

7 On Arthur's vision of Gloriana, whom he is pursuing, see

I.ix.13–15n. The 1590 text has Arthur's quest lasting seven years ('Seven times the Sunne'); 1596 changes this to one year.

12–16 The enemies – temptations embodying the seven deadly sins and attacks on the five senses – are described in detail in canto xi. They have besieged Alma's castle for seven years – the number of mortality and mutability, as Upton noted (*Var. Sp.*, II. 284; and see headnote to I.vii). Spenser also draws on his experiences as later recounted in his *View of the Present State of Ireland*. On the gnats simile, cf. I.i.23n. The cloud implies moral blindness; and the gnats/besiegers are overcome by being 'in the *Ocean* cast' because Maleger, their leader, will be conquered when Arthur throws him into water (xi.46). The north was associated with evil (iii.19n.); but the implied equation of Arthur and Guyon and the north wind might allude to, e.g., Ezekiel 26:7, God's vengeance upon Tyrus, because it rejoiced in the destruction of Jerusalem, by Nebuchadnezzar, 'a King of Kings from the North'.

18–19 Alma = soul (Italian), and she represents the rational soul (see st. 27n.) which 'includes the powers, and performs the duties of the two other, which are contained in it, and all three faculties make one *soul*, which is inorganical of itself, although it be in all parts, and incorporeal, using their organs, and working by them' (Burton, *Anatomy*, I.i.2.9, *ed.cit.*, 144). On the meaning of *alma* see also xi.2n. Her description again combines elements of virginal purity with Venerean attributes. On the white robe, compare I.x.12–13n. and I.xii.21–3n.; the pearl is dedicated to Diana–Luna (Agrippa, I.xxiv,54), and was also an emblem of beauty, as was the lily: Gilbert, *Symbolic Persons*, 249, and Ripa, 42. The 'yellow golden heare' is Venerean, as is the rose garland (I.x.29–31n., II.iii.21–30n.); but the hair is 'trimly woven' to suggest chastity (cf. Medina, ii.12–20n.). Alma represents the reconciliation of opposites as self-transcendence like the Dianan–Venerean Belphoebe, and Venus and Diana as moderating and mediating planets between Saturnian and Martian extremes (vii.1–2n., and Wind, 119, citing Ficino on Plotinus's *De amore*, identifying Venus with the soul).

21 Ninus and Semiramis were mythical founders of the Assyrian empire (I.v.48n.); she was supposed to have founded Babylon, which was situated adjacent to the tower of Babel (Smith,

III.776–7). Pagan history traditionally began with Ninus (Rathborne, 74n.). The Biblical account of the tower, to which Spenser alludes, is Genesis 11:3: 'thei had brycke for stone, and slyme had they in steade of morter'. Spenser's slime is *Egyptian* perhaps in allusion to the fertile Nile mud (I.i.21n.) or to the connection of Egypt with the passions (I.v.18n.). The tower of Babel was an emblem of human pride; as a punishment for building it God scattered mankind 'upon all the earth': previously there had been one language, now there was confusion of tongues (Genesis 11:1–9). Spenser also recalls the making of man from dust and his return to dust (cf. Genesis 2:7). The Babel myth is about fragmentation; the subject of this canto is the unified body and soul.

22   Spenser's mythological and astrological images of temperance yield to an ideal geometrical and numerical description. On the numerological tradition he draws upon, see Introduction to Book I. The 'frame' (= building, also constitution of the body) is composed of circle, square (quadrate), and triangle. Initially, these describe the physical shape of the body: head, torso, and the legs outstretched to form a triangle; but the figures are also symbolic. The circle is the emblem of perfection and eternity (e.g., Puttenham, *Arte of English Poesie*, II.xii) and so symbolises man's incorporeal nature; the triangle represents the imperfect body since it is geometrically 'most imperfect, and includes least space' (whereas the circle is 'the most perfect and most capacious' figure): Sir Kenelm Digby, *Observations on the 22. Stanza in the 9th Canto of the 2d. Book of Spencers Faery Queen* (1644; reprinted in *Var. Sp.*, II.472–78). The difficulty, as Digby noted, in geometrical terms is to join, or proportion, these incommensurate figures (a problem which was, however, solved by Archimedes by using a right-angled triangle: Fowler, 269. On the right angle as a symbol of reason, see i.57–8n.). The circle is perfect and masculine, the triangle imperfect and feminine, following the Pythagorean–Platonic view that the masculine is good, the feminine bad. In addition, the Pythagorean–Platonic tradition had it that the universe sprang from odd and even, male and female, numbers. The 'quadrate' is at once the material 'base' of the body, the four elements and humours, 'viz. *Choler, Blood, Phleme,* and *Melancholy*' (Digby, 475), and also the square of virtue (see i.57–8n.). In its former role it was corporeal; in its latter role, incorporeal (Fowler, 278). Furthermore, as Upton recognised (*Var. Sp.*, II.479), it might allude to the Pythagorean *tetractys* – the adding together of the first four digits $(1 + 2 + 3 + 4)$ to make 10: since ten was the number of perfection and completion this formula was regarded as embodying the fundamental musical and numerical principles of the universe; and since ten marks the return to the divine one, it is also circular (e.g., Agrippa, II.xiii). Finally, if the circle is the most capacious figure and the triangle the least capacious, then the square is literally 'twixt them both'.

Spenser uses seven in this stanza as the number of the mortal body (Macrobius, *Dream of Scipio*, I.vi.62–82: 'seven is the number by which man is conceived, developed in the womb, is born, lives and is sustained'; tr. Stahl, 112; and see I.vii headnote); while nine is the number of the mind and spirit (there are nine orders of angels, which correlate with the soul's nine senses, four inward and five outer: Memory, Cogitative, Imaginative, Commonsense, Hearing, Seeing, Smelling, Tasting, Touching: e.g., Agrippa, II.xii,208–9). There are, too, nine spheres in the Ptolemaic system; so nine is 'the circle set in heavens place' because the ninth sphere is the primum mobile, the celestial sphere. The quadrate or square is 'proportioned' by seven and nine, since $7 + 9 = 4^2$. The 'diapase' (= musical octave) is 'goodly' because it was a circular symbol of perfection, its first and last notes sounding together in unison. As such it sums up Spenser's ultimate vision of temperance as the coincidence of opposites and, at the same time, his Aristotelian notion of virtue as a mean between extremes, since eight is the arithmetic mean between seven and nine (hence they are 'compacted' into the diapason, eight). Lastly, the diapason governed the relationship between rational, irascible, and concupiscible. Agrippa was by no means alone in arguing that: 'As the Consonancy of the body consists of a due measure and proportion of the members: so the consonancy of the minde of a due temperament, and proportion of its vertues and operations which are concupiscible, irascible, and reason, which are so proportioned together. For Reason to Concupiscence hath the proportion *Diapason*; but to Anger *Diatessaron* [a fourth]: and Irascible to Concupiscible hath the proportion *Diapente* [a fifth]' (II.xxviii,277. In music the intervals of a fifth and fourth make up an octave).

23–6 The 'two gates' are the mouth and anal passage (see st. 32). The porch is the upper lip (see *Var. Sp.*, II.290 for Todd's note on the valuable marbles found in Cork), the portcullis is the nose. The vine and ivy can only be a moustache; but in this composite emblem of temperance they are also the attributes of Bacchus here rendered harmless (v.29n., xii.54n.). The barbican (watch-tower) has the porter of the tongue within it, which observes temperance with respect to speech; the 'warders' are the thirty-two teeth. Spenser elaborates on an already – to our eyes – grotesquely elaborate tradition: see Barkan, *Nature's Work of Art*, ch. III, esp. 154ff.

27 The journey through the body is a hierarchical ascent, following the Platonic division into belly (st. 27–32), 'breast, where is the heart, the seat of life' (st. 33–44), and 'head, in which the Intellect grows' (st. 45–60): quoted from Agrippa, II.vi,182, whose scheme comes ultimately from Plato's *Timaeus*, 69–73, where in the belly is the appetite for food and drink and the heart is the seat of courage. Compare, too, Burton, *Anatomy*, I.i.2.4. The three souls – vegetable, sensitive and rational – are implied as well. The vegetable, which man shares with the plants, is characterised by nourishment (which includes digestion and expulsion) – the aspect emphasised by Spenser here – and by growth and generation; the sensitive, shared by beasts, apprehends and moves (see st. 33–5n.); the rational 'is divided into two chief parts ... the *understanding*, [and] the *will*' (Burton, I.i.2.9, 144; and see st. 18–19n.).

29–32 'Mongiball' (Mongibello) is the Sicilian name for Etna; note the contrast with Mammon's furnace at vii.35–9n. Galen, *On the Natural Faculties*, III.vii mentions Etna in connection with the idea that digestion is similar to a boiling process. The 'Port Esquiline' is the anus: criminals were executed on the Esquiline in Rome, where there were also paupers' graves (Horace, *Epodes*, V.99–100 on the wolves and birds that haunt it, and *Satires*, I.viii.10ff.).

33–5 From the vegetable soul, Spenser moves to the sensitive soul. It is characterised by apprehending and moving faculties. To deal with the latter first: this causes external bodily movements and (Spenser's concern here) inward motion. It also includes appetite, under which come the concupiscible and irascible powers (Burton,

I.i.2.8). Anatomically, Alma's 'goodly Parlour' is the heart, 'the seat and organ of all passions and affections' (Burton, I.i.2.4, 133). Venerean–concupiscible preoccupations are the subject of st. 34 and the beginning of st. 35: note that Cupid has joined in the concupiscible power's quest for the 'pleasant and delightsome' (Burton, I.i.2.8, 141) by laying aside his bow, as at I Proem 3n.; while the rest of st. 35 depicts the irascible faculty in terms of Martian–Saturnian characteristics – annoyance, grief, etc. (compare Wrath at I.iv.35, who is followed by 'fretting griefe'; the gnawing of a rush as a sign of frustration is illuminated by *Var. Sp.*, II.293–4, which notes an instance of Henry II's extreme anger leading him to gnaw the rushes on the floor). These stanzas look back to the opposition of Elissa–Huddibras and Perissa–Sansloy at ii.12–20n. and, in terms of the book's larger structure, embody in little the extremes of Saturnian–Martian Mammon (e.g., vii.14n.) and Venerean Phaedria and Acrasia.

The tapestries on the walls of the parlour depict simple things ('easie to be thought', st. 33): i.e., these are simple impressions, and this takes us back to the apprehending faculty of the sensitive soul. Spenser alludes to the fact that perception is under the control of this faculty. But the apprehending faculty once more has two parts, outward and inward; and here Spenser allegorises the outward part which operates through the five outward senses and which 'have their object in outward things only, and such as are present, as the eye sees no colour except it be at hand, the ear no sound' (Burton, I.i.2.6, 137). The inward part comprises common sense (reason), phantasy (imagination) and memory: these are examined in detail at st. 48ff. and the wall decorations there are far more elaborate to show that we have moved beyond mere external sense impressions.

36–9 Prays-desire, who carries the poplar, emblem of Hercules, type of heroic virtue (v.31n.), is the root of Arthur's quest for Gloriana. The urges which impel him are heroic yet painful (his sense of the impossibility of fulfilling his quest), and Prays-desire embodies in yet another way the problem of the relationship of Saturn and Mars (sadness, disdain, rashness) to knightly courtesy and heroism (ii.12–20n.; vii.35–9n.; viii.33–53n.). The search for honour involves disdain and anger, but they must be tempered to accord with external circumstances. In confirmation of the parallel between Alma's castle and Mammon's cave, Prays-desire contrasts with Philotime. Her purple and gold signify social position and hence, again, desire for glory (according to Ripa, 202 Honour or Glory (*Honore*) is dressed in purple because it is the royal colour and sign of the highest honour. It is also a symbol of temperance, since it is produced by a just mingling of red and blue: *ibid.*, 480).

40–3 Guyon confronts the fountain of his own moral nature, Modesty or Shamefastness, the fear of performing a dishonourable or unworthy act, and the first of the parts of temperance according to the influential Macrobius (*Dream of Scipio*, I.viii.7, ed. Stahl, 122). Duessa has parodied modesty earlier (II.i.14–15n.); Shamefastness and Modesty reappear in the Temple of Venus at IV.x.50–1. We now see this virtue in its extreme and pre-social form. Modesty is usually described as a woman dressed in white, gazing at the ground, and accompanied by a turtle-dove (e.g., Ripa, 420). On the symbolism of blue, see I.x.14n.: another instance of Spenser's modification of traditional iconography. 'Castory' is a red substance obtained from the beaver. The bird has caused interpretative problems: Fowler, *E.C.*, XI (1961), 235–8 argues for the traditional dove; whereas earlier commentators suggested the jynx, the cuckoo, or owl: *Var. Sp.*, II.295–6. Spenser's phrasing might recall *Met.*, II.589ff., the tale of Nyctimene who seduced her father and was changed by Athena into an owl: 'though she is now a bird she still, conscious of her guilt, flees the light and the sight of men, hiding her shame in darkness'. But whether we take 'dight' as 'treat' or 'clothe', no one has yet satisfactorily suggested how Pan comes into it, unless he is just a synonym for 'Nature'.

44–5 The tour of Alma's castle reaches its climax in the head. In terms of the divisions of the soul (see st. 27n., 33–5n.), this is the inward part of the apprehending faculty of the sensitive soul: its three parts are explored at st. 48ff. As Upton suggested (*Var. Sp.*, II.297), the 'ten steps' signify completion and perfection (see st. 22n.). The turret is a symbolic analogue to the mount of contemplation at I.x.46–63n. Thebes was built by Cadmus, and its acropolis was known as the Cadmea. Alexander the Great totally destroyed Thebes in 335 B.C.; Hector's son, Astyanax, was thrown from the battlements of Troy by the Greeks to prevent him fulfilling a decree that he would restore the Trojan kingdom (*Met.*, XIII.415–17: 'Astyanax was hurled from those towers where he often sat watching his father fighting'). The use of gilding in Trojan architecture is mentioned in *Aeneid*, II.448.

48 Socrates was judged by Phoebus Apollo's oracle at Delphi to be the wisest man alive (Plato, *Apology of Socrates*, 21A); the 'sage *Pylian* syre' is Nestor, son of Neleus and Chloris of Pylos, who advised the Greeks during the Trojan War (Priam was king of Troy). For his longevity, see *Iliad*, I.250–2; *Met.*, XII.187–8.

49–58 Two of the men are named, the first at st. 52 (Phantastes), the third at st. 58 (Eumnestes = good memory). The second is identified as the reason at st. 54. We are now in the brain; and Spenser divides the mental faculties into three in accordance with the common medieval and contemporary scheme: front ventricle (or *cellula phantastica*), home of the imagination or phantasy; middle-brain (*cellula logistica*), home of the reason; the cold and dry back ventricle, where the memory is located (Klibansky, 68–9, 91ff., 265n.). Further, Spenser correlates these with the three parts of time and of prudence (see i.7n. and vii.1–2n.): Phantastes corresponds to foresight, reason with intelligence, while Eumnestes is memory. In Titian's well-known mid-sixteenth-century *Allegory of Prudence*, with its motto 'From [knowledge of] the past, the present acts prudently so as not to ruin future action', the notion is embodied in the familiar way by three human faces: that of an old man facing left (memory, the past), that of a middle-aged man painted full-face (intelligence, the present), and that of a young man facing right (foresight, the future): Panofsky, *Meaning in the Visual Arts*, ch. IV. Time himself is described by, e.g., Abraham Fraunce as follows: 'His face had three severall semblances: his browe and eyes resembling middle age; his mouth and cheekes youth; his bearde, olde age' (*The Third Part of the Countess of Pembroke's Ivy-church* (1592), 58^v–59^r).

Spenser's Phantastes–future–foresight is explicitly Saturnian, physically (dark, melancholic, etc.: see Klibansky, 290) and mentally (Saturn creates deep thinkers, and those who are superstitious and mad: Ptolemy, *Tetrabiblos*, III.xiii,341). At this point Saturnian astrological characteristics fuse with the usual descriptions of the phantasy, even down to the flies as symbols of delusion and idle notions (cf. I.i.36n., and cf., too, the quotation there from Burton on the phantasy being free in sleep and conceiving 'strange . . . shapes'). A centaur is half man, half horse;

a hippodame is a sea-horse (Spenser's mistake for hippocamp). The plenitude of Phantastes's imaginings also suggests the traditional notion that man contains all that is present in the external world (Marvell, 'The Garden', st. vi; Barkan, *Nature's Work of Art*, 28ff.). But Phantastes embodies an agonised and malign Saturn (see Fowler, 289–91 on 'house of agonyes', and Chaucer's *Knight's Tale*, 2450ff. on Saturn's evil influence), so that he complements psychologically what the equally Saturnian and malign Mammon represents in terms of appetite. Like Mammon, Phantastes is extreme and must be controlled; by itself, the imagination literally runs riot. And he is controlled when he operates as here in conjunction with reason and memory. His counterpart in the third room is also Saturnian, since Saturn is the god of old age and good memory (Curry, *Chaucer and the Mediaeval Sciences*, 129; Klibansky, 35n.; vii.1–2n.). Burton says that '*Memory* lays up all the species which the senses have brought in, and records them as a good *register*, that they may be forth-coming when they are called for by *phantasy* and *reason*' (*Anatomy*, I.i.2.7, *ed.cit.*, 140), and so Spenser gives his aged Good Memory a youthful aid in the shape of Anamnestes (Greek *anamnesis* = calling to mind). Memory as depicted here is in moral contrast to the Bacchic oblivion of Acrasia's Bower (xii.46–9n., 79–80n.). Ninus (st. 56) was reputedly a great warrior (see st. 21n.); Assaracus was a king of Troy and great-grandfather of Aeneas (cf. x.9 and 72–3n.); Inachus was the first king of Argos and a river god; on Nestor, see st. 48n.; and on Methuselah, see Genesis 5:25–7. The emphasis here and in canto x is a common Renaissance humanist one on the positive benefits of time, through which noble deeds are achieved, remembered, and emulated. The Saturnian Phantastes and Eumnestes are mediated by Reason, whose chamber mainly depicts legal judgements, traditionally under the patronage of Jupiter, who 'in his magisterial capacity ... possesses adequate knowledge pertaining to law, delivers just decisons, and judges with integrity' (Curry, *Chaucer and the Mediaeval Sciences*, 127, citing the astrologer Alcabitius). Moreover, Jupiter is influential in making men 'learned, ... geometricians, mathematicians, poets, orators, ... good in counsel, statesmen . . . magicians' (Ptolemy, *Tetrabiblos*, III.xiii,351–3): which just about accounts for the other details in st. 53. Jupiter's influence appears here, in the middle, because he was the chief planetary moderator of the excessive effects of Saturn (Klibansky,

271–2, citing Ficino, who talks about *ratio* (reason) resembling Jupiter).

CANTO X

1–4 Spenser paraphrases *O.F.*, III.1–4, in which Ariosto asks for a voice fit to sing the ancestry of his patrons, the Estensi. Spenser's argument is worthy of Homer (supposed to have been born in Maeonia, i.e. Lydia) and Phoebus Apollo, god of poetry, singing the victory over the giants who warred against the Olympians, piled Mount Ossa on Mount Pelion to reach the heavens, and were defeated on the Phlegrean plains (Vergil, *Georgics*, I.278ff.). The 'learned daughters' are the nine Muses: Apollo was often regarded as their father (see I.xi.5–7n.). Elizabeth is justly divine, since her ancestry reaches up in a line to heaven, like Zeus's golden chain (see I.v.25–6n.; this is the chain parodied by Philotime at II.vii.44–50n.); the rebel giants presumed unjustly to divine sovereignty (I.vii.8–10n.). The 'Northerne starre' (st. 4) is the Pole Star, the 'stedfast starre', emblem of constancy, of I.ii.1: the fame of Elizabeth's ancestors is 'enrold' above it as Redcrosse's name is exalted above the sun (i.32n.) and Braggadocchio's reaches to the moon (iii.38n.) because Elizabeth is supposedly descended from Arthur, who, it was believed, had conquered Norway, Iceland, Greenland, 'and many other Islands beyond *Norway*, even under the North pole' (Millican, *Spenser and the Table Round*, 47, quoting Hakluyt's *Second Part of the principall Navigations* (1589), 245).

5–69 Spenser's main sources for this account of British history are Geoffrey of Monmouth's *History of the Kings of Britain*, Holinshed's *Chronicles* (1577), Stow's *Annals of England* (1584), and the *Mirror for Magistrates* (for these and other sources, see Carrie A. Harper, *The Sources of the British Chronicle History in Spenser's 'Faerie Queene'*, Bryn Mawr College Monographs, Monograph Series, VII (1910)). Spenser's main impulse is patriotic. Here, as in III.iii and ix, the right of the Tudors to rule is traced back to Brutus, great-grandson of Aeneas, who, Geoffrey tells us, arrived in Albion (which he renamed Britain after his own name), defeated the native giants, and called his capital city New Troy, the

Troynovant of st. 46. Arthur reads as far as the reign of his own historical father, Uther Pendragon (st. 68). In epic terms, this historical panorama parallels Aeneas's vision in the underworld of his descendants, the central figure in which is Augustus, who will restore the golden age (*Aeneid*, VI.791ff.): Elizabeth's own function, according to contemporary political mythography (see II Proem 1–5n., and Yates, part II).

But there are moral implications in this historical account, too. The subduing of the giants is the subduing of rebellious impulses and of bestial passions within the individual (see I.vii.8–10n.); Brutus hands over the kingdom divided into three just parts (cf. the three souls, the three divisions of the brain at ix.49–58n., etc.) but intemperance asserts itself again (st. 17ff.; cf. the Lear story at st. 27ff.). Moreover, Berger, 92–9, 104, following Harper, *op.cit.*, 180, notes that the reigns read about by Arthur are divided by three interregna: at the end of Brutus's progeny (st. 36); at the death of Lucius 'without issew' (st. 54); and at the death of Maximian, who 'left none heire' (st. 61). At this point Britain becomes prey to 'Hunnes and Picts' until Constantine II – Arthur's grandfather – is chosen king 'by consent of Commons and of Peares' (st. 62). The wars that go on during these interregna (st. 36, 54) again suggest the warring passions; but since they are civil wars consequent upon the death of the sovereign without an heir, Spenser's allusion is primarily a political one, hinting at the vexed question of Elizabeth's own successor. And when Spenser's contemporaries read of the realm 'into factions rent' (st. 36), they would doubtless have recalled Henry VII's own pacifying function as uniter 'of the two principall houses of Lancaster and of Yorke: by whose longe discord and deadly debate, this realm many yeares was sore traveiled, and almost cleane decayed' when he married Elizabeth of York (E.K.'s gloss to *Shepheardes Calender*, 'April', 68). Constantly, because of the identification of body with body politic, we read on two levels; so that, for example, 'the greedy thirst of royall crowne' of st. 35 is a historical enactment of the ambition portrayed as a moral abstract in the person of Philotime at vii.43ff.

There is an even more obvious pattern to Spenser's account of Elizabeth's ancestors. At st. 50 we are told of Christ's birth; which means that, just as Book II as a whole moves from the classical view of temperance to a definition of Christian temperance and the necessity for divine love and grace (vii.65–6n.; viii.1–2n.), so does the account of the kings of Britain move from the pre-Christian (man in a state of nature) to Christian (the state of grace). The break comes in st. 50 because of the symbolic meanings of that number: see I.viii, headnote, where fifty, as a stanza-total, is connected with Arthur, the poem's main symbol of intervening grace whose interventions in the world of the poem re-enact Christ's one great redemptive intervention in human history. Christ's taking upon himself the mortality of 'fleshly slime' (st. 50) is an historical assertion of the inseparability of body and spirit in man that Alma's castle expresses emblematically (ix.22n.) and that Grille denies (xii.86–7).

70 Guyon, meantime, reads Spenser's own mythological account of Elizabeth's ancestry in contrast to Arthur's more 'factual' chronicle. It is in accord with the medieval–Renaissance habit of tracing royal genealogies back to Biblical or ancient mythological figures (Rathborne, 68ff.) and, unlike Arthur's, concentrates on the Welsh Tudor genealogy. Spenser's version of the Prometheus story is close to Natalis Comes, *Mythologiae*, IV.vi (who quotes Horace, *Odes*, I.xvi.13–16: 'Prometheus, as goes the tale, when forced to add to our primeval clay a portion drawn from every creature, put also in our breasts the fury of the ravening lion ' (tr. C. E. Bennet, Loeb edn (1925)). Having created man, Prometheus still had to give him a mind, so he stole fire from heaven, for which presumption he was chained on the Caucasus and had his liver perpetually gnawed by Jove's bird, the eagle (Lotspeich, 102–3). Prometheus was usually allegorised as Providence and the fire as soul and spiritual illumination (Allen, 176, 180, 193, 196, 231); and there was also a medieval and Renaissance tradition that Prometheus was a moral instructor with whom human civilisation began (Olga Ruggio, 'The Myth of Prometheus', *J.W.I.*, XXI (1958); and see T. P. Roche, *The Kindly Flame* (Princeton, N.J., 1964), 35ff.). 'Quick' means 'alive': in terms of Biblical mythology, he is Adam. Spenser's full allegory of the Garden of Adonis appears in III.vi: it is an earthly temperate paradise in which Spenser explores the cyclical pattern of generation, both human and cosmic. Elizabeth, like mankind in general, is the product of a combination of opposites: elf (a word often used by Spenser with disparaging connotations: E.K.'s gloss on *Shepheardes Calender*, 'June', 25; here signifying the flesh) and fay (spirit). Quick's search for a mate recalls Arthur's quest for Gloriana and its analogues (I.ix.13–15n.). What follows is an idealised version of the chronicles of human frailty that Arthur has just read; its function is to affirm Elizabeth's supernatural power and abilities as a ruler, to mythologise her out of the factual (or quasi-factual) realms of history so that we actually see her as Gloriana – at once a testament to man's constant search for glory (which redeems him from 'fleshly slime') and a manifestation of divine glory.

72–3 Elfin, whom 'all *India* obayd', suggests Bacchus in his role as lawgiver to, and civiliser of, India (see V.i.2). Augustus is compared to the triumphant Bacchus at *Aeneid*, VI.804–5; and Bacchus was identified with Osiris (Plutarch, *De Iside et Osiride*, 364E) who in turn was cited as the initiator of the Tudor line (Rathborne, 85, 92ff., 108ff.). On Cleopolis and Panthea, see I.vii.46n. and I.x.58n. As Rathborne, 111 notes, America was still popularly identified with India in the sixteenth century; so that Bacchus could be seen as conquering both (and see II Proem 2n.; and cf. the ambiguity of 'Indian' at xi.20–3n. below). 'Noble *Elfinan*' is probably Hercules: Spenser has him as the founder of Cleopolis because he was a type of heroic virtue and because his name was usually understood to be derived from *Hera* (Juno) and *kleos* (fame, glory): see v.31n.; Tooke, *Pantheon*, 257; Rathborne, 99ff., 111–13. He was supposed to have founded cities. In addition, the Libyan Hercules was listed second in the Trojan–Tudor pedigree which began with Osiris (Rathborne, 99).

The identification of Elfiline and Elfinell is difficult. Rathborne, 114ff. suggests Tros (who gave his name to Troy and virtually founded the Trojan empire) and Assaracus, Tros's son (see ix.49–58n.), respectively. The victory over the 'wicked *Gobbelines*' is then, in terms of classical mythology, the victory of Tros's sons over Tantalus, through which Troy gained its power in Asia Minor (Rathborne, 117). Elfant is, Rathborne, 118 suggests, Aeneas, founder of the Roman empire; Elfar might be Aeneas's son Ascanius or his grandson Silvius (*ibid.*, 118–19, with no explanation of the 'brethren gyants'), while Elfinor is Brutus (see st. 5–69n.). The bridge is a mythologised version of London Bridge (symbol of maritime and commercial supremacy), compounded of the magic bridge supposed to have been made by Vergil according to medieval legend, and the brazen bridge with which Salmoneus

spanned the city of Elis. In his pride he rode over it in his chariot
imitating the sound of Jupiter's thunder, and was killed by a real
thunderbolt (Rathborne, 120ff.; Starnes and Talbert, 217–18, 221).
Compare the 'Bridge, made all of golde, / Over the Sea' in
Spenser's *Ruines of Time*, 547ff. In excluding the names of Vergil
and Salmoneus, Spenser inplies man's divine aspect and
aspirations without the pejorative implications of pride.

74   The 'three sonnes' are the offspring of Brutus mentioned
earlier at st. 13. The number 700 has occurred earlier, too, at st. 36:
it signifies the reign of a just king (Bongo, *Numerorum mysteria*,
633f.; Fowler, 92n.).

75–6   The two sons of Elficleos referred to here are Prince Arthur
(who died in 1502) and Henry, Spenser's Oberon, who married
Arthur's widow, Catherine of Aragon, and succeeded to the throne
in 1509. Spenser omits Edward VI and Mary in accordance with
the view followed at Elizabeth's coronation that she was 'the only
true heire of Henrye the Eighth' (*Var. Sp.*, II.337). On
Elizabeth–Tanaquil–Gloriana, see I Proem 2n.

CANTO XI

On the appropriateness of the number eleven to the subject-matter
(the evil Maleger), see I.xi, headnote.

2   The image of the body politic establishes Alma as yet another
projection of Elizabeth, the virgin queen (cf. Medina, ii.40–2n.).
Alma in Latin = nourishing, and is usually applied to nature deities
(e.g., Ceres, Venus: Lewis and Short, *Latin Dictionary*, *s.v.*):
Spenser probably glances back to Elizabeth as Astraea, the virgin
goddess whose emblem was an ear of corn (II Proem 2n.). On
Alma as a Venus-virgin, see ix.18–19n.

5–6   Arthur, embodiment of magnificence and grace (I.vii.29n.),
fights the temptations that beset the temperate body. They are
infinite in number to symbolise the multiplicity of evil (I.i.15,
II.ix.13); but they are disposed in twelve troops to represent attacks
through the five senses (st. 7–13) and by the seven sins.

8–9   Spenser follows the traditional order of the senses – sight, hearing, smell, taste, touch (Aristotle, *De anima*, II.vi–xii). In general the creatures recall those encountered by Ruggiero outside Alcina's city: humans with cat- or ape-heads, centaurs, etc. (*O.F.*, VI.60ff.), though in Spenser they are specific emblems of each sense. Owls are known for their night-sight and are also associated with evil (e.g., vii.23); dogs were emblematic of vigilance (Tervarent, col. 95); the griffin has an eagle's head and lion's body: in itself it symbolises vigilance because it traditionally guarded gold mines (de Vries, 228–9); but the eagle, too, was an attribute of sight (Ripa, 447; for the reasons, see I.x.47–8n.). The lynx was thought to excel all other animals in sight (Ripa, *ibid.*).

10 The wild boar excels in hearing (Ripa, 449; Chew, 193), as does the deer (hart): Tervarent, cols. 67–8. The snake makes its appearance because of snake-charming: e.g., Psalms 58:4–5 ('the deafe adder that stoppeth his eare. Which heareth not the voyce of the inchanter, thogh he be moste expert in charming').

11 The hunting hound is an emblem of the sense of smell (Ripa, 448; Tervarent, col. 95; Chew, 194), as is the vulture (Spenser's 'puttock' or kite): Ripa, 449; Chew, 193. The ape is often associated with taste (Tervarent, col. 352), but also with vices in general (*ibid.*, cols. 354–5).

12 The ostrich can traditionally devour anything (Ansell Robin, 164–5); the toad was believed to be poisonous (*ibid.*, 135–6; the frog, incidentally, was a type of those who snatch at worldly pleasures: Evans, 200n.). On the pig and gluttony, see I.iv.21–3n.

13 The snail was an emblem of touch (Tervarent, col. 161), as were the spider (*ibid.*, col. 31) and hedgehog (*ibid.*, col. 212).

15 The 'two brethren Giants' are presumably the hands: A. Gilbert, ' "Those Two Brethren Giants": *Faerie Queene*, 2.11.15', *M.L.N.*, LXX (1955).

18–19 The similes are common: e.g., *Iliad*, XII.278ff. (snow and arrows) and IV.452ff. (water flooding from mountains). *Spumador* = golden foam (cf. Guyon's Brigador at ii.11n.). The foam signifies his fiery nature, as Upton noted (*Var. Sp.*, II.342), citing *Aeneid*, VI.881 ('foam-flecked flanks'); the gold suggests Arthur's solar role (I.vii.29n.). Horses 'of heavenly seed' deriving from the horses of the sun god are mentioned at *Aeneid*, VII.281–3. Zeus gave divine horses to Tros (x.72–3n.) in payment for his son Ganymede; Tros gave them to Laomedon (*Iliad*, V.265ff.). In some traditions, Ganymede's father is Laomedon. The horses of the sun are fiery and impatient (*Met.*, II.153ff.); and Spenser's line, which has no direct mythological precedent, might recall that Laomedon was helped by Phoebus Apollo to build the walls of Troy (*Met.*, XI.199ff.).

20–3   The captain is Maleger (Italian *malaugurio* = bad omen; also Latin *malus* = evil, deformed, and *male*, badly + *aeger*, sick). He symbolises bodily disease and spiritual malaise and so, ultimately, original sin, a physical result of which was mortality. See Woodhouse, 'Nature and Grace in *The Faerie Queene*'; and cf. Romans 7:24: 'O wretched man that I am, who shal deliver me from the bodie of this death' (Geneva gloss on 'bodie': 'This fleshlie lump of sinne and death'). Hamilton, 114 compares Ephesians 4:22: 'the olde man, which is corrupt through the deceiveable lustes' (Geneva gloss: 'all the natural corruption that is in us'). He is the horrifying truth that underlies Cymochles and Pyrochles, the depravity that Guyon has recognised within himself and been redeemed from through grace (vii.65–6n.; viii.33–53n.). He is also the disease of which the Bacchic Mordant died (i.35–56n.); so he rides on the Bacchic tiger (I.vi.20–6n.; Wind, 184). (But note that, like all deities, Bacchus has a good as well as a bad aspect: we have encountered Bacchus as lawgiver at x.72–3n.) The Indians (st. 21) might be American Indians (superstitious, cannibalistic, etc: Ripa, 338–9) or oriental Indians, whose country was especially under the patronage of Saturn so that its inhabitants were regarded as 'ugly, unclean, and bestial' (Ptolemy, *Tetrabiblos*, II.iii,143). The two countries were identified, anyway: x.72–3n. Maleger himself is Saturnian. His description at st. 22 reminds us that Saturn was the planetary god of old age, graveyards, and death (I.ix.33–4n.; II.vii.30n.). Hence, too, he has a skull helmet; though this is more obviously an emblem of Death himself (Chew, ch. VIII and figs. 141–8) and recalls, appropriately, the iconographical traditions in which a skull was depicted in the tree of knowledge as Eve picked the apple or in which the tree was itself a skeleton (*ibid.*, 2, and figs. 3–5). Dry and cold qualities are Saturnian (e.g., Curry, *Mediaeval Sciences*, 129–30); Saturn brings disease (*ibid.*; Chaucer, *Knight's Tale*, 2469); an ashy pallor is characteristic of his subjects (cf.

Chaucer, *ibid.*, 1361ff., and 2443: 'pale Saturnus the colde'). The snake is a Saturnian creature (Agrippa, I.xxv,56). Maleger's Saturnian characteristics are noticed by Berger, 85–8 and Fowler, 105. As a malign Saturnian figure he contrasts with the controlled Saturnian elements in the sensitive soul, imagination and memory (ix.49–58n.), and belongs with the poem's Saturnian images of evil, Mammon in canto vii and especially Despair in I.ix. Iconographically the two hags, Impotence and Impatience, recall Occasion (iv.4–5n.), since Impotence is the inability to act even when there is occasion to do so, and Impatience is a choleric tendency to act irrationally before the occasion presents itself – a failing shared by Amavia–Dido (i.35–56n.) and Phedon in canto iv. The parody middle-way between the two is Maleger; and the answer to the moral problem they pose (what virtue must one follow to enable one to act justly even though one has a fallen nature?) is prudence, which is not hasty, but decides at leisure (Ripa, 417). Impotence parodies memory; Maleger parodies the second part of prudence, intelligence; and Impatience parodies foresight: cf. vii.1–2n. and ix.49–58n. In view of this, Maleger's skull helmet takes on additional meaning, since a death's head was also an attribute of prudence, indicating the philosophical tendency of the prudent man, who ponders on mortality (Ripa, 418; the serpent, too, is a relevant emblem: *ibid.*, following Matthew 10:16: 'be ye . . . wise as serpentes').

26–31 Even Arthur is mortal and fallible, succumbing to the combined forces of Maleger, Impotence, and Impatience. Although he is the poem's symbol of grace, here he is the virtue of magnificence (I.vii.29n.) and himself needs the blessing of grace to enable him to survive. He rises, like Guyon in canto viii, 'as one awakt out of long slombring shade'. He is aided, too, by his sense of honour (the squire, Timias: I.vii.37n.): and see ix.36–9n. In *The Travels of Sir John Mandeville* it is recorded that the Tartars shoot behind them as they flee (ed. A. W. Pollard (1900), 165).

32–3 Arthur erupts like earth-bound fire aspiring (in accordance with contemporary meteorology) to its 'native seat', the sphere of fire, highest of the elemental spheres and believed to be situated under the sphere of the moon (Heninger, *Handbook of Renaissance Meterology*, ch. I). The image is a volcanic one (see I.vii.8–10n.; II.vii.35–9n.); but here symbolises just anger and divine vengeance.

Note the reference to 'disdaine' (see viii.33–53n.). The bear to which Arthur is compared in the bear-baiting simile of st. 33 is a choleric animal (Tervarent, col. 292); and his breaking of 'his caitive bands' contrasts with the unbinding of Occasion and Furor at v.18–19.

35–45 Arthur's fight with Maleger recalls Hercules's battle with the giant Antaeus, son of Poseidon (sea god) and Ge (earth). He gained his strength from being in contact with the earth and challenged all strangers to wrestle with him. He killed his victims and made a house to Poseidon out of their skulls (Smith, I.181). Compare Maleger's skull helmet at st. 22. The earth is Saturn's element (Agrippa, I.xxv,55). Hercules overcame him by holding him up in the air and throttling him. Hercules was an exemplar of heroic virtue and a type of Christ (I.xi.26–8n.), and his victory over Antaeus was seen as a victory over sensual desires (Lotspeich, 37; cf. Starnes and Talbert, 238). Arthur is appropriately compared to the Martian (and hence fiery) falcon in st. 36 (Agrippa, I.xxvii,58) and to Jupiter's eagle (st. 43), 'Embleme of Justice, and Clemency' (Agrippa, I.xxvi,57), attacking the Saturnian heron (*ibid.*, xxv,56); though the eagle simile is a common one (Horace, *Odes*, IV.iv; *Aeneid*, I.398–9). Jupiter moderates Saturn: see ix.49–58n. As Warton noticed (*Var. Sp.*, II.346), Spenser also seems to echo the fight of Grifone and Aquilante (Griffin and Eagle) with the robber Orrilo, who cannot be injured by the most savage blows, in *O.F.*, XV.67ff. Arthur's battle corresponds to that with Orgoglio in I.vii–viii; though in having three stages (st. 26ff.; 35ff.; 43ff.) it parallels Redcrosse's Christlike encounter with the dragon in I.xi. Arthur confronts Maleger 'with his naked hands', as Hercules overcame Antaeus, to symbolise the fact that he is man confronting the essence of his Adam-inherited mortality. The snatching up of a massive stone (st. 35) is common in ancient poetry: e.g., *Aeneid*, XII.896ff., where Turnus picks up a rock, used as a field-boundary marker, which is so big that twelve ordinary men could hardly have carried it. At st. 39, as *Var. Sp.*, II.346 notes, Spenser names four contemporary types of apparition: the 'magicall illusion' and 'aerie spirit' (see I.i.36n., 45n., 47n.); the spirit of the unburied body (the Catholic explanation of ghosts); and the 'hellish feend' called up by black magic: cf. again Archimago in I.i.

46 The defeat of Maleger by throwing him into a lake recalls and cancels out the parody emblem of temperance when Pyrochles, in the lake, continues burning (vi.42–5n.). Woodhouse, 'Nature and Grace', rightly sees the water as a symbol of baptismal regeneration and grace (cf. I.xi.29–30n.); and Hankins, 86–7 suggests a specific parallel with Luke 8, the account of the Gadarene swine in which Christ commands the devils to leave the man they possess: 'And they besoght him, that he wolde not commande them to go out into the diepe [Geneva gloss: hell]. . . . Then went the devils out of the man, and entred into the swine: and the herd was caryed with violence from a stepe downe place into the lake, and was choked' (verses 31–3). Hankins cites St Ambrose's interpretation (*Hexameron*, I.viii.32) of the lake as formlessness, the matter from which the world was created (the 'earth . . . without forme & voyde' of Genesis 1:2, covered with water). So that Maleger is thrown back into the chaos from which he originated. The man possessed by devils is called 'Legion, because many devils were entred into him' (Luke 8:30). The Geneva gloss on the name says that it implies 'an uncerteine and infinite nomber' (cf. Mark 5:9), and this perhaps recalls Maleger's infinite number of henchmen at xi.5. There are other similarities between Maleger and Legion: Maleger has a skull helmet and is difficult to control and overcome; Legion dwells among graves (Mark 5:3; Luke 8:27) and 'no man colde binde him, no not with chains . . . nether colde anie man tame him' (Mark 5:3–4).

47 Choleric Impatience rushes into the lake like the Gadarene swine and also like Pyrochles (vi.42); Impotence defines her moral being by committing suicide, like Amavia–Dido in canto i.

CANTO XII

1 The 'goodly frame' is at once the edifice of the Book of Temperance as a whole and the moral–physical frame of the knight of Temperance, Guyon, who is now reaching the goal of his journey, Acrasia (on architecture in Book II, see i.57–8n.; iii.21–30n.; ix.22n.). On Acrasia, see i.35–56n.; her 'magick mights' are a reminder that she is a Circe-figure (see st. 39–41n. below). The sea voyage to the Bower echoes the voyage of Charles and Ubaldo to the Gardens of Armida in *Ger. Lib.*, XV, where moral temptations in the shape of monsters are encountered; but both derive from the voyage of Odysseus, and particularly *Odyssey*, X (Circe) and XII (the Sirens, Scylla and Charybdis). There are additional hints in Spenser of Aeneas's voyage as recounted in *Aeneid*, III, and the voyage past the Sirens, Scylla and Charybdis, and the Wandering Rocks in Apollonius Rhodius's *Argonautica*, IV. The *Odyssey* and *Aeneid* voyages had by the Renaissance received elaborate allegorical treatment, in which the moral development of the protagonists was charted with extreme precision as they overcame various vices with the aid of reason and divine grace. In such readings, the sea symbolises passion and ungodliness (e.g., Allen, 93; Jean Daniélou, *Primitive Christian Symbols* (1964), 64, and ch. IV, 'The Ship of the Church', which discusses the image as a Christian commonplace). The ship symbolises the assailed State, Church, and individual; and the tradition that Spenser uses is that of the ship of the individual man piloted by reason or prudence (the Palmer's function at st. 3). See Allen, chs. IV and VI; George de F. Lord, *Homeric Renaissance*; B. Nellist, 'The Allegory of Guyon's Voyage: An Interpretation', *E.L.H.*, XXX (1963). An elaborate version of the metaphor Spenser has in mind appears in Quarles's *Emblemes*, III.xv: 'The world's a Sea; my flesh a Ship that's mann'd / With lab'ring Thoughts, and steer'd by Reasons hand', etc. It is accompanied by two glosses, one from St Ambrose ('The confluence of lusts makes a great tempest, which in this sea disturbeth the sea faring soul, that reason cannot govern it') and one from St Augustine: 'We labour in a boysterous sea: Thou standest upon the shore and seest our dangers: Give us grace to hold a middle course betwixt Scylla and Charybdis, that both dangers escaped, we may arrive at our Port secure.' See st. 3–9n. below.) In this canto the Herculean Arthur (xi.35–45n.) is replaced by the Odyssean Guyon, since the two were equated as moral heroes, e.g. by Seneca, 'De Constantia Sapientis', *Moral Essays*, Loeb edn (1928), I.51. One other notion governs Guyon's voyage: Acrasia, as a Venus figure (the false 'Pleasure' of st. 1), is associated with the sea, not only because Venus was born from the sea (Hesiod, *Theogony*, 188ff.) but because of the medieval moralising tradition in which Venus floats on the sea of delights or *libido* (Twycross, *Medieval Anadyomene*, 42ff.).

2 Guyon's final test – by Acrasia and her influences – begins on the third day perhaps because Odysseus sees Circe's house on the dawn of the third day after he and his men have arrived on her island (*Odyssey*, X.144ff.); and cf. vii.1–2n. The morning light 'trembling' on the waves suggests the fire and water emblem used earlier (v.2–14n.).

3–9 Cullen, 92–3, following R. C. Fox, 'Temperance and the Seven Deadly Sins in *The Faerie Queene*, Book II', *R.E.S.*, XII (1961), notes that Guyon is faced with all the sins on his voyage: gluttony (Gulf of Greediness), lust (Rock of Reproach), sloth (Phaedria and the Wandering Islands), avarice (Quicksand of Unthriftihead, Whirlpool of Decay), wrath in the form of 'wrathfull *Neptune*' (st. 22), envy (the doleful Maid), and pride (the mermaids of st. 31). The sequence follows the scheme of Flesh (gluttony, lust, sloth), World (avarice), and Devil (wrath, envy, pride): cf. I.iv.18–20n.

This first episode is based on Odysseus's voyage between two rocks, under one of which dwelt the monster Scylla and under the other, and lower, of which, in a gulf, dwelt Charybdis, who caused whirlpools three times a day: the steersman's function is of vital importance as in the Spenser instance (*Odyssey*, XII.217–21; and cf. *Aeneid*, III.420ff.). The Gulf of Greediness follows Vergil's description of Charybdis, which drinks down enormous waves and then spouts them up at the sky (*Aeneid*, III.420–3): it was interpreted as greed by, e.g., Landino (Allen, 150); while the 'Rock of vile Reproach', covered with the bodies of the lustful, is based on Scylla, interpreted as lust by Landino (*ibid.*) and others (e.g., Comes, *Mythologiae*, VIII.xii). In Spenser's version it reflects the ancient, medieval, and Renaissance preoccupation with the lodestone which attracts the iron in ships and so wrecks them; it was known as the '*Magnes* stone', or magnet, because it is found in the land of the Magnetes (Lucretius, *De rerum natura*, VI.906ff.). The wrecked ships and 'carkasses exanimate' also recall the Wandering Rocks of *Odyssey*, XII.59ff., from which no ship has escaped and which are washed by ship timbers and dead bodies. Moreover, only predatory sea-birds fly round them, and, Homer says, no birds can pass between them. There is an additional suggestion of the Sirens (see st. 30–32n. below), whose island was surrounded by the bones of their victims, and who were interpreted as rapacious courtesans (Twycross, *Medieval Anadyomene*, 37) and the bones as the death brought by lascivious thoughts (Allen, 231). Similarly, the attracting power of the rock is a literalisation of the drawing power of the Sirens' song. The cormorant signifies gluttony (Chaucer, *Parlement of Foules*, 362); and the bird passage might suggest Isaiah 34, God's vengeance on Edom, which will be laid waste and possessed by birds of prey (e.g., verses 11, 15). Spenser uses the whole episode as an emblem of the maintenance of the virtuous mean (cf. i.24n.). Comes and others applied this symbolism to Scylla and Charybdis: 'what else is meant [by them] but that which is written by Aristotle in his *Ethics*, that virtue is the mean between extremes, both of which must be avoided?' (*Mythologiae*, VIII.xii, cit. Lotspeich, 21, 106–7). On Tartarus, see I.vii.44n. The name is often used for 'hell', and in st. 6 Spenser refers to Lake Avernus, at the entrance to hell (*Aeneid*, VI.237ff.), which, incidentally, is also birdless, and from which ghosts ascend (Cicero, *Tusculan Disputations*, I.xvi).

10–12 The '*wandring Islands*' suggest Homer's Wandering Rocks (and cf. Apollonius Rhodius, *Argonautica*, IV.922ff.) conflated with the Isle of Fortune that keeps on changing its shape (*Romance of the Rose*, 5921ff.) and the common medieval fable of the illusory island that, when a ship is anchored on it, turns out to be a whale that then plunges under the waves (traditionally symbolising the allurements and deceitfulness of the devil: Evans, 122–3; J. H. Pitman, 'Milton and the *Physiologus*', *M.L.N.*, XL (1925)). There was a widespread contemporary belief in floating islands, a common authority for which was Pliny's *Natural History*: see *Var. Sp.*, II.356–7.

13 Latona was made pregnant by Jupiter, whose consort Juno became angry and persecuted her. She could find nowhere on earth to hide until the floating island of Delos permitted her to bear her children (Apollo the sun god and Diana the moon goddess) on it, because she was a wanderer on the land as the island was upon the sea (*Met.*, VI.184ff., 332ff.). At the time of the birth the island stood still, and a temple was subsequently built on it and dedicated to Apollo (*Aeneid*, III.73ff.). Berger, 236–7 suggests that this allusion to the birth of sun and moon hints at its Biblical analogue in Genesis 1:16. The creation of the luminaries occurred on the

fourth day of creation and, Berger notes, just as God separated sea
from land on the third day (Genesis 1:9) so Guyon, on the third
day of his sea voyage, encounters land. He also sees the fog of st.
34 as recalling not only the original chaos (see st. 33–4n.) but also
parodying the mist that preceded the creation of man: 'But a myst
went up from the earth, and watred all the earth. The Lord God
also made the man of the dust of the grounde, and breathed in his
face breath of life, and the man was a living soule' (Genesis 2:6–7).
This is likely, since the fog precedes Guyon's entry into Acrasia's
paradisal bower, and Acrasia manifestly denies man's spiritual
aspect by bestialising him.

14–17 On Phaedria, see vi.2–10n.; and on the Palmer's
opposition to her, see vi.19n. (in planetary terms it is an opposition
of Saturn and Venus: vii.1–2n.). 'Skippet' = skiff. Her hair is left
unbound to signify her wantonness (contrast Medina's braided
hair, ii.12–20n.).

20 The wheel is an emblem of instability and mutability:
Fortuna–Occasio is usually portrayed standing on a turning wheel
(e.g., Chew, 13, 27, 32–3, 37–45). On the labyrinth, see I.i.10–11n.

21–2 The threat here recalls Orgoglio at I.vii.8–10n., and the
giant Disdayne at II.vii.40–3n. There is a good description of the
sea god Neptune in his sea-blue chariot drawn by fiery horses at
Aeneid, V.817ff., where he is also followed by a retinue of
monstrous sea beasts.

23 The deformed creatures anticipate the deformed humans in
Acrasia's Bower (st. 39–40, 84–7). The 'spring-headed *Hydraes*'
combine the *hydrus* or water-snake (Ansell Robin, 149–50, and appendix) with the many-headed Lernean hydra which it was one of
Hercules's labours to destroy. Whenever he cut off one head, two
more grew in its place (I.vii.16–18n.). The 'great whirlpooles' are
spouting whales (Robin, 119–20; see st. 10–12n. on the whale as
the devil); the scolopendra is a sea-centipede which Aelian's
second-century *De animalium natura*, XIII.xxiii describes as
swimming as if rowing with its legs (see also Robin, 120ff.). The
'silver scales' seem to be Spenser's invention. The monoceros is the
narwhal or sea-unicorn (Robin, 76–7), though Spenser has
invented the 'immeasured tayles' to continue the idea of the
multiplicity and infiniteness of evil already suggested by the hydras'

heads and the legs of the centipede: compare the 'thousands thousands many more' of st. 25, and I.i.15.

24 The 'dreadful Fish' deserving 'the name / Of Death' is the morse (cf. Latin *mors*, death) or walrus (Robin, 122–3); the wasserman or water-man is a merman as is, presumably, the sea-satyr, which is mentioned in, e.g., Aelian, XVI.xviii (and see *Var. Sp.*, II.362–3). The ziffius or xiphias is a swordfish; and the rosmarine is yet another name for the walrus (Robin, 124). The ocean holds these monsters since it is traditionally the home of evil (e.g., Daniel 7:3, the four beasts that come from the sea).

26 On the Palmer's staff, see st. 39–41n.; and on Tethys, see I.i.39n. At IV.xi.18 she and Ocean are parents of 'all the rest ... Which afterward both sea and land possest'.

27–9 The 'dolefull Mayd' is a specific and equally extreme Saturnian (sad) opposite to the immodest, mirthful, and Venerean Phaedria of st. 14–17; and cf. Celeno's 'song of bale and bitter sorrow' at vii.23.

30–2 The mermaids are based on the Sirens of *Odyssey*, XII.39ff., 166ff., whose song Odysseus is able to listen to only because he has been bound to his ship's mast. His sailors, to prevent themselves being seduced, have had their ears plugged with wax pellets. Their song is in Homer a temptation to knowledge (they know past and future); but Guyon has already rejected this in Mammon's cave (vii.53–4n.), and so Spenser makes them a Venerean temptation to ease or idleness: cf. Phaedria at vi.2–10n., 15–17n. (for the Siren's song in *Ger. Lib.*, XIV), and 23n. (for the echo of Despair). Odysseus withstood the Sirens with the aid of prudence (Lotspeich, citing Comes, *Mythologiae*, VII.xiii). Sirens traditionally signify sensual pleasure (Twycross, *Medieval Anadyomene*, 36ff.; Allen, 93, 95, 188, 231; Starnes and Talbert, 108–10), and their music is the music that draws one to lechery: Twycross, 44–6. The mythographers generally agreed that there were three Sirens (*ibid.*, 36ff.); but Spenser has five mermaids to represent the five senses, as Upton first noticed (*Var. Sp.*, II.365). Sirens were originally bird-women (*Met.*, V.552ff.) but were frequently identified with mermaids (Starnes and Talbert, *ibid.*). It is perhaps relevant to the concept of *The Faerie Queene* as a national epic that the fish-woman (mermaid) seems to be peculiarly

British in origin (Twycross, 92ff.). The '*Heliconian* maides' of st. 31 are the Muses, who dwelt on Mount Helicon. Juno persuaded the Sirens to enter a contest with them which the Sirens lost. As a punishment they were deprived of their wings (Pausanias, *Description of Greece*, IX.xxxiv.3): Spenser's stanza is modelled on this incident and relates to the theme of bestial metamorphosis in the canto as a whole.

33–4 Like Odysseus, Guyon has to be warned by reason or prudence (the Palmer) to withstand the Siren music which conspires with external nature to seduce him. As Odysseus orders his men to set him free (*Odyssey*, XII.192–4), so does Guyon ask the boatman to slow down. Two of the elements here – sea and air – are projections of aspects of the mermaids themselves: the fish-tail (whose element is the sea) and the song (whose element is the air: e.g., Sir John Davies, *Orchestra: A Poem on Dancing*, st. 43). Guyon endures a musical parody of temperance, containing extremes (bass, treble) and mean (tenor/alto): cf. i.24n. and ii.12–20n. Zephyrus is associated with lust, though he is also (deceptively in this instance) the temperate wind of spring: see v.25–8n. The 'grosse fog' is a symbol of the blinding of the moral senses: cf. the darkness of Errour's cave (I.i.13–16n.), and I.iii.10–20n. and viii.30–4n. This is Acrasia's last attempt to scare Guyon away from her Bower and presents him with the ultimate fear of the unknown (st. 35). It does this by appearing to reduce the universe to 'one confused mas' – the primal chaos of *Met.*, I.5ff. and Genesis 1:2 (see st. 13n. and xi.46n.). At the same time it suggests the moral chaos awaiting those who enter the Bower of Bliss – the *akrasia* (bad mixture) that its goddess instils (Acrasia is a specific parody of Circe here, since according to Comes, for example, her name meant 'to mix', signifying that, as the offspring of Sun and Perse, an oceanid, she mixes heat and moisture, the origin of all living things: Allen, 226). Furthermore, in causing this chaos Acrasia, as a false Venus, wilfully perverts the essential function of love which, in Platonic accounts of the creation, was to form order (cosmos) from chaos (see Spenser's *Hymne in Honour of Love*, 57ff.). This fog episode follows the encounter with the mermaids as the smoke at *Odyssey*, XII.201ff., which announces the encounter with Scylla, follows the Sirens episode.

35–6 The birds are all associated with hell: on the owl, see

I.v.30n. and *Met.*, V.549–50 ('bird of ill omen', etc.); the night-raven is synonymous with the owl (Robin, 172–3) and also a bird of ill omen (Agrippa, I.liv,113 says that 'Owls, and night-ravens ... betoken ... death'); bats are traditionally evil and associated with death (de Vries, 36); the 'Strich' is the screech-owl (Latin *strix*; see Ovid, *Fasti*, VI.133ff., where they are descended from Harpies and attack and suck blood from babies); the whistler is a bird that portends death, often regarded as the plover (de Vries, 370); on the Harpies, see vii.21–5n. At *Aeneid*, III.245ff. Celeno speaks as a 'prophet of sad destiny' (*infelix vates*). The birds parody the creating spirit of Genesis 1:2.

39–41 The model for Acrasia's island is the island of Circe in *Odyssey*, X. The beasts – men degraded by their lusts (st. 85–7) – recall the wolves and lions that surround Circe's house and are men that she has bewitched (ll.212ff.). Immediately after this, Circe invites Odysseus's companions under the command of Eurylochos into her house, drugs them so that they forget their homeland, taps them with her wand, and changes them into pigs, though they retain the minds of men. Eurylochos, who refuses her invitation, returns to Odysseus, who is then offered a protective charm by Hermes–Mercury who is carrying his golden rod or caduceus. The charm is a plant called moly which, because of its protective function, was variously glossed as the wisdom, temperance, and grace which redeem one from the brutalisation of sensuality (Lord, *Homeric Renaissance*, 111–12; Allen, 92, 191, 227; L. L. Bronwin, 'Milton and the Renaissance Circe', *Milton Studies*, VI (1975), 22–4). Mercury himself was usually understood as wisdom or intelligence when in this kind of advisory role (cf. his descent to warn Aeneas away from Dido at *Aeneid*, IV.238ff.; Allen, 93, 138); and so the Palmer's staff combines the Odysseyan moly with Mercury's caduceus, 'the wand with which [in his role as *psychopompos*, or guide of the souls of the dead] he summons pale souls from Orcus and sends others down to wretched Tartarus' (*Aeneid*, IV.242–3). Spenser describes the caduceus at IV.iii.42; and it was interpreted by the mythographers as, among other things, an emblem of concord and peace (Ripa, 377–8). So it symbolises a harmonising and moderating power, and here asserts the full integration of the Palmer's and Guyon's personalities. Spenser probably regarded the wood as olive, in view of the olive garland at IV.iii.42 and the fact that the caduceus complements an olive branch in some personifications of Peace (e.g., Ripa, 377; and see ii.31n.). Spenser probably also recalls here Aeneas's golden bough (*Aeneid*, VI.187ff.) and the magic wand which will protect Ubaldo from Armida's animals (*Ger. Lib.*, XIV.73). Furthermore, as messenger of the gods and mediator between immortal and mortal, Mercury asserts mythologically the integration of the two that is a constant concern of Book II (e.g., ix.22n.; x.70n.); and as the god of intellectual inquiry it was his job, with his wand, to dispel clouds of mental obstruction (Wind, 122–3, citing Boccaccio, *De Genealogia Deorum*, XII.lxii): cf. the fog of st. 34.

42 The Bower of Bliss is a false and sensual earthly paradise in contrast to the paradise that is restored in I.xii. It is modelled on the paradisal garden of love in the romance tradition (e.g., *Romance of the Rose*, 1279ff.) but follows most closely *Odyssey*, V (the island on which Calypso kept Odysseus) and *Ger. Lib.*, XV and XVI, the garden and palace into which Armida has seduced Rinaldo: see R. M. Durling, 'The Bower of Bliss and Armida's Palace', *Comparative Literature*, VI (1954). It is, in effect, the pastoral equivalent to the artificial palace of Lucifera, another false Venus, at I.iv; and its opposite, symbolising the fructifying power of nature and the generative cycle, is the Garden of Adonis in III.vi presided over by a creating Venus. Other antitheses are the Temple of Venus in IV.x (a hermaphroditic Venus symbolising levels of ideal union) which is on an island and 'wall'd by nature gainst invaders wrong' (IV.x.6) and approached through a paradisal garden in which nature and art are in complete harmony (st. 21); and Mount Acidale in VI.x, the home of Venus and her Graces. More immediately, Acrasia in her Bower contrasts with the Venerean–Dianan Belphoebe in her natural setting, the wood, in canto iii (and cf. her grotto that is 'an earthly Paradize' at III.v.40). On the question of art and nature, see st. 50n. Armida's garden is enclosed (*Ger. Lib.*, XVI.1), as are, traditionally, all paradises (Greek, *paradeisos*, park); but Spenser inevitably recalls Song of Solomon 4:12 ('My sister my spouse is as a garden inclosed') and its interpretation as the Virgin Mary, the *hortus conclusus* (e.g., Eithne Wilkins, *The Rose-Garden Game* (1969), 117, 124, 173). Paradises are usually described as gardens of Venus, because she is goddess of gardens (Agrippa, I.xlviii,96).

44–5 The gate is 'framed ... of precious yvory' because of
ivory's Venerean connections (I.x.29–31n.) and in allusion to the
gate of ivory through which false dreams come (I.i.40n.), thus
neatly implying the falseness of all that Acrasia offers. The story of
Jason and Medea replaces those of Hercules and Iole and Anthony
and Cleopatra (among others) on the gates of Armida's palace at
Ger. Lib., XVI.3–7, with a probable echo of Chaucer's *Knight's
Tale*, 1944, where the enchantments of Medea and Circe are
depicted on the walls of the temple of Venus. Jason's task was to
fetch the golden fleece which was in the possession of king Aeetes,
brother of Circe, in Colchis; an expedition which he undertook with
the main Greek heroes in the *Argo*. When he arrived in Colchis the
king's daughter, the witch Medea, fell in love with him and
promised to help him in his task with ointments and other aids if he
would marry her. He obtained the fleece and escaped with Medea.
Part of their travels took them through the Euxine sea. They lived
together happily for ten years until Creon of Thebes betrothed his
daughter Creusa (or Glauce) to him. In revenge Medea sent a
poisoned garment and crown to the girl who, with her father, was
burnt by the fire that came from it. The 'boyes bloud' is the blood
of Medea's brother, Absyrtus, whom she killed as she and Jason
were fleeing from Aeetes with the fleece: she scattered parts of the
boy's body in the sea and Aeetes was delayed by stopping to collect
them. The story is told in detail in Apollonius Rhodius,
Argonautica, III and Ovid, *Met.*, VII. Medea destroys as Acrasia
destroys (see i.35–56n., and Hieatt, *Chaucer, Spenser, Milton,*
193); and 'the boyes bloud' recalls Ruddymane at i.40 and ii.3, a
parallel supported by, e.g., Thomas Cooper's *Thesaurus*, which
calls Absyrtus a 'yong babe' (cit. Starnes and Talbert, 112). The
story is a warning to Guyon, especially since he, like Jason, has just
completed a voyage: Jason obtained the golden fleece after various
trials (taming the bulls and killing the dragon that guarded it);
Guyon will overcome the golden Bower (st. 55, 61) and vanquish
Acrasia's animal henchmen. Acrasia corresponds in some ways to
Medea, whose aunt was Circe; Guyon must avoid the (moral)
dismemberment that Absyrtus suffered and that the young Verdant
(a parody Adonis, whose life-blood was spilt on the ground) suffers
at Acrasia's hands (st. 79ff.).

46–9 The Genius who is the 'celestiall powre' presides over the

Garden of Adonis at III.vi.31–3. He is the god of fertility and
generation: see Spenser's *Epithalamion*, 398–9, and the *Romance
of the Rose*, 16249ff. (Nature and Genius), 19335ff., and 19505ff.
(Genius talking about perpetuating the species). See also C. S.
Lewis, *The Allegory of Love* (1958), appendix I, and D. T. Starnes,
'The Figure Genius in the Renaissance', *Studies in the
Renaissance*, XI (1964). Agdistis was double-sexed, the offspring
of Zeus and Earth, and was worshipped as a nature deity
(Pausanias, *Description of Greece*, VII.xvii.10–12); the name was
also given to the earth mother, Cybele (Smith, I. 67), and was
identified with Genius in, e.g., Comes, *Mythologiae*, IV.iii
(Lotspeich, 61–2). But, Comes points out, *ibid.*, there are many evil
geniuses around who are opposed to the one good Genius and who
mislead men by means of phantoms into lust. These are the bad
personal geniuses of individual souls, which are presided over by
two such beings, one good, and one bad. Acrasia's Genius is one of
the latter (Lewis, *ibid.*; Augustine, *City of God*, VII.xiii). Genius
can, traditionally, be young (as perhaps here: 'comely personage')
or old (as at III.vi.31) and accompanied by a shallow bowl or wine
goblet (Gilbert, *Symbolic Persons*, 110–11). Mazer = a hard wood
used for drinking cups (*O.E.D.*). Flowers and unmixed wine were
offered to him (Tibullus, II.ii: 'Soft garlands must ornament his
hallowed locks ... he must be ... drunk with unadulterated wine');
so that Spenser's figure symbolises intemperance, since wine mixed
with water signifies temperance, (i.35–56n.). Hence Guyon,
with justified disdain (see viii.33–53n.), overthrows the bowl and
breaks the staff, which parodies the tree-shoot, emblem of fertility,
that is another of Genius's emblems (Gilbert, 111). It also parodies
the Palmer's staff. The wine bowl probably alludes to the
constellation known as the Bowl of Bacchus, important in
Macrobius's influential Neoplatonic account of the descent of the
soul through the planetary spheres as it journeys towards
the body. In *Phaedo*, 79C Plato talks of the soul 'staggering
as if drunk as it is being drawn into the body'. A clue to what
he means is, says Macrobius, 'the location of the constellation
of the Bowl of Bacchus in the region between Cancer
and Leo, indicating that there for the first time intoxication
overtakes descending souls with the influx of matter; whence the
companion of intoxication, forgetfulness, also begins to steal
quietly upon souls at that point' (*Commentary on the Dream of*

Scipio, I.xii.7–8; tr. Stahl, 135). There are additional overtones of Circe's wine of forgetfulness, drunk by Odysseus's men (*Odyssey*, X.233ff.; the identification of this wine with the soul's forgetting of its divine origins at birth is found in Plutarch, *Moralia*, Loeb edn, tr. F. H. Sandbach, XV (1969), 368–75. See Hieatt, *Chaucer, Spenser, Milton*, 178–80). Compare Excesse's wine cup at st. 56–7; and note the emphasis on memory, as opposed to oblivion, in Alma's castle (ix.49–58n.). At st. 46, finally, we are told that Genius's garment made him unfit for 'manly exercize': the suggestion of effeminacy here (lust leading one to abandon the heroic quest) is confirmed by what we see of Verdant at st. 79–80; and cf. v.35–7n.

50 Flora, goddess of spring and flowers, has pejorative associations, too: see I.i.48n., and ct. II.iii.21–30n. The earthly paradisal qualities of the Bower now become apparent; but warnings against accepting it at its face value as a true pleasant place or *locus amoenus* are there not only in the false Genius and the ambiguous Flora (goddess and harlot) but also in the over-enthusiastic role of Art, which is confirmed later at st. 59, where Art and Nature strive to undermine each other. The accusation that Nature is 'niggard' is untrue: according to the prevailing philosophy Nature was full and prodigal. Note the parody of the Aristotelian mean here: Art accuses Nature of deficiency and supplies it with excess. The relationship between the two had long been a commonplace of philosophical debate. Viewed simply, Nature is the great creating force; but with the Fall of man Nature herself fell, remaining good but not perfect. Art ideally complements Nature: it seizes on what is left unformed or imperfect and perfects it, as in the garden of IV.x.21 ('For all that nature by her mother wit / Could frame in earth, and forme of substance base, / Was there, and all that nature did omit, / Art playing second natures part, supplyed it'). But just as within fallen man there is an ever-present tendency towards the bestial, and within Nature evil, chaotic forces are always striving to emerge (Errour, Orgoglio, etc.), so Art, too, has its evil aspect: it can be 'curious' – not 'curious' or mysterious in a good sense but in a bad sense, as is the case with Mammon's cloak at vii.4 and Acrasia's fountain at st. 60, where there are suggestions that Art has co-operated by means of black magic with the supernatural powers of evil. Then, too, Art used wrongly can counterfeit Nature and, more than that, outdo her (the false Una in Book I, the Bower of Bliss itself). It is evil then because it misleads by appeal to the senses rather than leading the mind from the sensual to the ideal; it imitates the sensible rather than the intelligible. See especially Millar McLure, 'Nature and Art in *The Faerie Queene*', *E.L.H.*, XXVIII (1961).

51 'Joviall' = 'under the influence of Jupiter', the planet often, together with Venus, allotted to the sanguine temperament (Klibansky, 127, 187, 397), which was correlated with the first of the four ages of man (youth) and so with love and lust (*ibid.*, 300, 302, 369). The sanguine temperament also implies proportion and harmony, since it was regarded as the best and noblest of the four and as resembling the temperament of Adam before the Fall (*ibid.*, 103, 105, 369). Hence the Bower has an almost prelapsarian climate, protected alike from the rigours of winter and the excessive heat of summer: seasonal variation was a result of the Fall (see *Paradise Lost*, X.651ff.). Earthly paradises traditionally have temperate climates anyway: e.g., Chaucer, *Parlement of Foules*, 204ff., and *Ger. Lib.*, XV.53–4.

52 Rhodope was the wife of the Thracian king Haemus; in her pride at bearing a giant begotten on her by Neptune she called herself Juno and as a punishment was turned into a mountain (*Met.*, VI.87–9; Lotspeich, 105). The vale of Tempe in Thessaly is where Apollo loved and pursued Daphne; to escape him she was changed into a laurel (*Met.*, I.452ff., 568ff.); on Ida, see viii.3–6n., where it is connected with Venus; and on Parnassus, see I.x.53–4n. Note the interpretative problem posed here: not all the names mentioned have good associations; and, despite Acrasia's attempts, nothing 'with *Eden* mote compaire'.

53 On the bridling of the will, see v.1n. and our Plate 8.

54 For the vine as an emblem of Bacchus, see Vergil, *Eclogues*, VII.61; and Ovid, *Ars amatoria*, I.244 for the vine and Venus. Calypso's grotto (*Odyssey*, V.68–9) has a trailing vine. The offering of the vines of themselves to passers-by recalls an earthly-paradisal commonplace celebrated in, e.g., Jonson's *To Penshurst* which goes back at least to Hesiod's golden age in the *Works and Days*, 117–18 (the land gave up her fruits unasked). As described here, in

various stages of ripeness, Spenser's grapes echo *Ger. Lib.*,
XVI.11, where unripe and mature grapes cluster together; but
typically Spenser adds symbolic suggestiveness. Firstly, unlike
Tasso, he introduces a regressive progression from ripe to unripe to
artificial, in keeping with the artificial Bower itself which denies
time so insistently that Acrasia takes as her lover the Bacchic
Verdant, an eternal boy (st. 79–80n.). Secondly, the gems
mentioned are emblematic: the purple hyacinth or jacinth recalls
the unfortunate effects of love on Hyacinthus, loved by Apollo and
accidentally killed by the god's discus (*Met.*, X.162ff.).
Astrologically, the stone was dedicated to Jupiter (Agrippa,
I.xxvi,57; cf. st. 51n.); the ruby is associated with love and
happiness (de Vries, 394) and, as it is 'laughing', recalls laughing
Venus (see vi.2–10n.); the emerald belongs to Venus (Agrippa,
I.xxviii,59).

55–7 The gold grapes recall the golden apples of vii.54–5:
Mammon and Acrasia offer complementary temptations to
cupidity. This is the gold of artifice and not the gold of temperance
and virtue (I.vii.43n.) or the gold that symbolises the paradisal
golden age. The weakness of the boughs implies moral weakness:
they 'bow adowne' in compliance with Nature's fall as a sign of
their deviation from moral rectitude (cf. i.57–8n.). The figure of
Excesse is reminiscent of the voluptuous Pleasure/Venus in 'The
Choice of Hercules' (I.ii.36–8n.) and Lewdness, traditionally
scantily dressed and reclining (Ripa, 294–5; Chew, 74ff.).
Excesse's temptation is more explicitly sexual than Genius's, which
it parallels in the hope that, having now seen the Bower's beauty,
Guyon will the more readily succumb. She is modelled closely on
Circe, who also has a cup (I.viii.14n.). Durling, 'The Bower of Bliss
and Armida's Palace', notes an allusion to Ephesians 5:18: 'And be
not drunke with wine, wherein is excesse: but be fulfilled with the
Spirit'. The spilling of wine symbolises lust at III.ix.30; and in
staining the ground it parodies fertility gods like Adonis and
Hyacinthus who bled into the ground.

60–2 The fountain 'in the midst' inverts the 'river of water of
life' of Revelation 22:1 and Christ as the fountain (e.g., Geneva
gloss on Song of Solomon 4:15: Christ is 'ye true fountaine of all
grace'), while parodying the tree of knowledge 'in the middes of the
garden' (Genesis 3:3) and the tree of life 'in the middes' at

Revelation 22:2. Contrast, too, the well of ii.3ff. Its direct model is the fountain in *Ger. Lib.*, XV.55–62, which also has two wanton virgins (Spenser's st. 65 is virtually a translation of Tasso's st. 60, incidentally); though ornamented fountains were a popular feature of contemporary gardens. Spenser's fountain is made of a mysterious, unnamed substance, perhaps parodying the substance of which Alma's castle is made (ix.21, 23) and the 'altar of some costly masse, / Whose substance was uneath to understand' on which the hermaphroditic Venus stands at IV.x.39 'in the midst' of other altars (see Fowler, 'Emanations of Glory: Neoplatonic order in Spenser's *Faerie Queene*', in *A Theatre for Spenserians*, ed. Kennedy and Reither (1973), 70–1). But while this Venus sums up the ultimate mystery and delicacy of love, Acrasia merely offers an assertion of *libido*, the water of lust and sensuality. The Bacchic ivy reinforces its meaning (v.29n.); and the jasper recalls the Heavenly Jerusalem at Revelation 21:11 ('her shining was like unto a stone most precious, as a Jasper stone cleare as cristal').

63–9   The laurel is probably ironic, since it is an emblem of virtue (Daphne was changed into a laurel; see st. 52n.). Accordingly, Belphoebe's grotto is shaded by laurels at III.v.40. The episode of the 'naked Damzelles' follows Tasso closely (see st. 60–2n.), except that one of his women sings a song of temptation, offering a golden age of love in which martial arms are to be abandoned (cf. Verdant at st. 79–80). Just as Guyon, in his fallen frailty, succumbs slightly (st. 65, 68) until recalled by the Palmer, so do Tasso's knights have to overcome their desire with reason (XV.66). The 'faire Starre', translated from Tasso, st. 60, is the morning star, Venus–Lucifer (I.ii.4–6n.); and 'the *Cyprian* goddesse' is again Venus, worshipped on Cyprus and born from the sea-foam (see st. 1n. above). These details again follow Tasso, st. 60. The yellow hair is Venerean, and it is unbound (cf. Tasso, st. 61) to symbolise lust: compare st. 14–17n. and contrast ix.18–19n. The blushing of st. 68 parodies the blush of Modesty (ix.40–3n.).

70–1   The harmony here is characteristic of the *locus amoenus* (I.i.7–9n.), and Spenser closely follows Tasso, XVI.12 (birds singing, winds murmuring, strange harmonies coming from fruits, leaves, fountains, etc. in Armida's garden). The harmony is there, too, because Guyon is approaching the Venerean Acrasia, and Venus is the 'mother of harmony' (Martianus Capella, *De nuptiis*

Philologiae et Mercurii, ed. A. Dick (Leipzig, 1925), section 737, p. 372). There is a difficult interpretative problem in the genuine sensuous appeal of these stanzas, since uncorrupted elements are contributing to the music. The answer must be that these elements acknowledge that Acrasia, as a Venus, shares aspects of the good creative Venus. Starting off as a Venus Pandemos or Venus Genetrix, Acrasia breaks away at the point at which creativity spills over into lust: see vi.24n.

72–3 On Acrasia's lover, see st. 79–80n. With the phrase 'greedily depasturing delight', contrast III.vi.46, where Venus 'reap[s] sweet pleasure' of Adonis.

74–5 The song translates *Ger. Lib.*, XVI.14–15, where it is sung by a bird. It is in the tradition of *carpe diem* ('seize the day') songs, of which there are many ancient and Renaissance examples: e.g., Catullus, V (*Vivamus, mea Lesbia, atque amemus*; followed by Jonson in *Volpone*, III), and Herrick's 'Gather ye Rose-buds while ye may' (from *Hesperides*, 1648). The rose is a key symbol in many of these songs because it is an emblem of love and of mutability: see I.ii.36–8n.; Chew, 167 and fig. 121. Note the parallel between the 'bared bosome' of the rose and of the maiden at st. 66. The shock rhyme-word 'crime' confirms the harsh Christian verdict on concupiscence (i.35–56n.); while the lament for passing time, which it is the function of the artifice in Acrasia's Bower to defeat, reminds us that one of Acrasia's faults is regression, the refusal to acknowledge, and engage in, the temporal cycle. Contrast Venus at III.vi.40, who reluctantly realises that in the sublunary world 'All things decay in time'. The rose song looks back to Phaedria's lily song at vi.15–17, situated in a corresponding position at the end of the first half of Book II.

77 Acrasia lies on a bed of Venerean roses. The allusion in line 7 associates her with Arachne's presumption in challenging the virginal Athena (see vii.28–9n.); just so does Acrasia implicitly challenge the chaste Belphoebe, etc. Arachne's 'subtile web' also suggests, and connects Acrasia with, Archimago's 'web of wicked guile' at i.8; but it is cancelled out by the Palmer's equally 'subtile net' at st. 81, emblem of reason binding the passions. The veil is an attribute of Venus (e.g., Chaucer, *Parlement of Foules*, 267ff.); and

Spenser's description has a close similarity to Alcina in her transparent night gown at *O.F.*, VII.28.

78 Acrasia herself becomes an emblem of *libido*, like her fountain. In addition she parodies the virtue of Ovid's golden age, which had rivers of nectar (*Met.*, I.111), and the chaste Diana, to whom pearls were dedicated (ix.18–19n.; 'orient' = lustrous). The fire from her eyes is a Petrarchan commonplace; but combined with references to moisture it suggests the emblems of temperance and discord encountered at v.2–14n. and the familiar notion of generation from the reaction of heat and moisture (see st. 33–4n. on Circe, and III.vi.6ff.); though heat and moisture appear in Tasso's very similar description of Armida at *Ger. Lib.*, XVI.18 as she leans over Rinaldo.

79–80 Acrasia's lover – like Rinaldo – has abandoned the active warrior life for a life of slothful voluptuousness and effeminacy (see v.35–7n. and Introduction to Book II quoting Dio Chrysostom on types of lives). He is literally in a state of Bacchic oblivion (see st. 46–9n.) and is a Mars who has abandoned himself totally to Venus. This myth was open to various interpretations, most of which affirmed the rightness of the union as a coming-together of opposites (iv.16–17n.; vi.29–37n.); but here, simply, Verdant has yielded to the wrong Venus. He is described, conventionally, as a beautiful youth (cf. Adonis in Shakespeare's *Venus and Adonis*); and, as Fowler, 'Emblems of Temperance', has noticed, this is largely what makes him a Bacchus, since youth was traditionally 'green' (Italian *verde*) and Bacchus was depicted as a handsome 'eternal boy' (*tu puer aeternus: Met.*, IV.18). The river-knight Guyon releases the wine-god Verdant, symbolising the mingling of water and wine in temperance; so fulfilling Guyon's vengeance on Acrasia for killing Mordant, the equally Bacchic and youthful image of unregenerate man in canto i (see st. 35–56n.). Verdant's moral state is exemplified by No. XI of Quarles's *Hieroglyphikes of the Life of Man* (1638), which depicts the third of the seven ages of man, under the patronage of Venus. The engraving shows a Bacchic grapevine along with Venus's planetary sign, and there is this accompanying text from Seneca: 'Expect great joy when thou shalt lay down the mind of a child, and deserve the style of a wise man; for at those years childhood is past, but oftentimes a childishness remaineth, and what is worse thou hast the authority of a man, but the vices of a child'.

81–2   The net is based on the net which Venus's husband, Vulcan, made to catch her and her lover Mars in each others' arms. Having entrapped them, Vulcan invited the other gods in to look and laugh at their disgrace (*Met.*, IV.171ff.). See also st. 77n. Acrasia is bound in chains of unbreakable adamant which – a neat touch – is dedicated to Mars (Chaucer, *Knight's Tale*, 1990).

83   Guyon's pitiless rigour and wrath are Saturnian–Martian qualities used justly to overthrow Venerean concupiscence (e.g., viii.33–53n.). The destruction of the false paradise and release of Verdant parallel the defeat of the dragon and release of Una's parents – the restoration of the 'paradise within' – at I.xi and xii.

85–7   For the allusion to *Odyssey*, X, see st. 39–41n. In Homer, the sailors that have been turned into hogs are restored when Circe rubs a drug on them (see also *Met.*, XIV.300 where, like the Palmer, she uses her wand). They emerge from their metamorphosis younger, handsomer, and taller than before, unlike the men restored by the Palmer, who bear marks of shame at their degradation and concupiscence. Grille, though changed back, wishes, because of his depraved will, to forgo reason and understanding and remain a beast (see v.1n.). The story of Gryllus comes from Plutarch's dialogue in the *Moralia*, 'Whether the Beasts have the Use of Reason', in which Gryllus, one of Odysseus's companions, who had been changed by Circe into a hog (Greek *grullos* = pig), talks with Odysseus and refuses to be changed again into a man. The story became well known, in part through its influence on Giovanni Battista Gelli's *Circe* (1549; English translation, 1557), though there Odysseus, while talking with many creatures, does not actually meet a hog. The refusal to become a man again became an emblematic commonplace: e.g., Whitney, *Emblemes*, 82 on the Circe myth. Spenser invokes the usual associations of the pig with gluttony (I.iv.21–3n.) and sin (the Gadarene swine: see xi.46n.).

SELECT BIBLIOGRAPHY

Alciati, Andrea. *Emblemata*. Lyons, 1551.

Alpers, P. J. *Elizabethan Poetry: Modern Essays in Criticism*. New York and London, 1967.

Baring-Gould, S. *Curious Myths of the Middle Ages*. London, 1877.

Barkan, L. *Nature's Work of Art: The Human Body as Image of the World*. New Haven and London, 1975.

Bernheimer, R. *Wild Men in the Middle Ages: A Study in Art, Sentiment, and Demonology*. Cambridge, Mass., 1952.

Bible. *The Geneva Bible. A Facsimile of the 1560 edition*. Introd. L. E. Berry. Madison, Milwaukee, and London, 1969.

——*Excluded Books of the New Testament*, tr. J. B. Lightfoot, M. R. James, H. B. Swete, et al. London, n.d.

Bloomfield, M. W. *The Seven Deadly Sins*. Michigan, 1952.

Bongo, Pietro. *Numerorum mysteria*. Bergamo, 1599.

Burton, Robert, *The Anatomy of Melancholy*, ed. Floyd Dell and P. Jordan-Smith. New York, 1938.

Cheney, D. *Spenser's Image of Nature: Wild Man and Shepherd in 'The Faerie Queene'*. Yale Studies in English, CLXI. New Haven and London, 1966.

Comes, Natalis. *Mythologiae; sive explicationis fabularum*. Lyons, 1602.

Curry, W. C. *Chaucer and the Mediaeval Sciences*. Second edition. London, 1960.

Daniélou, J. *Primitive Christian Symbols*, tr. D. Attwater. London, 1964.

Douglas Waters, D. 'Errour's Den and Archimago's Hermitage: Symbolic Lust and Symbolic Witchcraft'. *E.L.H.*, XXXIII, 1966.

Ferguson, G. *Signs and Symbols in Christian Art*. New York, 1961.

Fowler, A. D. S. 'The River Guyon'. *M.L.N.*, LXXV, 1960.

——'The Image of Mortality: *The Faerie Queene*, II.i–ii'. *H.L.Q.*, XXIV, 1961.

——'Emblems of Temperance in *The Faerie Queene*, Book II'. *R.E.S.*, n.s. XI, 1960.

Gilbert, A. H. *The Symbolic Persons in the Masques of Ben Jonson*. Durham, N. C., 1948.

Heninger, S. K. 'The Orgoglio Episode in *The Faerie Queene*'. *E.L.H.*, XXVI, 1959.

——*A Handbook of Renaissance Meteorology*. Durham, N.C., 1960.

——*Touches of Sweet Harmony: Pythagorean Cosmology and Renaissance Poetics*. San Marino, Calif., 1974.

Hooker, R. *Of the Laws of Ecclesiastical Polity*. 2 vols. Everyman's Library. London, 1907.

Hopper, V. F. *Medieval Number Symbolism*. New York, 1938.

Jonson, Ben. *The Complete Masques*, ed. Stephen Orgel. Yale Ben Jonson. New Haven and London, 1969.

Kaske, C. V. 'The Dragon's Spark and Sting and the Structure of Red Cross's Dragon-Fight: The Faerie Queene, I.xi–xii'. *S.P.*, LXVI, 1969.

Kent Hieatt, A. *Chaucer, Spenser, Milton: Mythopoeic Continuities and Transformations*. Montreal and London, 1975.

Koller, K. 'Art, Rhetoric, and Holy Dying in *The Faerie Queene* with special reference to the Despair canto'. *S.P.*, LXI, 1964.

Lewalski, B. *Milton's Brief Epic: The Genre, Meaning, and Art of 'Paradise Regained'*. Providence, R. I., and London, 1966.

Lilly, W. *Christian Astrology*. London, 1647.

Lord, G. de F. *Homeric Renaissance: The Odyssey of George Chapman*. London, 1956.

Lucretius. *On the Nature of the Universe*, tr. R. E. Latham. Penguin Classics. Harmondsworth, 1973.

Macrobius. *Commentary on the Dream of Scipio*, tr. and ed. W. H. Stahl. Records of Civilisation, Sources and Studies, XLVIII. New York, 1952.

Meyer-Baer, K. *Music of the Spheres and the Dance of Death: Studies in Musical Iconology*. Princeton, N.J., 1970.

Millican, C. B. 'Spenser's and Drant's Poetic Names for Elizabeth: Tanaquil, Gloria, and Una'. *H.L.Q.*, II, 1938–9.

——*Spenser and the Table Round: A Study in the Contemporaneous Background for Spenser's Use of the Arthurian Legend*. Harvard Studies in Comparative Literature, VIII. London, 1967.

Mirror for Magistrates, The. Ed. L. B. Campbell. New York, 1960.

Nelson, W. *The Poetry of Edmund Spenser*. New York, 1963.

Panofsky, E. *Studies in Iconology: Humanistic Themes in the Art of the Renaissance*. New York and Evanston, 1962.

——*Meaning in the Visual Arts*. Garden City, N.Y., 1955.

Peacham, H. *Minerva Britanna*. London, 1612.

Ptolemy. *Tetrabiblos*, tr. and ed. F. E. Robbins. Loeb Classical Library. London and Cambridge, Mass., 1971.

Puttenham, G. *The Arte of English Poesie*. London, 1589.

Quarles, F. *Emblemes*. London, 1635.

Salmon, W. *Pharmacopoeia Londinensis; or, the New London Dispensatory*. London, 1678.

Seznec, J. *The Survival of the Pagan Gods: The Mythological Tradition and its Place in Renaissance Humanism and Art*, tr. B. F. Sessions. New York, 1961.

Steadman, J. M. 'Spenser's *Errour* and the Renaissance Allegorical Tradition'. *Neuphilologische Mitteilungen*, LXII, 1961.

Strong, R. C. 'The Popular Celebration of the Accession Day of Queen Elizabeth I'. *J.W.I.*, XXI, 1958.

Summerson, J. *Architecture in Britain: 1530–1830*. The Pelican History of Art. Harmondsworth, 1970.

Tooke, A. *The Pantheon, Representing the Fabulous Histories of the Heathen Gods and most Illustrious Heroes*. London, 1824.

Tuve, R. *A Reading of George Herbert*. London, 1952.

Twycross, M. *The Medieval Anadyomene: A Study in Chaucer's Mythography*. Oxford, 1972.

Whitney, G. *A Choice of Emblemes*. Leyden, 1586.

Whitaker, V. K. 'The Theological Structure of *The Faerie Queene*, Book I'. *E.L.H.*, XIX, 1952.

Woodhouse, A. S. P. 'Nature and Grace in *The Faerie Queene*'. *E.L.H.*, XVI, 1949.

Valeriano, P. *Hieroglyphica, sive de sacris Aegyptiorum aliarumque gentium literis, Commentatiorum Libri LVIII*. Frankfort, 1613.